The Harmony of the Soul

SUNY Series in the Philosophy of Psychology
Michael Washburn, Editor

The Harmony
of the Soul

Mental Health and Moral Virtue Reconsidered

Neal O. Weiner

STATE UNIVERSITY OF NEW YORK PRESS

Published by
State University of New York Press, Albany

For information, address State University of New York Press,
State University Plaza, Albany, N.Y., 12246

Production by Bernadine Dawes
Marketing by Bernadette LaManna

Library of Congress Cataloging-in-Publication Data

Weiner, Neal O.
      The harmony of the soul : mental health and moral virtue
reconsidered / Neal O. Weiner.
            p.   cm. — (SUNY series in the philosophy of psychology)
      Includes bibliographical references and index.
      ISBN 0–7914–1731–X — ISBN 0–7914–1732–8 (pbk.)
      1. Ethics. 2. Naturalism. 3. Ethics — Psychological aspects.
      4. Mental health — Moral and ethical aspects. 5. Virtue. I. Title.
      II. Series.
      BJ45.W45   1993
      171'.2 — dc20
                                                                                        93–20449
                                                                                        CIP

10 9 8 7 6 5 4 3 2 1

Contents

III   THE GOOD

Acknowledgments

Without the active support of Rosemary Baue, this book would have been forever a dead weight on my shelves—unfinished and disowned. I cannot thank her enough for her faith and generosity.

Charles Griswold, Marvin Kohl, Hugh McCann, and Alex Mourelatos took time from their many responsibilities to read draft versions. They gave me good advice, perhaps more of which I should have followed, and they gave me encouragement, which I much needed. I am very grateful to them both.

Henry Veatch did not even know me when, with typical grace, he consented to read the manuscript. Despite the eccentricity of my ideas and my obvious ignorance of so much that matters to him; despite the differences of that most critical of generations and the divergence of styles that come with it, he welcomed me with a generosity of spirit I had never before experienced. This sustained me in the dark moments and set before me a model of natural unselfishness that I will always try to follow.

To my wife, Barbara, I owe more than I can ever name. She is the foundation that makes all things possible.

For kindly granting permission to reprint from their publications, thanks to the following:

From *The Republic*. Reprinted by the permission of the publishers and the Loeb Classical Library from *Plato: The Republic*, vols. 1 and 2. Trans. Paul Shorey (Cambridge, Ma.: Harvard University Press, 1930).

From *The Gorgias*. Reprinted by the permission of the publishers and the Loeb Classical Library from *Plato: Lysis, Symposium, Gorgias*. Trans. W. R. M. Lamb (Cambridge, Ma.: Harvard University Press, 1961).

From *The Phaedo*. Reprinted by the permission of the publishers and the Loeb Classical Library from *Plato: Euthyphro, Apology, Crito, Phaedo, Phaedrus*. Trans. H. N. Fowler (Cambridge, Ma.: Harvard University Press, 1960).

From *The Presocratics* by Philip Wheelwright. Copyright © 1966 by Odyssey Press.

Introduction

> In the loneliest desert the second metamorphosis occurs: the spirit here becomes a lion; it wants to capture freedom and be lord in its own desert. . . .
>
> But tell me my brothers, what can the child do that even the lion cannot? Why must the preying lion become a child?
>
> Nietzsche

This book is a gesture at reconstruction. It is an attempt to revive certain traditional ideas by placing them on a contemporary foundation. In particular, it seeks to revive an undiluted version of virtue as conceived by Plato and Aristotle, and to place it on a scientific conception of nature by uniting it with the notion of mental health. Thus, in the broadest and most grand terms, what is sought is a reconciliation of value and fact, of ancient ways and modern. It could just as well be said that what is sought is a revival of the natural law tradition in ethics.

At the same time, this book is a thought experiment in philosophical likelihoods. It asks us to suppose what was once taken as the worst possible news for the human spirit—that human consciousness is a thoroughly natural thing and that we are mere parts of nature, not as different from the rest of animate nature as it has flattered us to think. It supposes that we are, in Nietzsche's symbolism, the earth and nothing more, or at least that we are by now so reconciled to the earth that it no longer bothers us to belong to it alone. It is then asked what really follows for the things we care most about—especially for ethics? What would become of ethics if we had no higher ideal to pursue than our own natural health? Would it die or be reduced to some thin shadow of its former self? The answer given is that it would not. It is claimed, in fact, that a reasonable naturalism would only repair our tattered moral consciousness.

This book is neither reductionist nor metaphysical. It does not claim that humankind is or can be explained as "nothing more than" matter and energy, chemicals, libido or economics. Neither is it linguistic. It does not claim that the word *good* can be analytically defined by some set of natural properties. Nor does it deny any of this. It merely *supposes* what once seemed metaphysically the worst. It argues that even if human beings are nothing more than healthy animals, only the best would follow.

To know that would be a great relief. But what if this naturalistic supposition should turn out to make more sense of what used to be called "spiritual" life than its alternatives? What if, given this supposition, even "spiritual" things should suddenly fall into place? Would we not then suspect that something went wrong when we first accepted the notion that there was some deep antagonism between nature (earth) and the noblest aspirations of the human spirit? Was that not what Nietzsche meant to show?

These worries are especially ours. It is surely true that at any time or place given individuals and even schools of individuals can conceive of nature as an amoral force and oppose it to value, which is then understood as some form of human construction. When this happens, as it did among the Greek sophists, for example, the conventional or the human can be identified with the spiritual, and the natural can be seen as a brute fact to be transcended by culture (Protagoras as pictured by Plato, Hegel, the early Marx). Or, the natural can be seen as the only true value in comparison to which the thin constructions of human consciousness pale into insignificance (Thrasymachus and Callicles as pictured by Plato, social Darwinism, certain common interpretations of Nietzsche). But even for western philosophy the general acceptance of a great gulf between nature and common moral values was a late development. From the earliest beginnings of Greek philosophy right up to the birth of modern times, the moral and the natural were generally thought to have an intimate connection. With all due allowances made for the exceptions, from the pre-Socratics to Thomas Aquinas, nature, or natural law, was understood by almost everyone to be the source of moral truth.

It is very hard for us who are so comfortable with the distinction between fact and value to sympathize with this early mode of thought. Apparently, nature was felt to be authoritative *both* because of its overwhelming positive presence—it simply was the way things were and had to be—*and* also because of its goodness—in that the way things were embodied a god's desire, or reflected the dynamics of a creative moral force. In all probability, these two reasons were not clearly distinguished. Or at least it so appears in the very first genuinely philosophical sentence to be preserved in the western tradition.

The unlimited is the first principle of things that are. It is that from which the coming-to-be [of things and qualities] takes place, and it is that into which they return when they perish, by moral necessity (*ananke*), giving satisfaction to one another and making reparation for their injustice, according to the order of time.[1]

Wheelwright's translation of *ananke* as moral necessity indicates that he thinks of Anaximander's *ananke* as both ineluctable factual necessity, that which simply must be, and also that which ought to be, the hand of justice in the course of history. There is an order of time, a plot, and it is controlled by a sense of what is owing or due. The things that are (presumably the elements in Anaximander's cosmology) are unjust to each other—they encroach on or oppose each other—and so must be punished by death or non-being, the return into the unlimited from which they came.

This concept of *ananke* mixes logical and/or causal necessity with the force of what is morally due or owing. Presumably, it reflects the same ambiguous conception of necessity that is found in the English phrase *have to* as in "I have to return the money I borrowed" and "You have to cross the river to reach New Jersey." In Plato this entwinement of necessities reached explicit formulation when, in the *Republic*, he insisted that from a strictly rational point of view there could be no truth (and hence no being) apart from the goodness that gave rise to it.

> This reality, then, that gives their truth to the objects of knowledge and the power of knowing to the knower, you must say is the idea of the good and you must conceive it as being the cause of knowledge and truth in so far as known.[2]

> the objects of knowledge not only receive from the presence of the good their being known, but their very existence and essence is derived to them from it. . . .[3]

Here is both the depersonalized notion of the creation of the world by a benevolent God (a clear mixing of the natural and the moral) and also the primary source of the medieval doctrine that *bonum* (goodness) was one of the transcendental predicates (i.e, a category, something that had to be predicated of all beings). It is ironic that in some quarters Plato's rationalistic dualism should be seen as the source of the devaluation of nature. In fact, it was an attempt on Plato's part to preserve the value-laden nature that he felt was threatened by the sophists' separation of nature and convention. For Platonism, at even its most rapturous extreme, nature is the moving image of an eternity (*Timaeus* 37d) that is itself determined in all its general structures by the idea of the good.

> Let us then state for what reason becoming and this universe were framed by him who framed them. He was good; and in the good no jealousy in

> any matter can ever arise. So, being without jealousy, he desired that all
> things should come as near as possible to being like himself. . . . Desiring
> then that all things should be good and . . . nothing imperfect, the god
> took over all that is visible and brought it from disorder into order, since
> he judged that order was in every way the better.[4]

If nature so conceived is not perfectly good, it is at least essentially good, and that makes *all* the difference. Perhaps Eliade is right when he says that Plato is the foremost philosopher of the primitive mentality—that Plato really did nothing but give abstract philosophical expression to the most basic tendencies of archaic thought.[5] But even if that is not so, it is still true that Plato's insistence on the goodness of being was not a peculiar sort of rationalistic fantasy *ex nihilo*. He was reaffirming in his own language the basic ontological vision of the pre-Socratics, and it seems reasonably clear that they in turn were giving philosophical/poetic expression to much of commonplace religious thought and feeling that preceded them (Cornford 1912).

Thales: All things are full of gods.

Anaximander: The infinite . . . seems . . . to surround all things and steer all.[6]

> The unlimited is the first principle of things that are. It is that from which the coming-to-be [of things and qualities] takes place, and it is that into which they return when they perish, *by moral necessity (ananke), giving satisfaction to one another and making reparation for their injustice, according to the order of time.*[7]

Heraclitus: It should be understood that . . . *strife is justice*, and that *all things* come to pass through the compulsion of strife.[8]

> All human laws are nourished by the one divine law, which prevails as far as it wishes, suffices for all things . . . [9]

Anaximenes: As our soul, being air, holds us together and controls us, so do wind [or breath] and air enclose the whole world.[10]

Parmenides: Nor will the force of true belief allow that, besides that which is, there could also arise anything from that which is not; wherefore justice looseth not her fetters to allow it to come into being or perish, but holdeth it fast.[11]

> [In his astronomy] Parmenides said that there were rings wound one around the other, one formed of the rare, the other the dense. . . . The middlemost of the mixed rings is the primary cause of movement and of coming into being for them all, and he calls it the goddess that steers all, the holder of the keys, justice and necessity (*ananke*).[12]

The precise interpretation of any of these lines can be debated, and there are certainly fragments of Heraclitus that pull in the opposite direction, but it seems impossible to deny the general tendency of all these thinkers in the direction of some sort of union between nature and goodness. Nor do we have to stay within the confines of philosophy to find this union. The plot of the *Iliad*, for example, is easily seen as an illustration of the same basic themes. There, despite the petty fury of the characters and the notable amorality of the subordinate divinities, the nod of Zeus, which governs the plot with an irresistible necessity (*ananke*), grants Achilles the revenge he hungers for, but only after he "pays the penalty" through the death of his friend. This is a tragic necessity, but it is also easy to see it as an act of primitive justice that balances the misery caused by Achilles's raging pride. In the *Iliad*, as in Anaximander and Heraclitus, there is strife, struggle, and apparent chaos, but the order of things is still controlled by a primitive sense of justice.

All of Plato and Aristotle can be seen as an attempt to preserve this union of the natural and the good in response to the challenge posed by the sophists' separation of nature and convention.

It is also worth noting that Judaeo-Christian creation mythology, at least as it has come down to us, is not essentially different. Yahweh's faceless transcendence does not amount to a devaluation of nature, as is claimed by recent popular philosophy. To the contrary, the text as we have it repeatedly insists upon the moral value of nature.

> And God said let the water under the heaven be gathered together unto one place, and let the dry land appear. And it was so. And God called the dry land Earth, and the gathering together of the waters called He Seas; and God said that it was good.
>
> And the earth brought forth grass, herb yielding seed after its kind, and tree bearing fruit, wherein is the seed thereof, after its kind; and God saw that it was good.
>
> And God saw everything that he had made, and behold it was very, very good.[13]

We ought to take seriously the suggestion that Biblical creation, the Homeric sense of history, most of early Greek philosophy, Plato and Aristotle were all in agreement that what is or happens is governed by some sort of moral law, and that the entire western natural law tradition was simply an elaboration of this original unity of fact and value.

And in the East, wherever the story of reincarnation is a part of religious or philosophical thought, the natural order still embodies certain principles of cosmic justice (karma). Certainly there is a moral meaning to the cycle of birth, death and reincarnation—to the notion that in each life-time one moves up or down the ontological scale in accord with earned merit. And the cycle of birth, death and reincarnation is, after all, the gen-eral formula for *all* the cycles of nature, the very same cosmic recycling that was the concern of Anaximander, too.

If it is true that the union of the good and the natural is a fundamental element of eastern religion, and if Eliade is right in his assessment of the archaic mode of thinking, then the possibility arises that only in the modern West is nature generally denied this high regard. Perhaps only for us (and even then, only for the most sophisticated of us) is nature a concatenation of amoral forces, a mere fact, devoid of moral authority. But even if this grander claim is not true, it is still true that when the modern west adopted these attitudes, it turned against its own philosophical traditions that stretched back from the scholastics to Anaximander.

At the level of the most basic philosophical attitudes, the modern West defined itself by a more or less self-conscious devaluation of nature. What before was taken as an embodiment of divinity, justice, spirit, purpose, eros or at least some kind of intelligence, came generally to be seen as mere stuff, ordered to be sure, but unreliably (Hume) or to no end that could be usefully discerned (Bacon, Descartes, Hume), or to an end that had only mathemati-cal/aesthetic value, but no concrete moral value (Galileo, Kant). As a rough generalization this is true despite the fact that many of the early scientists read theological meaning back into their scientific work (Kepler and New-ton, for example), despite the fact that a modern like Locke could fall back on a (very weak) notion of natural law ethics, and despite Rousseau's 'noble savage,' whom he himself ignored when, in *The Social Contract*, he set out to take the business of ethics seriously. The demise and/or semipermanent postponement of teleological thinking in the interpretation of nature came to be perceived as a precondition for the rise of science. This is a familiar point that was made by many authors well before the recent concern with the envi-ronment (Burtt 1924; Collingwood 1945; Stace 1952). But, from that moment on, the natural law tradition ceased to be the foundation of western moral philosophy (Strauss 1953; Veatch 1985).

The desacrimentalization or devaluation of nature that was begun by the scientific revolution was completed by what is called "the enlighten-ment." By the time it was over, one of the essential features of the modern European mind had been set—the banishment of teleological thinking from the putatively authoritative reconstruction of nature that is called "science." There were nostalgic conservatives among the philosophers (Berkeley, Leibnitz), neo-pythagorean mystics among the scientists (like Kepler), and there was always a protesting romantic counter-current

(Blake, Keats, Shelly, Rousseau, Novalis, D. H. Lawrence, Schelling) but it is undeniable that the general drift of things was in the other direction. As early as 1776, Hume could speak of the fact/value dichotomy and few would even remember that for the scholastics goodness was a transcendental predicate or that sober, learned men had once thought it obvious that the good, the true and the beautiful were all the same. In 1912 Russell wrote:

> Such an outline, but even more purposeless, more void of meaning, is the world which science presents for our belief. Amid such a world . . . our ideals henceforward must find a home. That man is the product of causes that had no prevision of the end they were achieving; that his origin, his growth, his hopes and fears . . . are but the outcome of accidental collocations of atoms—*all these things, if not beyond dispute, are yet so nearly certain that no philosophy that rejects them can hope to stand.* Only within the scaffolding of these truths, only on the firm foundation of unyielding despair, can the soul's habitation henceforth be safely built. Blind to good and evil, reckless of destruction, omnipotent matter rolls on its relentless way.[14]

Russell's attitude was not new. It is in the sophists, in Epicurus, and Machiavelli. Presumably, it has always been around in one form or another. What is new is that neither Russell nor his audience felt a need to prove it.

It is seldom recognized that in ethics the major consequence of the devaluation of nature concerns a change in the perceived relationship of human beings to their own desires. Nature is represented most poignantly in the human being by the body, and the body is a moral presence as desire—as the collection of what are called the "bodily desires," which is really the collection of *all* desires insofar as they stem from the natural forces that have made us. Whoever understands these desires, their relationship to each other, and the consequences of acting upon them is said to understand human nature and is thought to possess a kind of knowledge worth calling "wisdom."

Given the general view of nature held by the prescientific tradition, there thus arose for it a peculiar dilemma concerning human nature. On the one hand there was the well-known traditional suspicion of desire, the view of desire as wild, bestial and subhuman. But since nature was a moral order, and since the desires were a part of it, the tradition had also to conclude that human desire exhibited the same order that governed the rest of the cosmos. The desires simply had to be good, a priori, and consequently the good had to be the true object of desire. This is the basic meaning of the Platonic theory of desire (eros) and also of Aristotle's more cautious and qualified version of it.

then such being the case, must not love [eros] be love of only beauty, and not of ugliness?

[and] you hold, do you not, that good things are beautiful?[15]

Lovers of what is noble [*ta kala*—the same word that is translated as "beautiful things" in the *Symposium*] find pleasant the things that are by nature pleasant, and virtuous actions are such, so that these are pleasant for such men as well as in their own nature.[16]

Since for both Plato and Aristotle all "natural" or "true" desire is for the good, and since for both of them there is only one good for human life, there was in Plato and Aristotle no possibility of basic conflict between desires. All genuine desires had to form a coherent system of motivations toward that single good. This coherence of desire with itself and the moral good was understood as a harmony of the soul—a sort of psychological balance that has certain features in common with what is now sometimes called "centeredness" or "the absence of intrapsychic conflict." When, in the *Republic, Gorgias*, and *Symposium*, Socrates argues that true happiness and justice entail each other, he means it only for the person who has achieved this harmony of desires—not for someone who has merely forced himself to engage in morally correct behavior.

The original task of ethics was thus to understand, as far as possible, how this harmony of the soul was to be accomplished, and consequently ethics was at first concerned with matters of psychology and character (that is to say, with desires, virtues, vices, and their relation to happiness) rather than with abstract moral rules and their logical justification. The primary moral question was not, How must I behave in order to conform to the rules of correct behavior?, but rather, What must I do to bring my soul (my desires) into a coherent, balanced, harmonious condition so as to achieve real happiness and be just?

This faith in the harmony of the soul was derived from the Platonic commitment to the goodness of nature. It was a more or less self-conscious rational construction. It was certainly not understood to be an empirical fact, except, perhaps, in the case of extraordinary individuals such as Socrates is pictured to be in the *Phaedo* and *Symposium*. Empirically, the desires did not appear to Plato or Aristotle to be either harmonious or good, and so they are frequently treated with the disparagement that so often characterizes traditional philosophy. But that disparagement is only part of the picture, and it is unfortunate that it is the part that generally colors our impression of classical psychology.

Careful textual analysis shows that both Plato and Aristotle posited this harmony at the bottom of the human soul, a harmony that was *both* a gift of nature *and* a rare achievement of the very wise. The material is found in some of the less well-known parts of the *Republic*, the *Philebus*, and in passages scattered throughout the *Nicomachean Ethics*. In chapter 5, I will try to make that case in detail. But for now suffice it to note that even in the *Republic* the good, which is always one with itself, is said to be the sole motive force in the universe. If we include human behavior in this universe, then, since desire is the motivating force in human behavior, it inevitably follows that all desire must be directed toward that single good, and so must be in fundamental harmony with itself, appearances to the contrary notwithstanding. This extension of the Republic's moral ontology to human behavior is the explicit doctrine of the *Symposium* and *Phaedo* and it is hinted at throughout the Platonic corpus whenever the Socratic paradox comes up (Meno 77c, for example and throughout the *Gorgias*). Moreover, the inhabitants of the *Republic's* "city of pigs" are a perfect illustration of it.

> they will build themselves houses and carry on their work in summer for the most part unclad and unshod and in winter clothed and shod sufficiently. And for their nourishment they will provide meal from their barley and flour from their wheat, and kneading and cooking these they will serve noble cakes and loaves on some arrangement of reeds or clean leaves, and, reclined on rustic beds strewn with byrony and myrtle, they will feast with their grandchildren, drinking of their wine thereto, garlanded and singing hymns to the gods in pleasant fellowship, not begetting offspring beyond their means lest they fall into poverty or war.
>
> [and they will eat] the sort of things they boil up in the country. . . . But for dessert we will serve them figs and chickpeas and beans, and they will toast myrtle-berries and acorns before the fire, washing them down with moderated potations; and so, living in peace and health, they will probably die in old age and hand on a like life to their offspring.[17]

It is important to remember that it is this original, government-less, philosophy-less city, wherein desire and justice exist in natural harmony with one another, and not the city of the philosopher king, that is said by Socrates to be the "true" and "healthy" city.

> I understand. It is not merely the origin of a city, it seems, that we are considering, but the origin of a luxurious city. Perhaps that isn't such a bad suggestion, either. For by observation of such a city it may be we could discern the origin of justice and injustice in states. The true state I believe to be the one we have described—the healthy state, as it were.
>
> But if it is your pleasure that we contemplate also a fevered state, there is nothing to hinder.[18]

Later in the *Republic* (IX, 583b ff.) this dualism of the true city and the fevered one finds its psychological mirror in a theory of true and false pleasures designed to prove that the pleasures of justice are the only real ones. Thus, there turn out to be two kinds of desire and/or pleasure in the classical or Platonic theory—real and apparent. The harmony of the soul is constituted by only the real desires. Reason, in speculating about the ultimate motivating force of the universe, concludes that such real desires must actually exist and that they constitute a harmony. But Plato, Aristotle, and the tradition that both preceded and followed them, generally assumed that few would ever achieve the real harmony of the soul. For the vast majority of people, desire would always be at odds with itself, making real happiness and real virtue impossible. This assumed sad fact was the source of the traditional elitism, a fact that was to be accepted and dealt with benevolently, but which was not to be allowed to obliterate the ideal of harmony for those who could achieve it.

The insistence on the goodness of nature combined with the cold facts of human life thus forced the entire tradition to the paradoxical conclusion that for human beings the natural and harmonious are rare and hidden. This may be the meaning behind the paradoxical "know thyself" of Delphi. Because there are two selves (one hidden and harmonious, the other obvious and disordered), the self is not an easy thing to know. But even if that was not the meaning of the oracle, it was an idea that may have received philosophical elaboration at least as early as Heraclitus.

It pertains to all men to *know themselves* and to be temperate.[19]

To be temperate is the greatest virtue. Wisdom consists in speaking and acting the truth, *giving heed to the nature of things*.[20]

And yet:

Nature loves to hide.[21]

The hidden harmony is better than the obvious.[22]

You could not discover the limits of soul, even if you traveled by every path in order to do so; such is the depth of its meaning.[23]

Since by nature the desires are good, it follows that humankind, like every other animal, can be good, just, and happy merely by following its own desires. On the other hand, desire as we empirically know it, is wild and disordered ("bestial" as we sometimes say), and a life spent in its indiscriminate pursuit would be the most immoral and unhappy of lives. Only a dualism in which a hidden reality is the moral one can reconcile these views—and that is the view taken by the entire tradition from Heraclitus to St. Thomas Aquinas. The distinction that in Plato appears as the difference between real and apparent pleasures, is carried over into Aristotle as the difference between natural and unnatural desire. It reappears in Christian anthropology as the difference between man's fallen nature (which is manifest and commonplace) and his true, original nature as made by God (which appears on earth only in the personality of Jesus and the saints, as a foretaste of heaven).

> in the first state. . . . Adam had no passion with evil as its object. . . . For our sensual appetite, wherein the passions reside, is not entirely subject to reason, and hence at times our passions forestall and hinder reason's judgement, and at other times they follow after reason's judgement, according as the sensual appetite obeys reason to some extent. But in the state of innocence . . . the passions of the soul existed only as consequent upon the judgement of reason.[24]

> For it [original sin] is an inordinate disposition, arising from the destruction of the harmony, which was essential to original justice, even as bodily sickness is an inordinate disposition of the body, by reason of the destruction of that equilibrium, which is essential to health.[25]

For the tradition then, the normal and the natural conditions of the human psyche are decidedly not the same thing. For human beings, and presumably only for human beings, the normal condition is unnatural, which is essentially another way of saying that the human being is the sick animal. The other animals are what they ought to be merely by doing what they want, while humankind, by doing what it "wants" cannot achieve its own (true) desires, cannot be its own true self, and cannot even really be the thing it is. For human beings nature is an achievement that stands in need of art (or grace) for its completion. "Art perfects nature," said Aristotle. For human life, the name of this art was ethics. Its task was to restore people to their natural conditions, i.e., to make them well, and so ethics was a kind of healing, a kind of emotional therapy that was meant to bring happiness, moderation and a measure of tranquility into the lives of its practitioners.

This transformational, therapeutic vision of ethics is something very different from the justification of the rules of correct behavior that we now think of as moral philosophy. It is not exclusively modern to put the emphasis on law instead of virtue and obedience instead of transformation.

That emphasis is found in the Old Testament and Roman stoicism, for example, as well as in the social contract theorists and Kant. But the truly modern variant on it can be said to begin when, in the name of a principled and consistent empiricism, the possibility of a hidden, morally ordered, happiness-bearing human nature is no longer taken seriously. It begins when, without apology or reluctance, the natural, the normal, and the average are taken to be the same, and when, consequently, the nature of human desire is felt to be exactly what it seems to be—at best a confusing mixture of good and bad without moral rhyme or reason, and at worst a wild and violent thing—disordered, self-destructive, cruel and bloody, held in check only by the fear of punishment.

There are no new facts involved in the adoption of the modern attitude. The unhappy facts were always known. What changes is the paradigm for their understanding. The tradition saw the disorder of human desire as a deviation from our true nature and thus saw it as a form of sickness. But if the idea of nature as a moral order is not taken seriously, then there is no longer a need to hypothesize such a hidden nature. Human nature is then free to be exactly what it seems to be. The natural and the wicked can be the same; the healthy man can be a bad one.

The paradigm shift in moral psychology closely parallels the shift that took place in astronomy. The old paradigm insisted a priori that the planets had to go in circles because God would not make a universe in which anything less would do. A theoretical device (the theory of epicycles) was then thought up to explain the apparent disorder.[26] In psychology, the hidden harmony of the soul is the analogue to the hypothesis of circular motion. Its foundation too lay in the presupposed goodness of the natural order. To reject this presupposition was then to guarantee the conclusion that desire, happiness, goodness, and frustration are exactly what they seem to be to common observation. This is precisely the point made by Machiavelli when, in a passage frequently taken as definitive of the modern attitude, he states that life as it really (i.e., naturally) is, is so far from life as it ought to be that one needs to choose between moral propriety and a successful life in this world when, that is to say, he claims that the rules of nature do not dance to a moral tune.

> But my intention being to write something of use . . . it appears to me more proper to go to the real truth of the matter than to its imagination; and many have imagined principalities and republics [and we add, "hidden harmonies of the soul"] that have never been seen or known to exist in reality; *for how we live is so far removed from how we ought to live, that he who abandons what is done for what ought to be done, will rather learn to bring about his own ruin than his preservation.*[27]

For Machiavelli, as for most of what is called common sense, the world, i.e. nature, health, success and 'worldly' happiness, requires immorality, which is precisely the point denied by the traditional theory of the hidden harmony of the soul. Hobbes, in another passage often taken as definitive of modernity, put the same point somewhat differently. First, he misunderstands the traditional notion of the harmony of the soul as an inert absence of desire. Then, he attacks it as, presumably, another meaningless scholastic impossibility. But in any case, he makes it clear that for him happiness lies elsewhere—in what is usually called "success."

> The felicity of this life consisteth not in the repose of a mind satisfied. For there is no such *finis ultimus*, utmost aim, nor *summum bonum*, greatest good, as is spoken of in the books of the old moral philosophers. Nor can a man any more live whose desires are at an end, than he, whose senses . . . are at a stand. Felicity is a continual progress of the desire from one object to another; the attaining of the former, being still but the way to the latter.[28]

So understood, happiness is nothing more than the possession of the means to satisfy the endless succession of empirical desires that happen to constitute the psychology of a given individual. It can and has been endlessly argued whether such "success," even were it attainable, would really be worth calling happiness; but no one has ever confused it with morality.

This endless succession of satisfactions was happiness as Kant understood it.

> Without any view to duty, all men have the strongest inclination to happiness, because in this idea all inclinations are summed up.[29]

And because he understood it this way, he gave it little moral significance.

This entire line of thought is epitomized with marvelous generality in Hume's distinction between is and ought. Therein Hume distills the philosophical kernel from Machiavelli's assumption that the rules of life have little in common with the rules of morality. And once the laws of nature (that which is) are in this way seen to be amoral, it becomes necessary to build one's ethics on some other foundation. Hence Kant's attempt to rid ethics of anthropological speculation and to found morality on a priori principles; hence what is called "deontological" ethics, i.e., ethics that has as little as possible to do with the empirical realities of nature.

Utilitarianism, the other great thread of moral philosophy in the scientific period, seems at first to be quite different. Certainly it cares very much to know the specifics of human nature. It defines the moral good as the means to happiness. Therefore it needs to know all about desire and its satisfaction. But everything then depends on the operative conception of happiness. If a crudely hedonistic notion of happiness is used, utilitarianism becomes a grotesquely unsatisfying moral philosophy. It becomes more acceptable as its notion of happiness becomes more subtle. If it were to employ the Platonic/Aristotelian notion that true justice really is true happiness and that there is a kind of secondary justice that constitutes the means to this ideal condition, then, in its ultimate principles at least, it would be indistinguishable from Platonism. There is no reason why utilitarianism could not be developed in this direction. When it is combined with a strong notion of alienation, something like this happens. But in general, and despite Mill's own discussion of the "higher" pleasures, the value-free notion of nature has guided the development of utilitarianism, so, the intimate union of justice and happiness has not been a part of it. In general, utilitarianism has taken the empirical condition of human life as definitive of human nature and human happiness.

Utilitarianism and deontological ethics continue to be discussed with great subtlety and refinement in academic philosophy. At the level of general educated opinion, however, there holds sway a tolerant, liberal form of relativism, which, while granting a maximum of freedom for the subjectivity of individual pleasure, limited only by the need to prevent overt harm to others, has nothing to offer as to how that freedom should be used. Instead of understanding desire and happiness more deeply, our popular, educated culture has tended to turn freedom itself into the substance of moral truth, and, as has been so often said, that is simply not enough. One needs not only to be free *from* oppression, one must be free *for* something. But for what?

For virtue? At the level of both academic and popular philosophy there is some reason to believe that it may be time for a reconsideration of the moral possibilities offered by the classical theories of virtue. A growing group of academic philosophers has become suspicious of the is/ought distinction and the so-called naturalistic fallacy that rests on it. With this suspicion has inevitably come a revival of interest in the traditional concepts of virtue and the virtues. Peter Geach (1956), Elizabeth Anscombe (1958), Philipa Foot (1978), James Wallace (1978), N. J. H. Dent (1984), and Henry Veatch (1985) are some of the more well-known names, but Alasdair MacIntyre was probably the most influential when he argued that the postenlightenment deviation from matters of character (virtues and vices) to matters of rule or law was a mistake that had lead to the contemporary dead end of moral philosophy (1981, chapter 5). The solution, he says, lies in reviving the notion of virtue, with its traditional emphasis on character, emotion, and the concept of human flourishing.

I take MacIntyre's attempt to revive virtue as undoubtedly a major step in the right direction, and so also his general criticism of the excessively high enlightenment standards of rationality as producing, on the one hand, an irrelevant academic search for demonstrable moral truths, and, on the other, a popular disbelief in the interpersonal nature of any moral truth at all. But in what is this new ethics of virtue to be grounded? Is there some modern way of reconstituting the union of nature and goodness that used to provide the foundation for the harmony of the soul?

The harmony of the soul was and still is a very commonplace, primitive faith that projects into human psychology the entire problem of evil and the justification of the ways of God to man. As already noted, in Plato, when this faith was first called upon to defend itself rationally, it relied on metaphysics and epistemology, on a moral interpretation of the principle of sufficient reason. A significant portion of early modern philosophy was metaphysical debate over these points wherein Leibnitz (chiefly) played the role of Plato. The rationalists lost, however, and the ground was cleared for a view of nature that was free of both rationalistic constraints and commonplace moral sentiment. We will not renew that metaphysical debate here.

It is interesting, however, now that the project of clearing away metaphysical and sentimental cobwebs has gone on for some three hundred years, to see that many elements of the old teleology have re-emerged, at least at a semipopular level, within the scientific culture. I do not refer to the many romantic, anti-intellectual reactions against the scientific deconstruction of emotion-laden, value-bearing nature, but rather to the peculiar way that the language of virtue and the presupposition of the harmony of the soul has entered the semiscientific language of medicine.

From Jung on there has been a consistent and coherent thread of thought within psychotherapy that has insisted that the idea of mental health is *also* a moral (and perhaps even a spiritual) ideal. Erich Fromm (1947, 1961), Karen Horney (1950), Carl Rogers (1961), Abraham Maslow (1962), Scott Peck (1980, 1983), and many other psychologists, both scholarly and popular, illustrate this particular line of thought, making it either their explicit thesis or their more or less explicit presupposition.

What is especially interesting is that this way of thinking has gone out from the world of books and by now resides comfortably in popular thought. For better or worse, the language of therapy has to a large extent taken over the language of virtue. Vices like gluttony and bullying are thought of as character disorders, and are commonly discussed through a semitechnical, quasimedical vocabulary. Gluttony becomes a compulsive eating disorder, with another disorder, anorexia, at the opposite extreme. Intemperance becomes symptomatic of the addictive personality. Excessively rigid temperaments are labeled "anal-sadistic," and excessively compliant ones are called "oral-masochistic." The astonishing fact is that at the very moment when relativism seems to dominate the popular philosophical discussion of ethics, real, concrete virtue-ethics has reappeared in popular language in the form of psychological medicine.

Of course, there is also much resistance to this blending of medical and moral language. Traditional Freudians still view morality with psychotherapeutic suspicion; behaviorists (with their crude, allegedly naturalistic reductionism) will have none of it; and positivists like Thomas Szasz do all that they can to purge the medical model from psychiatric theory and practice—all of which will be discussed thoroughly in the chapters that follow. Wherever the is/ought dichotomy is still felt to be unbridgeable, wherever science and values are still thought to belong to different universes of discourse and wherever positivism and existentialism are still the dominant philosophical moods, the synthesis of moral and medical language is resisted. But popular thought, which generally has little use for such subtle (perhaps oversubtle) distinctions, has short-circuited these reservations and run roughshod over the is/ought distinction just as it has always done. The result is that a semi-moral/semi-medical way of thinking about what the self ought to be has become dominant in many circles, and might well be said to constitute an original American contribution to popular ethics, the moral equivalent of jazz. What, we ask, is the significance of this development from the point of view of traditional philosophical naturalism?

If there is any value that can be described as natural, surely it is health, and health was always the fundamental idea of traditional naturalistic ethics. In it virtue is understood as the healthy condition of the human being. Indeed, the whole concept of flourishing is a medical concept that is indistinguishable from full, vibrant health.

Socrates: You admit the existence of bodies and souls?

Gorgias: Of course.

Socrates: And do you not consider that there is a healthy condition for each?

Gorgias: I do.

Socrates: And a condition of apparent but not real health?

Gorgias: Of course.

Socrates: [Then] to the pair, body and soul, there correspond two arts— that concerned with the soul I call the political [or ethical] art;... but the art that cares for the body comprises two parts, medicine and gymnastics.[30]

The same point is made more simply in the *Republic*.

> Virtue, thus, as it seems, would be a kind of health and beauty and good condition of the soul, and vice would be disease.[31]

Recall again the quotation from Aquinas.

> For it [original sin] is an inordinate disposition, arising from the destruction of the harmony which was essential to original justice, even as bodily sickness is an inordinate disposition of the body, by reason of the destruction of that equilibrium that is essential to health.[32]

Physical health is *prima facie* the one clear natural value—a norm given to us by the forces that made the body. It does not seem to be created by us; it does not seem to be culturally relative; and it is certainly specific enough to provide concrete, noncontroversial therapeutic goals. (See chapter 1 for an extensive discussion of all these points.) It is then only to be expected that if morality is understood within nature, it will be conceived as a kind of health of the soul.

From the positivistic point of view, this is merely an extension of the medical model to behavior, but such a view, if it is meant to have historical validity, incorrectly presupposes that behavior was first viewed nonmedically. Historically speaking, the overwhelming likelihood, to judge from Greek moral philosophy and the medical practices of traditional peoples, is that the medical "model" of the soul came first and that it took a great deal of philosophical effort to divorce health and goodness. In this regard it is of no small interest that the words *integrity* and *health* come from the same linguistic/conceptual root. "Integrity" comes from the roots "integer" and "integral." Etymologically "integrity" means to be "one," "not broken into pieces," "whole" "unbroken," "working." "Health" in turn comes from "hale," which in old English meant precisely the same thing—"whole," "not broken up."

It appears that one or another variant on the medical model held general sway until the scientific revolution accustomed people to the artifice of a nonteleological anthropology. From then on, of course, the idea of healthy behavior seemed metaphorical, but the fact is that Freud and his humanistic followers were step by halting, unintentional step, renewing in modern form the most ancient foundation of ethics.

This does not mean that medicine and morals can be run haphazardly together. The reunion of health and virtue depends on how literally it is still possible to understand the idea of a healthy soul. The possibility is clouded over by the usual sort of unclarity that surrounds the simplest notion of health, and the much greater obscurity that derives from all the loose and frequently naive talk about mental health. This all needs to be gone through and worked over with great care. That is definitional, or conceptual task of this book, and it is worked out in parts I and II. Therein the definition of physical health is explored, clarified, and then extended to the psyche, without, it is claimed, any importation of metaphorical meaning.

But one can go only so far through the clarification of definitions. One can show in a very general way what mental health is, defend its legitimacy, its naturalness, and explain how the offered definition relates to the common standards of mental health used in psychotherapeutic practice. But the case for a new harmony of the soul requires more than this. Once the meaning of health is understood, the question becomes whether or not its concrete embodiment in real human beings is congruent with the demands of ethics. To a large extent, this is an empirical question—the sort of thing steered away from by most philosophers. But the question must be asked. There is good reason to believe, given current scientific developments, that the harmony of the soul is no mere verbal construct (or at least, good reason to believe that this conclusion is more likely than its opposites).

In the functionalist rationalism of the theory of natural selection, for example, we find one seed of this new synthesis. Another lies in the emergence of ecology as a sort of functionalist bio-cosmology. So also for socio-biology, with its struggle to reinstate the natural as a respectable category for the study of human behavior; and for the anthropology that has corrected our prejudiced conception of "primitive," "archaic," or "natural" man. And Freudianism, in addition to reinstating the categories of health and illness in the study of human behavior, has also recreated the notion of a hidden structure of the soul (the unconscious), a structure that humanistic psychology has suggested might yet be a harmony.

Some of these theories are more controversial than others. Some are more properly "scientific," some are tinged with politics, some have been overworked, and some have been too enthusiastically promoted. Here too there is much to be sorted out, but even so, taken together they add up to a most remarkable possibility. As a result of these scientific developments, the pieces are now available for a synthesis that would resurrect the harmony of the soul and restore to nature a measure of its former moral authority. The possibility arises of basing virtue on a nonmetaphysical, nontheological, natural teleology, that would amount to a resurrection of moral psychology—a reconstitution of the harmony of the soul on the most modern of foundations.

Our question thus becomes, What if that which has been judged metaphysically the worst were really true? What if humankind is a purely natural thing with no transcendence beyond nature of any kind (neither Platonic/ontological nor phenomenological/ existential)? The goal is to show that even under these circumstances only the best would follow. To do this we must obviously give free reign to a ruthlessly naturalistic anthropology, referred to here as the reconstruction of human nature "within the naturalistic brackets." Essentially, this reconstruction assumes that the content and ⟨ dynamics of human emotion, including the unconscious and the familiar mechanisms of defense, are the controlling forces in human behavior, and that they are themselves controlled by the same forces that control all other structures of living things. Roughly speaking, anthropology within the naturalistic brackets will simply assume that human behavior is governed by thought, thought by emotion, emotion by psychodynamics, psychodynamics by protoplasm, protoplasm by DNA, and DNA by natural selection. On these assumptions, we hope to show that the harmony of the soul as elaborated by the tradition is a very real thing, or to show at least that the supposition of a hidden, moral human nature is more reasonable than any alternative.

Of course, there is no intention in this of proving the relevant scientific theories. That is done or not done by the sciences themselves. Here, we simply work with the current theories. Philosophy can, however, clarify operating assumptions, remove confusions, and point to connections across broad expanses. Philosophy cannot prove the theory of natural selection or its extension into sociobiology, but it can point out that sociobiology is the logical development of naturalism and that, at least in its broadest outlines, it must be assumed if we wish to see where the naturalistic assumptions really lead. Nor can philosophy settle the intra-disciplinary wrangles of psychology. But philosophy can help to clarify the idea of the unconscious and its relation to the philosophical notion of true desire. And philosphy can show how the predominance of unconscious motivation not only does not pose a threat to moral freedom and responsibility (as has been commonly thought), but in fact goes a long way toward helping us to understand how freedom can be achieved (see chapter 7). It can also show how the moral interpretation of the unconscious can make good sense of certain other troublesome ethical problems (conscience and the peculiar nature of ethical knowledge; also in chapter 7).

It goes without saying that this attempt to work within the naturalistic brackets is not intended as a strict deductive proof of the harmony of soul using the scientific theories as basic assumptions. The matter is far too complex for that. There are simply too many possibilities that cannot be decisively excluded, too many turns in the argument where choices have to be made without definitive evidence. The goal is, therefore, simply to tell a likely story—a rational story, which, while not really proving its conclusion, might still show the harmony of the soul to be a likely possibility. In this regard, the task is a bit like the one that Plato set for himself in the *Timaeus*. Our concern is not the cosmos but the psyche. The substance of our reasoning is empirical, not metaphysical. But the goal is to this extent the same—to show that a hidden harmony is a likely possibility. It would please me to show that it is the most likely of possibilities, but I would be content to show only that it is more likely than it has been respectable to think for many years. This would make the harmony of the soul a worthy object of rational faith—an open door through which a sane and sensible person might choose to walk.

I
The Body

1
Health
A Tattered Absolute

Philosophy's interest in health has been tied to its interest in teleological explanation. For Plato and Aristotle, health was an important topic because it presented the clearest possible example of fulfilled natural purpose. Even so, it was not systematically explored by them, and in modern philosophy it was essentially a non-topic. Until quite recently, it was discussed only as a side issue in the controversy about purpose and function in biology.

The theory of natural selection drove teleological explanation out of biology and toward psychology. Behaviorism meant to drive it out from there as well. The philosophical question concerned the role left for function in the explanation of biological activity. Could one have function without purpose? Only Skinner went so far as to deny the usefulness of function altogether. Nagel was more typical in *The Structure of Science* when he argued that there were natural functions in biological phenomena, but that they did not entail any special type of causality since they could be fully accounted for in nonteleological language.[1] At the other end of the spectrum were traditionalists like Hans Jonas and Teillard de Chardin who sought to maintain biology as a special field of teleological explanation.

Function, not health, was at the center of these debates. Health proper was not an issue until the seventies. At that time the tremendous increase in biomedical technology (birth control; genetic engineering, etc.) combined with the legalization of abortion and the rapid expansion of the mental-health movement combined to stretch the logical limits of medical practice as it had been understood, thereby prompting a crisis in its basic concepts. The philosophical discipline of medical ethics was born, and part of its discussions concerned the very meaning of health. The idea was then submitted to more intense philosophical scrutiny than it had ever received before.

Health care rests on a plethora of assumptions hardly ever brought to the surface. Today, perhaps because we live in an age that tries to question everything, these assumptions are challenged, and justifications are demanded.[2]

The aura of unquestioned naturalness that had supported the concept of health was comforting, but conservatives were alarmed at the powerful new techniques that were exercised in the name of health, and progressives wanted to be free of the limits imposed by a nonhumanistic, allegedly naturalistic outlook. The debate came down to two fundamental questions. The first was the inevitable argument over whether there really is some one thing called "health." The second was whether or not health, however defined, was a natural norm or a value more or less created by human desire and/or social forces. The conservatives, Kass (1975) and Boorse (1975), took proper function as the meaning of health and argued for the traditional point of view—that the functions are defined by nature and are more or less simply read off from it by an unbiased use of human intelligence. Kass's Aristoteleanism was unabashed.

> Health is a natural standard or norm—not a moral norm, not a 'value' as opposed to a fact, . . . , but a state of being that reveals itself in activity as a standard of bodily excellence or fitness, relative to each species and to some extent individuals, recognizable if not definable, and to some extent attainable. If you prefer a more simple formulation, I would say that health is "the well-working of the organism as a whole," or again, "an activity of the living body in accordance with its specific excellence."[3]

Englehard (1974, 1976) and Margolis (1966, 1976) took the alternative view. First, Englehardt tried to loosen the connection between disease and function by claiming that "there is not one single set of criteria for calling something an illness."[4] Then, he attacked the naturalness of natural function, arguing that functions are environmentally relative. He concludes:

> Our ideologies and expectations about the world move us to select certain states as illnesses because of our judgement as to what is dysfunctional or a deformity and to select certain causal sequences . . . as being of interest to us because they are bound to groups of phenomena we identify as illnesses. Although there is a stark reality, it has significance for us only through our own value judgement, in particular through our social values. Through these we construct a world of communal action and reaction . . . including the arts and sciences of medicine.[5]

Margolis reached a somewhat less relativistic conclusion by a slightly different route. He granted that the notion of function is primary for the understanding of health and disease.

> A diseased state, on any plausible theory whatsoever, is . . . defective or deranged with respect to some condition of healthy functioning, . . . or suitably related to such a state even if there is no complaint.[6]

The problem concerned the way functions are assigned.

> The ascription of "natural functions" to human persons cannot possibly be provided in the context of psychiatry in a way that ignores the culturally prepared goals of human societies. And if the functioning of the human animal . . . [physical health] may be fairly said to be inseparable from the functioning of the human person [mental health], and if, natural norms are not simply straightforwardly discovered, then we need to provide a rather different rationale for the ascription of functions from what has so far been sketched.[7]

He goes on to recommend that we view medicine as

> ideology restricted by our minimal requirements of the functional integrity of the body and mind.[8]

"Minimal" is the key word here. It would seem to render the notion of natural function irrelevant to all controversial questions. As soon as the matter becomes interesting, ideology (and politics) would presumably rule supreme.

Margolis and Englehardt were hardly alone in deconstructing the naturalness of natural functions. The debate took place in what was essentially still the sixties, and many others, from Foucault to Laing and Szasz, announced similar views, although with far less care.[9] In general, all the old arguments that had been used against objective values and objective truth were now aimed at health. Sedgewick put the matter in its bluntest form.

> All departments of nature below the level of mankind are exempt both from disease and from treatment until man intervenes with his own human classifications. . . . The blight that strikes at corn or potatoes is a *human invention* for if man wished to cultivate parasites (rather than potatoes or corn) there would be no 'blight', but simply the necessary foddering of the parasite crop.[10]

The times were extremely anti-authoritarian, and the privileged, natural status of the idea of health seemed to many just one more tool with which a repressive society beat its nonconforming members into shape.

The theme was even a part of the popular movie *One Flew over the Cuckoo's Nest*.

The basic questions remain the same. To deal with the problems set before us, we need a definition of health; that decided, we must then ask whether health is determined by natural or social forces. The first of these questions inevitably boils down to understanding the relation between biological function and the other criteria of health—normal structure and painlessness or lack of discomfort.[11] And since the meaning of health, like so many things, is revealed best by its absence, and since so much medical practice proceeds in this negative way, it is easier to get at it indirectly, through illness and disease.[12]

Consider a hand that cannot grasp things—a hand that is twisted, bent, or painful. In one way or another, the entwining of these three criteria (dysfunctionality, deviant structure, and pain) constitute the meaning of illness. The first two claim to represent objective fact; the third at first presents itself as pure subjectivity. Their interrelations are complex, and each is quite properly taken as an index of illness in day-to-day medical practice. Traditionally, however, dysfunctionality has been assumed primary. With what justification?

Linguistic analysis alone leads to this conclusion (Margolis 1976: 241). We are committed, however, to working within the naturalizing brackets, and this gives us something more to work with. Within the brackets, all things are shaped solely by the laws of nature, and for organic beings the relevant laws comprise the theories of evolution and natural selection. We assume then that the body is a kind of organic clay, entirely molded by evolutionary pressures. Consequently, we assume, with certain qualifications, that the body's details are as they are because of some direct or indirect contribution they make to the survival of the species. We assume no purpose in nature, no mind behind the operation of diffusion, mutation, variation, and selection. We may assume that nature is ultimately determined or we can allow for randomness. It makes no difference. Still the body evolves as if it were designed for life and reproduction.

This is the minimal order that structures organic nature, and on this "as if" teleology hangs the priority of function. It is tempting to conceive this "as if" teleology very simply—to imagine that each detail of bodily structure is what it is because of a certain well-defined role it plays in the reproduction of the species. This role is then understood to be its function, and the body is understood as a system of such functions, each related to life and reproduction as means to ends. Eating would be for the sake of living; grasping things would be for eating them; the hand would be for grasping, and so on.

This picture is not wrong; it is merely oversimple. The rough idea of an "as if" teleology simply has to be correct if the theory of natural selection means anything at all, but the order it gives rise to is imperfect for several reasons:

1. An organ may have more than one function. Consider, for example, all the things done by the hand besides grasping (Wright 1973: 141).

2. Because a single genotype can have multiple phenotypical effects (pleiotropism), not all of which need be functional, a physiological structure may be selected without its making any direct contribution to life or reproduction (or even if it is in one respect dysfunctional) simply because it is genetically linked with another organ that makes a contribution significantly greater than any burden imposed by the first. For example, the genotype that gives rise to sickle-cell anemia also confers resistance to malaria (Lewontin 1984: 262).

3. Genetic drift (the isolation of eccentric breeding populations) occasionally allows less functional or even dysfunctional elements to become generalized within a limited sphere for a limited time (Simpson 1958: 15; Lewontin 1984: 263; Gajdusek 1964: 356).

4. The level of selection (DNA molecule, individual, family, or tribe) is not always clear, and so it is not always clear whose survival serves as the ultimate "as if" end (Lewontin, 1970).

5. Selection can operate only relative to a given environment. Consequently, environmental changes confuse the issue of what is to count as an organ's proper function. In Africa, protection from malaria is much more important than in North America. What then is health for Americans whose blood cells are adapted to an African environment?

The sum total of these considerations complicates the picture significantly, but only by making it harder to discern exactly what an organ's natural functions are, and by allowing some (presumably minor) structures to arise for which there may be no function. This does not invalidate the basic primacy of function. Structure arises, to be sure, without regard to function, and in that sense function follows form. But a structure remains because of (almost) nothing but its function or its linkage to a function. In the end, normal structure is still almost always derived from normal functioning, and normal functioning is still almost always a means to the supreme function—the life and reproduction of some molecule, individual, group, or species in the appropriate environment. To understand, as best we can, the detailed working out of these matters is to understand, as best we can, the health of any species. That the matter is complicated and uncertain should not be allowed to obscure the basic primacy of function that is vouchsafed by the naturalistic brackets.

It is worth noting here that while the "as if" teleology is ruthlessly mundane vis-à-vis the goal of reproduction, this need not be discouraging to those with higher aspirations for human physiology. Function need not be narrowly interpreted. Play, for example, obviously makes an indirect contribution to survival and reproduction, but this does not mean that in play one must be thinking about these things. In fact, the more one thinks about them, the less one is playing. One plays for its own sake, and the reproductive benefit just happens somewhere down the line. Because of complex genetic linkages in an individual, and because of the division of labor (function) in social life, even celibacy and homosexuality can (and in some cases probably do) have roles to play in relation to reproduction.[13] Certainly reason, and probably art and religion, while pursued for their own sakes by some, nevertheless contribute to DNA's hunger for reproduction. In this regard they are no different from sex itself, which, while generally and properly pursued as an end in itself, a form of play, nevertheless admirably serves the goals of nature.[14]

From within the naturalizing brackets, life is for the sake of reproduction, but this does not mean that the connection to reproduction of every bodily organ is univocal, direct, universal, or that the activity must have that functional meaning for the consciousness that engages in it. Nevertheless, the relationship to reproduction remains decisive. A healthy organ is still one that does the thing(s) it has been genetically "designed" to do.

What then is the relation of normal structure to normal functioning? Normal structure is selected and maintained by virtue of its close causal connection to normal functioning. Since organic forms are extremely complex and took a great deal of time to evolve, it is unlikely that structural novelties will enhance function. Deviation from the structural norm is thus an excellent indicator of illness, and that presumably is why the bulk of medical practice proceeds by structural comparison. Swellings, bruises, lesions, breaks, gaps, discolorations, and a nearly infinite number of structural deviations constitute the workaday criteria for disease identification. But the same argument shows that structural deviation is not identical to illness. If no functional impairment came from the fat within the arteries, arterial sclerosis would not be an illness but merely a deviant arterial lifestyle. It is an illness *because* the flow of blood is impaired and because this flow is the presumed function of the artery.

To rule all deviation unhealthy would be to commit an act of medical bigotry. When even a novel deviation is fully functional, it is healthy, and when a deviation has been subjected to evolutionary pressures for a long period of time, it is likely to be functional. Peg teeth among Eskimos, for example, or enlarged lungs among Peruvian Indians constitute such functional adaptations of structure to a specific environment. They are merely new kinds of functionality, not dysfunctionality.

This applies also to the deviations within a breeding population as well as deviations of one population from another. If structural variations within the population correspond to a division of labor that makes the group as a whole more likely to survive, and if the variations are ancient, they are most probably alternative versions of health. Consider, for example, the structural differences by gender in every species, and the differences between the "castes" of bees. There is no reason in principle why such a division of labor might not extend to still smaller groups (groups defined by left-handedness, for example, or variations in size and musculature). But in general, only those deviations that have been selected over a long period of time have much chance of being part of an alternative version of health.

Decisions of this kind should be made solely on grounds of the variation's functionality, with appropriate allowance made for the legitimate possibility of divergent healths. Health is not a mere average physiological condition. But neither should these decisions be made by an equally mechanical toleration of everything. Only a worked out functional hermeneutic of the body as a whole made up of parts and as a part within a social whole can make the appropriate detailed determinations.[15]

Pain is the other criterion of illness, and it is certainly our most immediate and pressing awareness of it. A child who breaks his arm is not primarily aware of its dysfunctionality. What he knows is his pain. His tears are a demand for pain relief, and not, at first, a plea for the restoration of function. But he is in pain because he is ill, not ill because he is in pain.

There are no illnesses that do not normally cause some kind of pain (or at least discomfort or excessive effort), and there is almost no bodily pain that does not indicate some kind of illness. This happy correlation of pain and illness has long been noted,[16] and its evolutionary explanation is obvious—were dysfunctionality generally pleasant or normal function painful, the survival potential of the species would be significantly reduced. The painfulness of dysfunctionality is a great motivator towards health, even if, all things considered, one should not care to live or reproduce.

Even this correlation is not perfect, however. Childbirth, which is clearly functional and healthy, is painful, and some illnesses bring with them certain short-term pleasures (delusions of luxury in a man dying of thirst, for example). These (rare) exceptions are important, because they prevent us from defining health through the simple subjectivity of pleasure and pain. A large, functional and (to some people) unattractive nose is not unhealthy, even if it does cause a certain kind of discomfort. And if someone were painlessly dying we would not think him healthy, even though we might admire his tranquility. In those rare cases where we must define health *either* through function *or* painlessness, as in childbirth, we unhesitatingly choose function. Painlessness is our most immediate and untutored criterion of health, but the two are not identical.

Pain and structure have evolved with function to be the most reliable imaginable symptoms of illness. In practice, it is essential to use them as indices of illness, and these correlations constitute excellent rules of thumb. But still they are only rules of thumb. Within the naturalistic assumption there can be no doubt that function is the lead element—the core meaning of health and illness.

This leaves us with the question of the role of ideology and social needs in the specification of functions. Some functions seem straightforward and utterly uncontroversial—for example, the grasping of the hand— but even here the matter is complicated by the fact that the hand is also for the perception of texture, for caressing, for hitting, for molding, and for many other things, including waving goodbye. Do social values decide which function is most determinative of health? Further, there are organs of which we do not yet know the function, and those about which we have made mistakes. The heart was once considered the seat of thought. Its true function was not understood until the circulation of the blood through the capillary system was accepted. Functions, as previously explained, have to be discovered by complex empirical reasoning that needs to take into account not only all that is known at the time about the interrelations of the organs within the bodily ecology, but also the possibilities of group variation and of a physiological division of labor within groups. Mistakes, sometimes politically or morally motivated, are as possible here as they are in any other matter. But does this mean that social needs can really determine the very meaning of health?

None of these points entails the conclusion that functions are not natural, that they are subject to relatively ephemeral social needs or that they are determinable by mere ideology. It follows only that functions are not always easily known, that many are not known, and that some may never be known. But within the limits of empirical fallibility our mistakes are, in principle, correctable, and where they are not *de facto* correctable, we can still know enough to be aware of our ignorance. That we blunder does not show that health is socially constructed in any important sense of those words. To the contrary, that we sometimes recognize our errors suggests that a trans-cultural knowledge of controversial bodily functions is a very real possibility.

After the 18th century, masturbation was often held to be a disease, and in the prewar South there was the putative disease of drapetomania that caused slaves to run away from their owners.[17] Without a doubt, social values influenced the "discovery" of these "diseases," but it does not follow from this that they were real diseases.

Masturbation is presumably not an illness, but the fact is that it was not for purely moral reasons that this error was made to begin with. There were crude, nonmoral, mistaken biological reasons for it. It all depends on what one takes the function of the sex organs to be. If it is reproduction, then *prima facie* masturbation seems dysfunctional (as does celibacy). Combine this crude functionalism with a prudish mentality, and you get a ready acceptance of the alleged disease of masturbation. But there is a nonmoral, nonpolitical, nonphilosophical reason for the wrongness of this conclusion.

That the sex organs are "for" reproduction does not mean that their proper functioning must always result in reproduction or that they might not have other functions too. Sex organs are also presumably "for" elimination and "for" creating certain kinds of interpersonal bonding.[18] Although masturbation does not fulfill any of those other purposes, neither does it significantly hinder them (contrary to what was once thought). It is not even remotely dysfunctional, and therefore it is not an illness.

In the case of drapetomania, the slaveowner's viewpoint is plausible only if the tendency for slaves to run away is dysfunctional, and that, in turn, is possible only if it were the natural function of the black population to be the slaves of whites. And although racist theories have frequently said such things, there is simply no empirical evidence to back it up. From the cold, morally indifferent viewpoint of natural section, the enslavement of one race to another could even possibly create a natural function only if the races had evolved together (and not just coexisted) over a very long period of time in a community in which the one was almost invariably the slave of the other. As a matter of historical fact this simply did not happen in the American South (or anywhere else, for that matter, although the caste system of India probably comes the closest). Slavery was forced on African blacks in spite of their natural tendency to take perfectly good care of themselves in their customary environment, and it did not last long enough and was not systematically selective enough to effect a significant genetic change in the population.

We are disposed towards these conclusions by moral considerations, but they are really based on matters of relatively simple fact, interpreted through nothing more than the theory of natural selection. This is not ideology. Although one can say that there was a social need in the South for docility as the natural function of blacks, that need did not create a true health function. Natural function and social function are simply not the same thing.

Or consider the even clearer case of the Chinese men who bound and thereby crippled the feet of their women as a sort of sexual ornamentation. If the people of this culture were to claim that the function of a woman's foot was not to run or walk but to please the male sense of domination, can we really say, quite apart from aesthetics and morality, that their judgement was as correct as ours? Obviously there are good reasons for believing that the function of a woman's foot is walking rather than hobbling, reasons that are entirely independent of any moral conception of the equality of the sexes.

A large part of the basic rationale behind these conclusions was made clear by Larry Wright in his 1973 article "Functions." He distinguished between the function of something and "other things that it does which are not its function" (e.g. rapid communication in the case of a telephone vs. its taking up space on the desk, disturbing one at night, etc.; or, the heart's pumping blood vs. its production of a thumping noise or making wiggly lines on electrocardiograms). Wright notes correctly that it is part of the meaning of "function" that in order to call Y the function of X, we have to believe that "X is there because it does Y" (Wright 1973, p. 157). This serves neatly to distinguish functions from other things that the object can accidentally do or might be good for. The foot "is there" because it enables locomotion, not because it provides gainful employment for shoemakers. *A fortiori* it distinguishes functions from accidents that are actually dysfunctional, like foot-binding.

But one might pursue the matter further. How do we know that locomotion is the reason for the foot's being there? Might not Chinese men legitimately project their desire onto the universe and claim that women's feet are there because they can be so delightfully bound and thus give pleasure to men? Might not they even appeal to the arguments above and claim that this is a natural division of labor between men and women? This is an empirical question. Again, the answer comes through the theory of natural selection regardless of moral or political considerations. While it is not impossible that a function that aids the survival of the individual (walking, running) could be selected against in order to promote the reproductive good of the species (attracting male suitors by appearing weak and non-threatening), it is not plausible to think so in this case since: (1) the walking function of the foot is older than the entire mammalian order, while the binding custom is a recent, easily eliminated overlay that was confined to certain classes in certain parts of China; and (2) the social group in general would be far less able to survive if half its members make this rather great sacrifice in mobility merely to attract the same men who would have had to come their way in any case. If the foot grew of itself into the crippled shape, if the custom were spread across all those with a genetic heritage similar to the Chinese, or if the sacrifice of mobility were, all things considered, a more plausibly successful reproductive strategy, then the possibility would be worth thinking about. But as it is, it is interesting only as an extreme-case philosophical example.

More generally put, the recognition in biology that a certain organ "is there because it does Y" depends on various factors having to do with the details of evolutionary theory. In addition to those already mentioned, we must list also the appropriateness of the structural details of the organ in relation to its alleged function. One wants as many as possible of its parts to have a clear role to play in relation to the alleged function without useless redundancy.

Given this criterion alone, no neutral observer familiar with even the grosser details of the foot's structure—the multitude of muscles and bones all apparently designed to move in just such a way, to support just such a kind of weight, to bear up under just these conditions and so poorly under others, and familiar also with the utter absence of a single structural detail that makes the foot especially suitable for crippling (a structural weakness that collapses at just about puberty, for example)—no one familiar with all this can be brought to believe that the foot's natural function is to make a woman appear attractive by manifesting her weak, halting, feeble, crippled gait. Of course the feet of women can be used that way, just as watches can be used for target practice and nails can be hammered with a screwdriver, but there is nothing in the internal structure of the foot, the watch, or the screwdriver that makes them especially suitable for these purposes. Thus, these are seen as acts of violence—assaults on the integrity of the functional unit—and they are recognizable as such regardless of our moral predispositions.

For the body, the theory of natural selection is the essential etiological presupposition for the assignment of functions, and it is applied to specifics largely through a physiological/functionalistic study of the relationships of parts to wholes. It is not that we merely see that grasping is a thing the hand factually does. If the assignment of function were crudely empirical in this way, it would be relative to current usage. Factually, the hand also waves goodbye; factually, the foot is bound. But the degree of adaptation of the parts to the socially constructed functions is very low compared to their adaption to grasping and walking, and so, all else being equal, that is their natural function.[19] In problem cases one just keeps on adjusting the interpretation of the parts to the interpretation of the wholes, of the wholes to the parts, and of those wholes to still larger wholes until one comes up with an explanation that harmonizes everything with everything. By definition, that is truth in matters of this sort. Obviously, it is an ideal we work towards, not a fact that we possess.

This is the hermeneutic of the body, and its working out is the business of biology, at least so far as biology is the ground of medicine. The theory of natural selection is what anchors the entire process. It is the guiding assumption that gives sense and direction to more concrete work. And this of course, is precisely the thing we accept when we agree to work within the naturalizing brackets.

Physical health is thus a natural value. It is given to us, and not in any important sense created by us. In general, it is the same for all people, but there are some differences between groups and some variations within groups. At whatever level we conceive it to operate—species, group, or individual—it is a given. We conform to it or we deviate from it, but we do not make it what we wish it to be. Thus, though it is not timeless, though we are never sure of it, and though we may be quite ignorant of certain specifics, health has some of the characteristics of what gets called an "absolute."

This is the essential truth of the matter, but it ignores a complicating factor—that all evolution (and, therefore, all right-functioning) is relative to its environment. Once the earth's atmosphere had no oxygen but consisted of a poisonous (to us) mix of gases. Certain species of life thrived in this primitive atmosphere. For them, oxygen was poisonous. When the atmosphere changed, they were forced either to adapt or die. For creatures in such a shifting environment, real health is impossible. They are simply caught between one adaptation and another—a period of adjustment, as it were, fish out of water. For them, it is a question of doing the best they can.

In such transition periods it is impossible to tell a priori what course of action would be most conducive to health values. There are always two possibilities. The organism can alter itself in order to better fit the new circumstances, or it can alter the circumstances so that doing the things it was "designed" to do will continue to be functional.

When a coal miner refuses to work on the grounds that air saturated with carbon dust makes him ill, or when he insists on making the new environment more like the old (better ventilation), he chooses to change his environment. If he undertakes breathing exercises, diet, or medication as a way of coping, then he opts for altering himself. In this case it is clear enough that it would be best to find another line of work. Doing so returns him to the original environment, and only in that environment is real health possible. But if such a return is out of the question, the decision can be reached only by a cost-benefit analysis in which the total health gain (all things considered) is weighed against the total health cost. There are no precise rules for making such calculations, and in many cases the relevant medical knowledge simply does not exist. In transition periods, it is simply not clear what health requires.

True health thus presupposes a relatively stable environmental background against which there has been ongoing evolution for many thousands of years. Different natural environments, if they remain stable for a given population for a long enough time, will produce different meanings of physical health for different human groups. These differences are just as natural and just as independent of human will as any other assignment of function by natural selection. They are relative, but to the environment, not to our wishes or conventions. Also, it must be said, the differences are very small compared to what is common. It may be healthy for Eskimos in the arctic to have a somewhat lower body temperature, or for Peruvian Indians to have somewhat larger lungs. But for all of us, the heart pumps blood, the lungs transfer oxygen, the brain thinks and the feet get us from one place to another.

There is a further sort of relativity within the naturalizing assumptions. The natural environment is only part of the background against which human evolution has occurred. We are social animals. Without social life there would be no language, no education, no transfer of technical achievement from one generation to another, and no extensive cooperative activity. Clearly social life is as important to the survival of the human species as are fins to a fish or claws to a lion. Since we survive by intelligence, language and the transfer of knowledge from one generation to the next, and since these are thoroughly social activities, it is clear that sociality is our greatest tool in the effort to survive. Socially, we are the dominant species; as individuals, we are the weakest—naked, defenseless, ignorant—lacking even the instinctive wisdom of animals.

This means that wherever there are human beings there is society. Consequently society must be part of the background against which evolution occurred. If ever there were unsocial creatures that one might want to call "human," we have for so long lived socially and our success as a species is so dependent on society that we must be as adapted to it as is a turtle to its shell (indeed, society *is* our shell). We have lived in some primitive form of it for at least 1.5 million years. We have lived in social forms complex enough to support religion and the transmission of medical knowledge for at least 60,000 years.[20] In some stretched sense of the word, we may have once "created" society, but by now society has created us as much as has the natural environment itself. The adaptation to society need not be perfect, but it has most certainly occurred.

Health then is relative to those social structures *that have been stable enough to allow natural selection to work in a single direction over a very long period of time.* From this it follows that the only specific form of social organization to which we are biologically adapted is that of the hunter-gatherer society, the only social form that existed until the invention of agriculture some 12,000 years ago. More or less human hunter-gatherer societies existed for at least 1.5 million years before that, and it was obviously against that primitive social background that the human body evolved and to which it is adapted. All other specific socio-economic and/or political forms (from agriculture to urban life, from feudalism to modern technical industrialism) are newcomers that have arrived too late and (in some cases) departed too soon to make a real change in the definition of health (Farb 1978: 89).

Whenever urban, industrial, capitalist, socialist, or (for that matter) feudal or agrarian society makes demands on us to which we are not adapted, we are caught in the fish-out-of-water syndrome, and in many cases it is simply not clear what health requires. One ought not make too much of this. It *does* mean (again) that we do not always know what health is, and it *does* mean that our adaption is (partly) relative to the social environment. The critical point, however, is to understand that this does not make it relative to whatever social form we happen to find ourselves in. The coal miner, for example, is not a person who would be adapted to breathing clean air if he were born into a hunter-gatherer society or dirty air in an industrial society. The environment against which evolution has occurred for a very, very long time is normative. The newcomers are just problems to be dealt with as best we can.

Whenever therefore questions about the definition of health require for their solution an understanding of social structure, it is not to our own society that we ought to look, but to those of hunter-gatherers. The muscles of men's legs and their general physical structures are adaptations for the purpose (among others) of running down animals. If then one asks how much ability to run is required of us by health, the answer is a great deal more than urban people have any clear use for (which is why running is such a good exercise). The answer to the question of how much meat is healthy to eat is not found by taking an average of contemporary eating styles. In all probability we are adapted to eat about as much meat as hunter-gatherers did. While there is much variation on this matter, the bottom line is that they ate a great deal less meat than we do—not enough less to satisfy vegetarians, but enough to help explain why our diet causes so much illness.[21]

The specific forms of social life change quickly, but evolution is slow, rooted in millions of years of the distant past. It is traditional, and in this sense conservative and inherently nostalgic. The meaning of bodily health changes very little over vast periods of time. This is often frustrating to progressives who for moral or technical reasons might like to see rapid change. Nonetheless, it seems clearly to be so, and we can expect constant friction between progressives (of the left or right), who take their point of reference from the present, and health values that must inevitably be rooted in the past.

In the end all this means that given the naturalizing assumptions, the body has a functional integrity that is not to be dealt with lightly. Its health is not an absolute in the true sense of that word—a value known for certain and valid for all individuals at all times and places. Health is certainly not a Platonic ideal. It is uncertain, conditioned, and subject to a degree of variation from group to group and individual to individual. Further, in its purest form it can exist only in the original environment and so must be adapted in messy ways to current circumstances. But just as the naturalistic brackets give us an "as if" teleology, so they may be said to give health as a messy sort of "as if" absolute. Despite the element of relativity and uncertainty, within any practically usable time period the meaning of health is still something given, unalterable, more or less knowable, and pretty much the same for all. It is subject to ancient social needs, but not to those of the moment. It is a tattered, empirical ideal, but it is autonomous and natural. It is a reality that simply has to be recognized by our moral, political, and economic agendas.

II
The Soul

2
Behavior

The roots of the word *psychiatry* mean the healing of the soul. If this is a metaphor, it is certainly a rich one—rich enough to generate a wide variety of hopes and fears. We use the word here in its etymological sense, to be synonymous with "clinical psychology" or "mental-health therapy in general," despite the fact that in current medical usage it has a much narrower significance. Given the word's conceptual history, it is no wonder that there is confusion over psychiatry's goals.

That psychiatry has won a respectable place in the medical establishment does not mitigate the confusion about the meaning of mental health. In fact, it was probably the general acceptance of the mental-health movement that allowed the debate about its goals to begin in earnest. During its infancy, when psychoanalysis was considered an exotic European import and was the most visible form of mental-health therapy, psychiatry had a special need to dissociate itself from philosophy, religion, and morality. Because it sought recognition from a skeptical medical establishment, it took pains to appear as scientific and narrowly medical as possible.[1] An eccentric petitioner in the age of positivism could hardly afford an internal debate about its own ends—especially when those ends inevitably overlapped with traditional moral, political, and religious concern. It is understandable that the tendency was to say little about mental health in general and to concentrate instead on the most blatant cases of specific illnesses.

But the question about the meaning of mental health was too obvious and too important to go long unasked. As the controlling ideal of the mental-health establishment, it is, in fact, reshaping our moral thought as surely as if it had led a successful revolution. Indeed, there has been a revolution. It has already been noted how the language of medicine has partly dis-

41

placed the language of morality. Matters of character—fastidiousness, promiscuity, gluttony, addiction, ambition, etc.—which used to be thought of as moral, are now routinely treated as medical problems. Fastidiousness, for example, is now treated as a mild form of compulsive behavior, or promiscuity as a symptom of low self-esteem. This is not merely a change of vocabulary. Along with it has come a redrawing of the normative lines. What a previous generation saw as proper ambition is now a compulsion. What was once considered moral integrity, is now viewed as a pathological judgementality. The so-called sexual revolution was only the cutting edge of this general shift of values that might more properly be called the "therapeutic revolution."

With this extension of therapy into "normal" living, it was inevitable that the unasked questions about therapy's goals should come to the surface. By appeal to what standard does the therapist judge that so much attention to cleanliness is normal, and beyond that lies neurosis? How much ambition makes a workaholic? Where does flexibility end and craven wimpyness begin? Whatever the standard is by which such matters are measured, therein lies the real working meaning of mental health.

The problem is clearly illustrated if we consider the definitions given for various illnesses in the *Diagnostic and Statistical Manual of Mental Disorders III*, the standard reference work in pathology for the mental-health field. Almost invariably these definitions include undefined words such as "unreasonable," "excessive," and "inappropriate." Thus a symptom of the dependent personality disorder is said to be "the inability to make everyday decisions without an excessive amount of advice or reassurance from others."[2] The obsessive-compulsive personality disorder is characterized by "adherence to . . . overly strict and often unattainable standards,"[3] and the passive-aggressive type "unreasonably criticizes or scorns people in positions of authority."[4] In such definitions everything depends on how "excessive" and "unreasonable" are defined, and obviously there must be some positive behavioral ideal in the mind of the therapist who applies them or she could not give them any useful meaning. But what is that ideal?

If one searches the literature of psychiatry for an answer to this question, one finds a bewildering array of definitions of mental health that at first glance seem so vague and/or mutually contradictory that it is easy to conclude that there really is no commonly accepted standard. We pass over as not helpful the notion of mental health as the mere absence of pathological symptoms (Jahoda 1958: 10) and arrive at a profusion of positive definitions that is initially quite numbing. We find definitions that range from the staid "adjustment" (Menninger 1947) and/or "normality or nondeviant behavior" (Scheff 1966) to the exuberance of "spontaneity" and/or "freedom" (Rogers 1951), while passing through such alternatives as "rational living" and/or "mastery of the environment"; "the ability to love and work" (Freud and others. See Jahoda 1950: 55–6); freedom from guilt" and/or "the absence of intra-psychic conflict" and/or "the replacement of id-functions by ego-functions" (Freud);[5] "integration of the parts of the self" (Jung); "happiness" and/or "satisfaction" (Boehm 1955); "flexibility" (Kubie 1954) and/or "the possession of a democratic character structure" (Adorno 1950); "being one's true self" (Horney 1950); "the realization of one's full potential" (Maslow 1968); "the possession of a productive character" (Fromm 1947); and many others.[6]

This seemingly wild profusion of ideals is more than a little distressing to those who desire conceptual clarity at the foundations and tends to confirm the suspicion that the whole business of mental health is a metaphor gone wild. We ought to bear in mind, however, that these definitions were not meant to be philosophically precise formulations, but rough guides to practice. Consider how we might react to the following definitions of physical health if they had been collected from a variety of theorists and practitioners: "the body's doing what it is supposed to do," "the harmonious interworkings of the different bodily organs," "a body that can live an reproduce itself," " a good strong heart," " a body that fits into its overall ecological niche," "painlessness," "a vigorous constitution," "a body that can perform the tasks required of it by society," "a body in homeostasis," "a structural ideal," "a functional ideal," etc., etc. This wealth of formulations would not bother us because we are fairly sure it comes merely from the overemphasis of one aspect or another of a more or less common goal. The situation may be no worse for mental health, and if the previous chapter succeeded in harmonizing a variety of superficially contradictory explication of physical health, there is reason to hope the same can be done for the health of the soul. In the chapters that follow an overall view of mental health will be developed within which most of these definitions find a fair and appropriate place.

Needless to say, however, there are those who have drawn the negative conclusion. Szasz (1961) led the way by in declaring that mental health is simply not the true business of psychiatry. It is, he claimed, a mere metaphor—the medical model a more or less transparent disguise in which moral judgement illicitly inserted itself into a non-medical, interpersonal arena. Many, many others have followed him in this, most notably Foucault (1965), though Foucault's criticism is really directed more against the political abuse of the medical model than against the model itself. These thinkers have had considerable influence on the way the mental-health movement now thinks about itself, and it simply must be admitted that the ensuing degree of disagreement simply does not exist in the non-psychiatric medical community.

Is it the metaphorical character of mental health that is responsible for this, or are there other explanations? The confusion could also stem from unclarity of language, from the failure to think thoroughly enough about the literal meaning of health and its relation to the person, from the lack of a unifying theory of the person, from the intrusion of moral and/or political and/or metaphysical bias into medicine, or as is almost surely the case, from all of these at once.[7]

We proceed as before, asking first what mental health would be if there is such a thing, and then whether, within the assumptions of the naturalistic brackets, it really does exist, and, if so, how specific we can be about its nature. The first point is essentially a matter of shifting the general conclusions of the previous chapter from the body to whatever it is that is called "mental" in the phrase "mental health." The second question asks whether evolutionary pressures structure the mental subject matter in a way analogous enough to the physical to create something worth calling "mental health."

THE GENERAL MEANING OF MENTAL HEALTH

We know what physical health is. It is the right functioning of the bodily organs as that is understood through the theories of evolution and natural selection, with all due allowance made for the possibility of group and individual variation and the disparity between the original and current social environment. This amounts to a tattered harmony of organic functions. Now we want to know what mental health is. Surely the most straightforward way to answer the question is simply to shift the general form of this definition from the physical to the mental, whatever that might be. Mental health, if there is such a thing, must then be a tattered harmony of mental functions (Boorse 1976: 63, Flew 1973). The question then reduces itself to the issue of what is meant by "mental."

To answer this we do not need a logically or philosophically correct explanation of the difference between the physical and the mental. That would land us immediately in matters too great to disentangle. All that is really needed is an analysis of the mental-health subject matter that will roughly identify the kinds of things actually dealt with by psychiatry. More ultimate questions about the relation between the mental and the physical can simply be set aside, and if this leaves it unclear where exactly to draw the line between mind and body, that is acceptable so long as the conceptual unclarity reflects the vagaries of actual psychiatric practice.

What is dealt with by actual psychotherapeutic practice seems to be identified by the interweaving of two criterial elements, one of them behavioral and the other motivational. Of these two, the behavioral is the most tangible and in *some* respects the more important.

Mental-health therapy obviously deals with human behavior, and in the name of simplicity it is tempting to hope, following philosophical behaviorism, that the traditional distinction between the physical and the mental would turn out to correspond to a distinction between two types of behavior—a shift from the "behavior" or activity of specific bodily organs or body parts to the behavior of the human organism as a whole, i.e., to the behavior of persons. This seems to be what was suggested by Margolis in the passage previously quoted, and its attractiveness is understandable. The sexual organs, for example, have certain very limited functions that are required of them by physical health, but it is not these organs that fall into and out of love, get married, divorced, have children, and treat them well or poorly. The sex organs do not even make love. Whole persons do these things, and it is the entire complex of such generalized human behavior that is dealt with by psychiatry. At the same time, failures of specific body parts (dysfunctions of the liver, heart or reproductive system, for example) are usually treated as ordinary physical illness.

Unfortunately, the matter is not so simple. In some rough way this emphasis on the generalized behavior of the person as the defining quality of the mental has got to be correct, because what makes this generalized behavior the behavior of a person, as opposed to the behavior of an animal, is precisely that it is under the influence of whatever it is that we mean by "mind." By "persons," in other words, we may mean something like "creatures with minds," so that the definition of "mental" as "the general behavior of persons" probably begs the most important question.

But whatever the logical virtues of the definition, it does not take account of an important distinction that actually exists in psychiatric usage. It is true that the generalized behavior of persons is usually considered the subject matter of mental-health therapy and that the "behavior" of specific body parts is usually referred to as physical medicine. But some generalized behavioral abnormalities are assumed to be caused by electrochemical processes not essentially dissimilar to the causes of physical illness, while others are thought (by some at least) to be caused by a peculiar configuration of human motivations. In actual practice, the etiological question is important for the matter of classification, and it intersects with the purely behavioral criterion in crucial ways. If, for example, the nonfunctionality of even a very specific body part is thought to be rooted in the emotions rather than in some physical cause, the matter is classified by all as a mental-health problem—a psychosomatic problem, as we say. At the same time, even the most general pattern of abnormal human behavior, if it is thought to be caused by physical processes not essentially different from the causes of physical illness, is classified by some psychiatrists as a physical illness and by others as mental (Boorse 1976: 67).

What seems indicated is that the mental-health subject matter is, in practice, identified by both a behavioral and an etiological criterion. Regardless of the solution of the implied metaphysical and/or scientific difficulties, it does seem fair to say that behavioral disturbances of whatever type, if thought to be caused by motivations, are more generally (and more properly) called "mental illnesses" than are those thought to be caused by physical events. Motivations, after all, are the kinds of things that have been traditionally classified as mental while chemical events are not. Thus, if a behavioral problem is understood to be caused by a motivation, there is a much stronger tendency to call it a mental illness than if not.

Taken altogether, these points suggest that the notion of mental health as employed in therapeutic practice seems to be woven from two criteria—the notion of general human behavior as opposed to specific organ functions and also the notion of a motivational etiology rather than a physical one. When these two criteria overlap, we get paradigm cases of mental illness. When we have one criterion without the other (generalized behavior with an alleged physical cause, or specialized behavior with an alleged emotional cause) we get cases about which there is likely to be debate of one sort or another. Finally, when both criteria are absent (specialized behavior and physical cause) we have undebated examples of physical illness. For the sake of simplicity, in all that follows we will deal only with the paradigm cases of mental illness—cases of generalized human behavior that is taken to be governed by motivations of some sort. Whether or not this class of behavior can be ultimately reduced to material causation is not at issue here.

The matter can be further refined. Motivation is generally assumed to consist of two elements: affect and cognition. It is presumed, for example, that it were not for the affective or emotional element, there would be no "psychic energy" to count as the motive force, but without various specific cognitions that energy would not, as it were, know how to aim itself. (One may want to eat, for example, but if one does not know that the thing on the table is food, there is no motivation to eat it.)

As part of the reaction against Freud, there has been a tendency among certain psychiatrists to move the locus of therapeutic concern from emotion to cognition. Szasz, for example, urged us to view mental-health problems as translation problems and the therapist as a kind of language instructor.[8] So also those who speak of therapy as a matter of acquiring new skills ("social skills" as they are sometimes called). This way of viewing the matter essentially turns illness into simple ignorance and therapy into straightforward cognitive development. Since ignorance is cured by education and not medicine, as traditionally understood, the purely cognitivist view is attractive to those who wish to avoid the stigma of the medical model.

I can see no reason to insist a priori that the pure cognitivists cannot be right. It may yet turn out that, in some important sense, Socrates was right to insist that all behavioral error is really ignorance, and therapy may really boil down to some form of intellectual quest. On the other hand, the great contribution of the Freudian school was to point to the problem of motivated ignorance (i.e., the unconscious), which, if taken seriously, indicates that the locus of the problem is not in any kind of simple miscognition or lack of skill, but in the affect that wills it. Unless this motivated ignorance is taken into account, the understanding of mental illness will be relatively thin and will certainly be irrelevant to what remains a large portion of actual psychiatric practice.

It is difficult to untangle the ultimate relations of affect and cognition in any concrete motivation. If a man forgets his wedding anniversary, it at first appears a simple error of memory, a sort of miscognition. But we may have reason to suspect that beneath the forgetting lies a dissatisfaction with his marriage, which is a matter of the affects. Going farther, it may turn out that the critical point is not so much the dissatisfaction as the fact that the dissatisfaction is unacknowledged (or unconscious), which makes the problem again one of cognition. This specific miscognition, however, is the failure to acknowledge one's own emotions, and miscognitions or blocked cognitions of this sort are generally understood to be governed by a *fear* of facing the presumed truth, which reinstates the primacy of emotion. But then this fear seems to be rooted in the belief that we will be better off not knowing the truth about ourselves, which is again a matter of cognition. And so on. It seems always possible to hypothesize affect behind miscognition and (mis)cognition behind affect until ultimately one reaches the Socratic view that since everyone desires his own happiness, all self-defeating behavior must be some sort of miscognition.

It is not clear how useful it is to carry the argument out in this way. Whatever the ultimate truth, it seems reasonably clear that the vast bulk of actual mental-health practice concerns precisely that point where affect and cognition intersect (especially in regard to the recognition of one's own emotions) and in the consequent behavioral "choices" one makes in dealing with the world. Straightforwardly cognitive matters are generally not part of this; they are thought to belong to education, and in education of that sort extensive discussion or expression of one's own feelings is not appropriate. There is good reason, therefore, to limit the definition of mental health to precisely this area of intersection between affect and cognition.

Thus the paradigmatic cases of the mental-health subject matter would seem to be the general behavior of the person insofar as that behavior is understood to have its origins in motivations that arise from the area of intersection between cognition and affect. Whether cognition or affect is the ultimate cause is a question that can be left open here, just as we can leave open the question of the ultimate relation of mind and body. For our purposes it is only important that the unclarities this introduces into the definition accurately reflect the uncertainties that exist in actual practice.

THE EMPIRICAL REALITY OF MENTAL HEALTH

If this is a useful way to understand the mental-health subject matter, then the next question is whether or not in real human beings this complex of behavior and motivation is the sort of thing that is structured so as to be properly called "healthy" or "ill." If we stay within the naturalistic brackets, then the answer must clearly be affirmative.

From within the naturalizing brackets we must make the same assumptions about the behavioral/motivational complex that we make for the function/pain complex in the case of specific organs. We must simply assume that the entire complex is what it is through the operations of natural selection—that behavior, emotion, and cognition have been formed for the sake of life and reproduction just as if they were parts of a "psychological body" wherein emotion relates to general behavior just as pleasure and pain related to the functioning of specific body organs. Just as natural selection required us to accept an adaptedness of organ functions in relation to the overall functions of the organism, so here we must assume that there is a suitability of general behavior in relation to the same overall functions. And finally, just as the naturalistic brackets gave rise to a tattered harmony of organ functions with each other, and also with pleasure and pain, so here we must presuppose a harmony of general behaviors with each other and also with the emotions that motivate them. If we understand the word *soul* as simply a shorthand for "general behavior that is motivated by emotion and cognition" then it is an inevitable consequence of the naturalistic brackets that there exists a certain harmony of the soul and that it constitutes the meaning of mental health. It is undoubtedly a tattered harmony—perhaps an especially tattered harmony[9]—but from within the naturalizing brackets we are simply forced to conclude that it is no less real than the harmony of the body.

The bracketing of the body is just barely controversial. For most people it is a blandly accepted fact, and it is opposed only by those (mostly fundamentalists) who refuse to acknowledge the controlling role of natural selection in the genesis of human beings. The bracketing of human motivation, however, arouses the most passionate controversy, and, interestingly, it is often the very people who are most contemptuous of the fundamentalists who themselves adamantly refuse to surrender to nature the remainder of the person. Let science and nature have the body, but there remains a strong tendency to insist on the motivational autonomy of the person and the emotions that drive her. This ambivalence about the relation of the different aspects of the person to natural causation can easily be seen as the contemporary form of mind/body dualism, and it requires considerable discussion to allay the related fears.

It is not, of course, that those who balk at the naturalization of the person wish to preserve an immortal soul. The problem is that the naturalization of selfhood is deeply offensive to many well-motivated moral, political, and metaphysical sensibilities; it rubs against both the traditional notions of a transcendent soul and the contemporary notions of creative selfhood. It reminds us of crude reductionism and the comfort it gave to those with the lowest moral and/or social ideals. It is thus unpalatable to many who have felt it their duty to uphold the freedom and dignity of the person, and because it suggests that nature, not nurture, has made us what we are, it arouses the suspicion of all who fear a biological determinism and the racism, sexism, or quietism that has often come with it.

These fears are completely understandable. Still, they are at bottom unfounded, and although it will take many pages to explain why, a few remarks should be made at the outset. It must be remembered that the point here is not to prove the validity of the naturalistic brackets. Our question is hypothetical. We want to know what really follows from the reductions. It is not part of this question to prove that social conditioning and/or individual creativity really do not transcend the forces of nature. Our task is simply to assume that they do not and to show that nothing terrible follows—to show that only the best of conclusions follow from the worst of possibilities.

This may look like an argument for the categorical correctness of the naturalistic brackets, but it is not. In the introduction, for example, it was suggested that the concept of moral freedom is not incompatible with a thoroughgoing naturalism, and later we will argue that the idea of "brutish" nature is essentially a simple misrepresentation of empirical fact. These points are not made to prove that the naturalistic reductions are correct, but only to show that what is usually feared from them does not really follow.

In the same spirit we will here say something about the political fears that were roused by the latest attempt to carry out a naturalistic bracketing of the person—the storm of protest that was aroused in the late seventies by the appearance of sociobiology. In this discussion we are in no way attempting to prove the correctness of sociobiology. But since the naturalistic brackets force us to assume sociobiology, or something very much like it, we can try to show that it is not the monster it has sometimes been pictured to be.

The old style biological determinism (such as found in Spencer's *Social Statics*) that gave rise to social Darwinism and other racist and/or imperialist theories was based on the mistaken view that there existed a simple, one-to-one correlation between genotype and observed behavioral phenotype (Sahlins 1976: 5). Such theories always result in the conclusion that observed social behavior is in some simple, direct way determined by inherited chemistry. Thus, they make the status quo appear inevitable, and so lead to the acceptance (eager, complacent, or resigned) of the condition of the oppressed. This is the essence of what has given all naturalistic reductions such a bad name among the left (or rather, among *all* advocates of radical change). Indeed, Richard Lewontin, an articulate and polemical left-wing critic of sociobiology, whose sting is all the sharper because he is himself a leading geneticist, declared the pacification of protest as the real reason for the attractiveness of sociobiology. "The general appeal of sociobiology," he said, "is in its legitimation of the status quo" (Lewontin 1984: 236)—as if sociobiology had no purely theoretical appeal that could be generally appreciated and no defenders who are not from the right.

The first point that needs to be made is that contemporary sociobiology simply does not maintain this one-to-one correspondence of genotype and phenotype. Lewontin himself reluctantly admited this.

> sociobiologists . . . at times retreat to the position that they are only claiming that genes determine a possible range of human behavior. (Lewontin 1984: 236)

Other critics of sociobiology more readily granted that men of the caliber of Wilson, Trivers, Hamilton and Fox do not maintain the simpleminded correspondence of genotype and phenotype that leads to racism, nationalism or fascism, and do not consider the "limited biological determinism" view merely a position to which they retreat.

> All sociobiologists grant that within the genetic potential, environment makes a large difference to behavior. (Searle 1978: 168)

In fact, the standard illustration of the genotype/phenotype relationship offered by sociobiologists themselves (Wilson 1978) was the chameleon that is born with a genetically determined set of possible colors, some of which will be actualized in one environment, others in other environments. Environment, including the social environment, is the trigger, and it goes almost without saying that different environments may cause the same genotype to express itself in ways that are phenotypically different. But there are limits. The chameleon's color is phenotypically flexible, but no natural environment can produce a pink chameleon with lavender stripes, and no socially contrived environment can produce one that will not do the chameleon a certain harm.

This whole matter was neatly summed up when Wilson spoke of genetic nature as merely "keeping culture on a long leash." He cited the example of the sexual instinct and its relation to Shaker culture, which was celibate. The sexual instinct is surely real, and surely it is genetically founded. But culture, Wilson said, is not forced to institutionalize the sexual instinct in any specific way. It can even repress it or deny it totally, as did the Shakers. But then the range of genetically founded human possibilities force culture to pay a price—physical extinction for sure in the case of the Shakers, and also whatever psychological and/or physical harm might come from the outright denial of so basic a drive. If the price is great enough, as it was for celibacy, we can be assured that the practice will be eventually altered or the culture will die (Wilson 1978: 178).

"Genetic determinism" is the wrong label for such a position. One should speak instead of genetic predispositions, of the ways they react with each other in various environments, and of the price that may be paid by social forms that choose to alter their normal phenotypical expression. If the predisposition is less critical than the sexual, the price will surely be less dramatic than it was for the Shakers. All things considered, it *may* in some circumstances be wise to pay it. Sociobiology says only that for a very wide range of human behaviors there is such a predisposition and a price for evading it. In the end, this is nothing more than a way of saying that although the human psyche is very flexible, it is not a perfectly plastic material that can be shaped in any way a social reformer might see fit.

Unlike the baboon or the horse, man can imagine things different from the plot laid down for him. . . . If [we] accept that all behavior is culturally learned and that [we] can learn anything, [we] can invent any kind of society and culture for [ourselves]. If [we] believe that [we] have a species-specific repertoire of behavior that can be combined successfully only in certain ways, then there is a definite limit to what this animal can do, to the kinds of societies in which [we] can operate, to the kinds of culture [we] can live with. But there is no end to [human] dreams. (Fox 1989: 19)

Is sociobiology then a rationalization of the status quo? The sociobiological position does limit our dreams, but that is not the same thing as defending the status quo, which in some cases may already be an imposition of unsuitable social arrangements onto a relatively unreceptive genetic material. It has to be borne in mind that the social environment against which human evolution occurred is that of the hunter-gatherer band (Wilson 1975b), not contemporary social forms, so that it is just as likely that sociobiological health considerations could count as much against the current status quo as for it. All that is contained in the general idea of sociobiology is the idea that human beings are not infinitely malleable and cannot be shaped in accord with any ideologically or technologically motivated program. Apparently, this modest position was too much for some progressives.

But Lewontin also attacked the sociobiologist's real position. The view that cultural possibilities are limited by genetic mechanisms seemed to him tautological, which may be part of the reason he does not think the sociobiologists really believe it.

> Although sociobiologists, when challenged by geneticists, at times retreat to the position that they are only claiming that genes determine the possible range of human behaviors, sociobiology is emphatically not simply the claim that human society is of a nature made possible by human biology. All manifestations of human culture are the result of the activity of human beings; therefore it follows that everything ever done by our species . . . must be biologically possible. But that says nothing except that what has actually happened must have been in the realm of possibility. Whatever it is, sociobiology is not [this] simple tautology. (Lewontin 1984: 236)

Is the sociobiologist's real position not so much wrong or reactionary as it is tautological? Does the claim that human biology sets the limits of possibility within which human culture must work, reduce to the fatuous remark that what is possible is possible?

Suppose that the sociobiological position really is the relatively simple claim that the human genetic constitution is such that only certain combinations of human behavior are possible in a given social environment. An example of this might be the claim that a society cannot force slavery on one segment of its population and at the same time expect that segment of the population to work as efficiently, happily and responsibly as those who freely choose their work. Such claims are clearly not tautologies. In fact they are as subject to empirical confirmation or refutation as any other social generalization.

Or suppose that the sociobiologist goes a bit further and explains the incompatibility of certain behavior patterns through genetically determined, behavior-specific instincts or drives (Wilson 1978: 38) such as the conflict of the sexual instinct with Shaker culture, or the nursing instincts of infants with certain kinds of infant-feeding devices and schedules. Now instincts have been criticized on the grounds that they are nothing more than the behavior they are alleged to motivate, as when, for example, without further elaboration, one offers as the reason for a specific form of behavior an alleged drive for exactly that. If that were all there were to the matter, then indeed an instinct would be no different from Molliere's 'dormative potency'. But that is not all there is to the matter. First of all, there is the possibility of linking the alleged instinct in predictively fruitful ways to many other theories in genetics and molecular biology. And secondly, even were that lacking, it is no tautology to say that such drives exist if it is added that they can be frustrated, repressed or socially (mis)interpreted, and that when this happens a certain empirically observable psychological and/or social price must be paid. This is not merely to put a 'mystical' instinct behind the observed behavior. Rather, it is to treat the instinct as a theoretical entity, like the atom, that gives rise to concrete observable predictions that would not otherwise be made—predictions of frustration or anxiety that are alleged to be caused by the suppression of the instinct. Thus, even were the idea of an instinct as the explanation for the behavior it gives rise to tautological, it is not tautological when used to explain behavior that is alleged to stem from the suppression of instinct. It is true, of course, that all that has ever been done by our species must be biologically possible (including celibacy, breast feeding, bottle feeding, pacifiers, and misguided attempts to wean infants at too young an age, or to make them nurse in a mechanically regular way), but to claim that this proves sociobiology a mere tautology seems utterly to miss the point.

Perhaps Lewontin meant only to assert the behaviorist slogan that there are no instincts, but that is a different matter—essentially of a peculiar kind of metaphysical prejudice that lacks any empirical support whatsoever and is in fact contradicted by evidence that could hardly be clearer—the nursing behavior of newborns, for example. If that is what is meant, then certainly the burden of proof is on the other side.

In any case, whatever the final truth about instincts, the principal point here is that the mere assertion of their existence simply does not entail a defense of the status quo because it does not entail a one-to-one correspondence between genotype and phenotype. Instincts may be repressed and/or molded in various ways, and because of that fact sociobiology can lead to results quite critical of the status quo, as it would have done in the South in 1840, for example.

While a theory of instincts or drives may be unpopular with a wide variety of philosophical schools (behaviorism, existentialism, etc.) there is no reason to see in the sociobiological version of it a vicious biological reductionism, a radical denial of human flexibility, or a radical denial of power to social conditioning. It is merely an attempt to return to biology some role in the understanding of human behavior. Few really believe that social forces are so omnipotent as to be able to specify any manner of behavior and emotion that might be thought just or advantageous or profitable. Few deny that some reasonably specific emotions are formed by evolutionary pressure and are, therefore, instinctual—hunger, thirst, the sexual impulse, the infant's attraction to the breast, the urge to speak, to walk, etc. Almost everyone recognizes that there are limits to how far we can stretch this human material, that those limits are set by nature, and that a price is paid for exceeding them. The real problem, and it is a great one, is to define the precise limits of that flexibility and to determine the exact cost of its violation.[10]

There are deeper, nonpolitical reasons for rejecting the naturalization of the person. These are metaphysical and epistemological reasons that are rooted in either old-fashioned transcendentalism, phenomenology, or linguistic analysis. All this is left aside here since our purpose is not to prove the correctness of the naturalistic reduction but merely to understand it in accord with the most current empirical theories and to see where they lead. It does need to be said, however, that while the philosophical revulsion against naturalism used to have a great deal of popular support, the climate of opinion has now changed in important ways. The fearful, contemptuous attitude toward nature that has characterized the modern West and which culminates in the transcendence of the self over nature in existentialism; the certainty of nature's grubbiness and of the human superiority over it and, consequently, our willingness to alter nature as an expression of our creative force; the entire techno/scientific dream of domination over "dumb matter" and the sense of our dignity as lying in our superiority and freedom—all this has been questioned by the now commonly accepted failure of the enlightenment dream. In many quarters, the naturalization of humankind no longer seems threatening. Instead, it is the supposed human superiority to the natural that seems to be the threat, and one hears once more of the need to view the human being within the fold of nature.

But what could this mean? It cannot mean the rejection of all that science has learned about nature. That is the Luddite mentality. Nor can we simply return, like the neo-Thomists and those enchanted by Greek, eastern or primitive concepts of nature, directly to the world as it was conceived before the scientific revolution. To do that would be to adopt a

peculiar kind of romanticism that would put the (scientific) mind at war
with the heart. Consequently, it can never achieve more than a temporary
or idiosyncratic outburst of anti-scientific sentiment. The nature back into
which man is to be put can only be the nature as known by modern science,
and this can only mean a willingness to work out an anthropology of
human emotion within the naturalistic brackets. Or at least we must be
willing to hear of such a possibility and see where it really leads.

[margin handwritten note: But nature as told by modern science may not be the whole story of nature.]

In any case, if we do not make some such assumption as this, there is
simply no real meaning that can be given to the idea of mental health. It
will be a mere metaphor, more or less thin as the analogy to the body holds
or fails. The body is healthy only because of certain "as if" functions to
which it has been molded by evolutionary pressure. Without that pressure
there would be no objective reference point from which to define "right
function." If we refuse to naturalize the person, we will have only the concepts of pain and adjustment through which to define mental health.
Despite their inherent subjectivity, a painless, distress-free life and/or a life
of social adjustment are real goals and can certainly be pursued, but there is
no reason to do so under the auspices of medicine. If that is all there is to
the alleged notion of mental health, then either psychiatry is just one more
servant to the consumer society, or, worse, it is a form of social control. If
we will not view the person from within the naturalistic brackets, then let
us admit at the outset that there is no such thing as mental health. There
may be education; there may be adjustment; there may be spontaneity, happiness, flexibility, and control, and different people and different societies
may value these personal differences differently. But unless the person as a
whole is somehow formed by evolutionary pressures, there is simply no
such thing as the proper functioning of the elements of personhood and,
consequently, no such thing, properly speaking, as a healthy personality.

A LIMITED SPECIFICATION OF MENTAL HEALTH

If we place personality within the naturalistic brackets, then it is clear that
in the limited way previously described, behavior must be predisposed by
the operations of evolution and natural selection. This formation of personhood must apply also to the motivations behind the behavior. The person is
a complex of behavior and emotion, and it goes without saying that any
attempt to understand mental health through behavior alone must fail. The
critique of a purely behavioral approach is well known.[11] Even if we had a
list of certified healthy behaviors, a person whose only motivation for
doing them was a joyless release from fear, a person who enjoyed none of
them for their own sakes and who was essentially doing these right things

only to escape pain of one sort or another, would obviously not be a healthy person, just as a heart that pumped blood, but did it painfully, would not be a healthy heart. Health cannot be merely doing the right thing. The healthy thing must be done for the appropriate motive, and this means, at least in some matters, that it must be more or less enjoyed.

While this is correct, and while we will say much more about motivation in this regard (see chapter 3), there has been a tendency to exaggerate its importance in some of the definitions of mental health. Perhaps this represents an overreaction to behaviorism. But in any case health cannot be defined through motivation alone, as some psychologists, especially those in the humanistic tradition, have a tendency to do. Motivations, conceived as "inner," are invisible to any but the agent and, if conceived as unconscious, are unknown even to him. All that we directly experience is behavior (our own and that of others) plus our own conscious motivation. Definitions in terms of motivation alone, therefore, such as "spontaneity," "absence of intrapsychic conflict," "self-acceptance," "lack of unconscious motivation," "guiltlessness," etc., all of which say much the same thing, are essentially useless unless some theoretical correlation is made between the motivation and the behavior it is alleged to give rise to. Lacking that, any motivation could give rise to any behavior, and we would never know mental health or illness when we saw it. For the theory of motivation to be useful, therefore, some assumptions about the behavioral correlates must be made, and these overt, empirical correlates (be they as subtle as a smile, a tone of voice, the display of a certain attitude, or as obvious as love-making, talking, dancing, refraining from murder, holding a job) are the things that we recognize when we recognize mental health. In them lies the working muscle of any definition.

The naturalistic brackets drive us to similar conclusions about the primacy of behavior. It is primarily on behavior that evolutionary pressures work. So long as one engages in a certain amount of a certain kind of heterosexual behavior (whatever the motivation) one's genes will be preserved. Considered utterly in isolation from all other factors, there is no reproductive differential between sexual activity performed for love and the same amount of sexual activity performed from fear or the desire to dominate. Consequently, in this very limited sense and to this very limited degree, evolutionary pressure is indifferent to motivation. Therefore, we are more sure that behavior has been formed by evolutionary pressures than we are about motivation. In the long run it is not so simple, and, as will be argued in the next chapter, motivations too are formed by evolutionary pressures. But the formation of motivations is secondary—a means to the formation of behavior—and therefore the matter is never as certain. It is very clear that hunger is our basic motivation for eating, and it hardly seems controversial that it has been formed for this purpose by evolutionary pressure. But it is even clearer that unless we eat we die.

The attempt to develop some reasonably concrete specification of mental health must then begin with behavior. If we had a certified list of all the behavior that constitutes mental health, one half of the business of defining mental health would be accomplished. Because only genuine empirical research across a very wide spectrum of the social sciences could work up such a list with real rigor or specificity, it is not available to us. Nevertheless, certain broad matters seem straightforward enough to allow us to make a gesture—a *mere* gesture—at illustrating what such a list might be like.

There are certain broad ranges of behavior that are so clearly necessary for the survival and reproduction that evolutionary pressures simply must have formed us to engage in them, and so they simply must be a part of the mental-health inventory. Eating, sleeping, and some sort of productive labor, for example, are simple requirements of life, and there is little doubt that people who cannot engage in them are ill.

A particular species of behavior (say eating) is what we will call an *arena* of behavior for the entire organism—a coordination of eye, nose, hand, lip, tongue, jaw, tooth, throat, stomach, etc.—in relation to a specific thing or things (food). Just as the activity of a particular bodily organ may or may not fulfill its "as if" function, so we may say that activity within a given arena may or may not fulfill the "as if" functions of that arena. Often we will be unsure what the functions of the arena are, but in the case of eating it seems clear enough that the primary "as if" function is to get nutrition into the body. This is for the simple reason that nutrition is necessary for life and there is no other way of achieving this in the original environment than by eating. If such behavior diminishes to the point where this function is inhibited, we have a behavioral illness (anorexia, perhaps, or some other diagnosis, depending on the specific style of the deficiency). If one eats so much as to become obese, thereby harming the capacity for survival and reproduction, it is called a "compulsion." If one customarily eats more than is needed for nutrition and then regurgitates it, it is the clinical condition called "bulimia."

The idea of human life as composed of various arenas of behavior leads to the idea of the psychological body, i.e., the collection of all the arenas of human behavior conceived on analogy with the organs of the physical body. As the latter is a unity of organ functions harmoniously related to the ends of life and reproduction, so the psychological body is to be understood as an organic unity of behavioral arenas subordinated to the same ends. In the end, mental health can be nothing but the right functioning of this psychological body. Its harmony will be at least as tattered as the harmony of bodily functions.[12] It will be relative to the original environment and it will be subject to individual and group variation, just as was the body's. It will also be subject to the special problems that concern the nuances of motivation (to be discussed later). But one way or another the harmony of this psychological body—this balanced personality—must be the meaning of mental health, if there really is such a thing.

It goes without saying that even with an arena of behavior as clear as eating there are questions we cannot answer. We do not know, for example, to what extent social interchange over the meal (a highly ritualized and very important matter in almost every society) is a part of the function of eating. Nor do we know how much sensitivity to the pleasures of pure taste should be involved. *L'homme ne mange pas, il dîne*, goes the aphorism, pointing to an entire world of subtle matters surrounding this most commonplace and uncontroversial of activities. We simply do not understand the full functional significance of food, and it would surely be wrong to view it only as a source of biological nutrition. But we do understand the rough, general truth. That is hardly debatable. For the more subtle matters, hypotheses can be offered, evidence can be brought to bear, reasons given and progress can be made, just as one can make progress in interpreting the body's functions.

The clearer the relation between a given arena of behavior and the "as if" ends of evolution, the clearer the meaning of health for that arena. Arenas constituting the necessary, life-sustaining functions of the individual (like eating) are the clearest; arenas that are necessary for life but not absolutely required of every single individual (like work), are less clear, since a genetically based division of labor may have excused some from the business of labor, producing, thereby, a sort of natural leisure class. (While conceivable, this seems about as likely as that natural selection should produce a body organ that made no contribution to life. Consequently, work is only marginally less clear than eating.) Arenas of activity necessary only for reproduction (like sexuality and child care) are still more unclear, since not every single member of the community need engage in them. Also, there are other, indirect contributions to reproduction that can be made, such as happens among bees and ants, for instance. Thus, heterosexual activity in the sexual arena is, at least for most people and for a certain period of their lives, right functioning. Whether or not there are others who have been genetically excused from this function by virtue of a division of labor—exclusive homosexuals, the young, the elderly, priests—is an empirical question that can be settled only by specific research.

Aside from behavioral arenas that are absolutely necessary for either life or reproduction, there are others that may merely enhance those goals.

Play is one such arena. We assume we are predisposed to engage in it, and so to be unable to do so is very probably a genuine behavioral illness. Related to it are the production and enjoyment of art, music, religious activity, chatting, dancing, storytelling, and so forth. From within the brackets, there can be no doubt that these behavioral arenas arose because of some contribution made to life and reproduction, but it is not clear what exactly this is. Consequently, it is more or less unclear what exactly a healthy engagement in that behavior would be. Were it, the theory of health would become a theory of aesthetics and religion too.

Perhaps someday there will be an all-encompassing theory of the psychological body within which even aesthetics and religion will have their places. That is something to be hoped for. It would amount to an entire philosophy of life based on the concept of health. Till then, slow, uncertain progress can be made about such matters by thinking about them in the right way. The empirical evidence gathered by the social sciences is, of course, critical. But the right conceptual scheme (the right "paradigm") is needed to digest the overwhelming plethora of information that has already been gathered.

The trick is to ask questions of the data based on the concept of the psychological body—to think of each arena of behavior as a psychological organ and of the totality of these organs as a delicately balanced, organic whole that encompasses all the life-sustaining behaviors of the individual (eating, sleeping, drinking, loving, obeying, commanding, working, learning, talking, playing, laughing, fighting, etc.). We then ask of these behavioral arenas the same basic question we ask about physical organs. How are they supposed to relate to the general task of survival and reproduction of the species in the original environment?[13] Hypotheses will be offered and will be accepted or rejected for approximately the same reasons that we accept or reject hypotheses about body functions. First, we want to know how the alleged function would have made some real contribution to survival in the original environment. Second, we want to know how well the alleged function fits the activity that we find currently going on in the relevant arena. Third, we want the reconstruction to be worked out so that there is a minimum of mutual interference between the various functions, for here as with the body we can only assume that evolutionary pressures tend to weed out survival strategies that are in fundamental conflict with each other (just as they have arranged it so that healthy bodily organs do not interfere with each other).[14]

In short, we should be disposed to consider the behavioral arenas to be mutually dependent, delicately interrelated, and, like the bodily organs, balanced against one another in relation to the overall organic functions. Such a balance is understood to be health. In the case of the behavioral arenas, it is psychological health. It is also what used to be called "a well-ordered, well-balanced life"—the harmony of the soul.

For the soul as for the body, this harmony is not a gross empirical fact. It is a paradigm that gives meaning to the empirical data. The paradigm is not derived from simple observations, nor is it contradicted by them. It is, in a certain limited sense, an *a priori* ideal, or hermenuetic device,but it is an ideal that is demanded by the naturalistic brackets and the theory of evolution.

Relation to the overall function of the organism, the fit with known behavioral facts, and a harmonious fit with other activities are the three criteria to be employed in thinking about the proper functioning of any arena of activity, and with them we can approach the enormous task of working out a concrete, full and useful definition of mental health. Needless to say, this is a huge task (possibly the entire goal of social science) and not likely ever to be completed. But it is most certainly a direction in which we could work, and there is no reason why, in a stumbling, partial, tentative, and uncertain way, we cannot make progress.

This is, of course, not the direction social science has taken. As an overreaction to the crudely judgmental social theories of the nineteenth and early twentieth centuries, and out of respect for the fact/value dichotomy, much recent social science has attempted to be entirely nonjudgmental. More recently still, value judgments have been re-allowed, but no objective foundation has been supplied for them. Social science of both types has stressed the diversities of people rather than an underlying common human nature. The request for a reconstruction of the psychological body obviously goes counter to this trend. In effect, it is a new way of asking for the redirection of attention toward a common human essence. It is understood that this essence is not to be found by a crude empirical cataloging of the diversities of human behavior, nor by averaging them. This is not true of physical health, and it is not true of mental health. Health is always a reconstruction of the empirical data guided by the tattered "as if" teleology of the naturalistic brackets.

Without claiming anything even remotely like thoroughness, we can now make a gesture in the direction of such a reconstruction by providing a very roughly reasoned list of the behavioral arenas that constitute mental health. Such a list would bear gross similarities to that propounded by Malinowski (1944). The guiding overall assumption would be provided by the naturalistic brackets: that human behavior, like all organic characteristics, arises from an "as if" teleology with reproduction as its ultimate end.

We can divide the arenas of behavior into two broad groups and be absolutely sure that both of them are required by health. First and foremost are the activities that are necessary for the conception and rearing of the next generation (the activity of reproduction and all the subordinate activities that are necessary for it). Second, there is the business of self-maintenance and all that is subordinate to it. The former concerns, at a minimum, heterosexual sex, love (of one sort or another) and marriage (of one sort or another); family, nurturing, child rearing, education, and in general, all the behavior that simply must be performed to bring the next generation to adulthood. From nature's point of view, these are the ultimate human activities, whatever our subjective wishes or values might be, and to them everything else, including self-maintenance, is biologically subordinate.

But before one can take care of the young, before one can reproduce at all, one has to be able to take care of one's self. All that relates to the care of one's self we call self-maintenance, and under it we would have to list, hunting, gathering, building, exchanging, cooperation, sharing, and learning (all of which roughly equal work), not to mention such nearly automatic activities as eating, drinking, elimination, and sleeping.

We may think of a third group of activities that are equally necessary for both reproduction and self-maintenance: among these would be (for humans) speech (i.e., rationality, deliberation, and technical achievement) and "sociality," by which is meant the minimal behavioral conditions for the possibility of social life.

If we had a complete list of the activities necessary for life and reproduction, then we would have gone as far as we can in the way of a casual enumeration of the specific meaning of mental health. The definition would still be very incomplete. All that empirical research could learn about the specific ways of engaging in these behavioral arenas, their relationships to different natural and social environments, and also *all that could be learned about the possibilities for group and individual variations* would be needed to complete our understanding. Also, all that could be learned about arenas of behavior that merely enhance life and reproduction but are not strictly necessary for them would be needed. Lacking such empirical specification, we nevertheless present the following very crude, nearly minimal outline as a way of illustrating the goal (see table 2.1). It must be borne in mind that this is merely a list of activities that must somehow be performed by the social group if that group is to survive and reproduce. *It is not, ipso facto, a list of activities that are required for the health of every member of the group,* though some of them clearly are of this nature and others may be.

Table 2.1.

Reproduction—Maintenance of the Next Generation

Heterosexual sexuality
Capacity for some (unspecified) form of marriage (i.e., mating)
Capacity for participation in some form of family life
Nursing (literally and in the extended sense)
Protection of and provision for the young
Some degree of self-sacrifice on behalf of the young
Education

Self-Maintenance

Eating
Sleeping
Elimination
Hunting
Gathering
Building
Exchange
Cooperation
Self-assertion (This would presumably include self-assertion to the point of aggression in certain cases—against plants and animals at a minimum (for food), and possibly against certain highly threatening people, i.e., violence exercised in self-defense.)

Reproduction and Self-Maintenance

Sociality (This represents the whole complex of activities, whatever they may be, that are truly necessary for social life, including, presumably, a certain respect for others, for one's traditions, and a required minimum of peacefulness.)
Speech
Educability
Play and recreation

LOVE AND WORK

Inadequate as they are, this table makes clear how the substance of mental health is determined by two broad arenas of activity, self-maintenance and reproduction. Each is served by many subarenas. These subarenas would presumably be broken down into still more subordinate means, and so on, without any clear limit. As the means become more specific, so presumably will the possibility for individual variation become greater. Eating is certainly required of everyone, for example, and it is likely that we are all predisposed to ritualize the matter in one way or another; but we are not all required to eat the same amount of meat or to eat with chopsticks. No matter how well worked-out the list may be, therefore, it will never constitute a simple template against which the behavioral details of a human life can be straightforwardly measured. The more specific behavioral arenas will constitute more or less rough generalizations about the nature of mental health. There will be deviations from these generalizations that really are illnesses, and others that are simply the peculiar phenotypical configuration of a given person's health. Thus, if one wished to offer a general definition of health from the behavioral side alone, it would be best to stay away from specifics and call it the ability to maintain oneself combined with the ability to help in the task of reproduction, while keeping mum on exactly how these activities are to be performed in any individual case.

It is of interest that this turns out to correspond to one of the best known definitions of mental health—the ability to love and work (usually attributed to Freud). In a rather straightforward way, what we have called "self-maintenance" is simply work, the activities an individual must engage in to keep on going. Most essentially, it is the providing of food, but it is also various crafts, learning, obeying, commanding, and all the other activities that one must at one time or another engage in just to provide the necessities of life (though not necessarily in all social or natural environments). By the same token, what we have called "reproduction" includes most of what is meant by love, not only in the narrow sexual sense, but also in the broad sense of caring for others—of sexual partners for each other, without which there is no stable ground for the rearing of children, but especially of the strong (usually the adults) for those who are weak and cannot, at least at the moment, offer anything in return (usually the children). And just as work/self-maintenance is generally self-centered, so is love/reproduction generally other-centered. Interpreted in this way, Freud's definition leads to a rough idea of mental health as a balance of self-interested and other-regarding activities—a definition that obviously makes a lot of common sense. I do not know to what degree Freud himself might have understood his definition in this broad way, but it is unlikely to be altogether accidental that his definition corresponds to the basic moral dichotomy that lies at the evolutionary heart of the human psyche.

One wonders also whether it is accidental that this same dichotomy corresponds to the traditional stereotypes of gender. Most of what is associated with reproduction (sex, children, family, love, generosity, self-sacrifice, nurturing, education) constitutes the traditional feminine stereotype of all "advanced" cultures, while most of what is connected with work constitutes the corresponding male stereotype (strength, cunning, mastery, hunting, self-assertion, etc.). Could the basic dichotomy in the "as if" goals of organic life be mirrored in a genetic division of labor between the sexes? This division, if true, would give to the sexes fundamentally different values and outlooks on life while at the same time binding them together in a biologically founded mutual need through the institution of the family.

This is, of course, just the traditional view of the matter. Nothing here said proves it to be true (nor does the often-cited nonuniversality of the stereotype disprove it. Genotypes specify only a range of possible behavior). But should the traditional view turn out to be correct, it certainly does not amount to a denigration of the female stereotype. In fact, it shows precisely the opposite. From nature's point of view all of the functions that make up what we call "life" are but servants of DNA's urge to reproduce itself. Life is for the sake of the egg, not vice versa. Thus, from nature's viewpoint the stereotypically male function (work) is but a means to the stereotypically female function (reproduction), so that the male provider is essentially a servant to the mother and child.

Because the stereotypically female activities include greater doses of generosity and self-sacrifice, they are also superior from a traditional religious/moral point of view. This makes the higher premium set on male virtues puzzling, but it is presumably rooted in the failure (or refusal) of men and women to draw their values from within the naturalistic brackets. Instead, writers of both sexes have tended to take stereotypically male virtue as normative, a tendency that is no doubt aided by the fact that current social conditions reward most highly the work virtues of self-assertion, calculation, and control. The radical feminists, of course, are the exception to this tendency.

It is important to repeat that none of this is meant to assert that the traditional stereotypes are in fact genetically founded. But even if they are, and even if the feminine virtues were to receive what would therefore be their just recognition, it would still not mean that all men are genetically bound to strenuous self-assertion while all women are forever destined for lives centered on children and characterized by high doses of maternal generosity. It would entail only the blandest of generalizations—that most people will be predisposed towards the behavior traditionally associated with their gender. There will be individual variation in this as in all other matters. Some women will be genetically disposed to work and some men will be disposed toward nurturing of one sort or another. Even if genetically founded, the stereotypes are still mere generalizations, not universals. This does not make them therapeutically useless. It means only that they must be applied to specific cases with great sensitivity to the possibilities for individual variation.

Moreover, as has been repeatedly said, genotypes specify only a range of phenotypical behavior. Choices within that range are made by the environmental triggers, both natural and social. It is possible, therefore, that change of social environment can have some real effect on the gender roles. But this is not to say that gender roles are mere social clay. Nor is it to say that the stereotypes as we know them are forever fixed by nature. It is, though, to utter a truth that ought to be banal, that we are a mixture of both nature and nurture and that social programs that do not pay sufficient heed to both our sources will inevitably fall into promoting ill health of one sort or another.

HEALTH VALUES AND THE STATUS QUO

A few final points: Those familiar with the traditional ethics will see in the biological foundation of human behavior a revival of the natural law theory of ethics, and indeed that is the whole point towards which we are driving. But since in modern times such theories have been associated with neo-Thomism, where they are frequently used to argue against progressive measures (birth control, abortion, legalization of suicide and euthanasia, for example), they are viewed with disfavor by many. The theory of health here advocated has much in common with these traditional natural law theories, and so it may be suspected that we are moving toward a health-oriented defense of the religious view on these issues.

But the theory here advocated is much more flexible than neo-Thomist orthodoxy. To use suicide as an example: though the urge to self-maintenance is paradigmatically natural and healthy, and though most suicide is therefore unhealthy, it does not follow that every suicide is an illness or an unnatural act. If a young person in full health falls into depression and kills herself, all feel that something is deeply wrong; it is easy to view the matter as a species of mental illness. But when an elderly person who can no longer participate in any but the most minimal life activities makes the same choice, i.e., simply hastens the impending inevitable, few feel it is the same sort of thing.

Health values and common moral sentiment are likely in harmony here. Certainly the urge towards self-preservation is natural and healthy, but only for the sake of life and reproduction. As the number of remaining life functions approachs zero, it is quite reasonable to say that the meaning of suicide changes from a negation of life to its affirmation. Consequently, from the point of view of health, it is as wrong to condemn all suicide as it is to say it is simply a matter of personal choice. As is so often the case in such matters, the truth (if health is its measure) lies somewhere in between. So also, one suspects, for such issues as birth control and abortion.

This raises the question of whether the sociobiological approach to mental health will turn out to support or undermine the status quo on a wide variety of political issues. The answer, it seems, is not simple and will probably not satisfy those who are strongly progressive or strenuously conservative. Presumably, it will be with mental health as it is with physical health. Because we do not live in the social form to which we are genetically adapted, health values will be radical on some issues and conservative on others. On the gender issue, for example, if progressivism is the view that gender stereotypes have no biological ground, then the sociobiological approach to mental health is likely to end up relatively conservative. From within the naturalistic brackets, and although it is a complicated issue that requires many qualifications, it is not likely that anything as ancient and universal as gender role differentiation could be a purely social construct. If, however, the progressive view simply requires equal pay for equal work, or equal educational opportunity, then there is no conflict at all between it and sociobiology. Lastly, if one takes the stand of radical feminism (that there are, in general, genuine, natural, irremovable differences between men and women; that women's virtues are the equal if not superior to men's; and that what is needed is a restructuring of society so as to give appropriate recognition to women's values), then the sociobiological approach to mental health could turn out to be its great support.

For the reasons already given, in the South of 1850 health values would have been radically egalitarian. As repeatedly said, this potential for radicalism in sociobiological theory stems from the fact that its social frame of reference for all questions of health is the generalized hunter-gatherer band. From this stems the radically conservative, radically nostalgic orientation that will prevent the medical approach to human behavior from ever being a mere apology for the status quo. If anything, the approach should be criticized for its peculiar kind of radicalism. Its danger is a romanticism of the primitive, not contentment with the status quo.

But this too is an oversimplification. While the naturalistic brackets *do* commit us to an essentially nostalgic health functionalism, it need not be crude. If, for example, there were a pan-environmental genetic disposition toward the specific behavior of ritual dancing, this would not mean that health requires us to dance to rain gods. We would need only to find suitable phenotypical expressions in the contemporary environment. Genotypical adaptations need not be very specific. Throwing baseballs is probably as good as throwing spears, and the rock concert or grand waltz may be as good as the rain dance. Going to the movies may or may not be as good as listening to the tribal storyteller, just as lots of bread, sugar or salt may or may not constitute a healthy diet. It all depends on how we reconstruct the original diet and the original role of storytelling. These are empirical matters, to be judged by the sciences of nutrition and literary anthropology if and when the evidence comes in. But in any case, the possibility of substitution for nonspecific adaptations is always there.

Lastly, there is the fact that in certain conditions health itself may require us to do things we are not naturally adapted to do. Contraception, for example, employs technological devices to which we are not adapted and which are certainly harmful to one degree or another. But in conditions of extreme overcrowding, all things considered, contraception may allow life to be more natural than it would be without it. Once the primitive conditions have been left behind, further technical advancement may actually bring us closer to the natural and the healthy. Thus there is here no Luddite, antitechnological grumbling. A high-tech electronic device might well be more healthy than its low-tech mechanical counterpart, and the low-tech counterpart may be more conducive to health than agricultural slave labor. A life of high culture may be more natural and more healthy than an untutored life of working-class drudgery (as is in fact the case, to judge from the reports of anthropologists on the extent of leisure in hunter-gatherer societies (Lee and DeVore 1968). Everything depends on the specifics of the reconstruction of the psychological body and its relation to current conditions. These are empirical questions, and while we may be able to discern certain broad outlines of some matters in advance of more complete knowledge, we should be wary of quick answers to specific questions.

3
Motivation

the man who abstains from bodily pleasure
and delights in this very fact is temperate,
while the man who is annoyed at it is self-
indulgent.

Aristotle[1]

In health as in ethics, it is not enough simply to do the right thing. However
carefully we might draw the list of behavioral arenas, and however precisely they might be codified, mere conformity to them could not count as
health, any more than a heart that was forced to pump blood (by a pace-
maker, perhaps) could be called a "healthy heart."

The naturalistic brackets force us to assume that we are fully adapted
to our behavioral functions, and this in turn means that the entire psychological body, "inner" and "outer," must be formed by natural selection. Our
motivations, then, must be as adapted to our behavior as our behavior is to
life and reproduction. The "inner" person—pleasure, pain, feeling, desire,
enjoyment, emotion, drive, instinct, libido (whatever it is that is said to
"move us," however, it is understood, even if ultimately it should be
reducible to some subtle concatenation of behavioral dispositions)—all
this the naturalistic brackets force us to assume is at bottom just as much
shaped by natural selection as is the behavior it gives rise to.[2]

Thus we assume that whatever healthy behavior is, our pleasures and
pains are adapted to it, and this means that healthy behavior is generally
more enjoyable than its dysfunctional counterpart, just as *generally* we find
the healthy functioning of the body more pleasant or more enjoyable than
its alternative. We will see, however, that we must go farther. It is not just

that healthy behavior is more enjoyable and less painful than its opposite. For the most part, functional behavior is positively pleasant, so that a life rich in positive pleasures and a healthy, functional life are very much the same thing.

It goes without saying that life as we live it does not manifest this snug harmony of pleasure and function. What is functional (work, for example, or even love) is often painful, and if dysfunctional behavior were not *in some way* more enjoyable than healthy behavior, there would be no reason to engage in it. Although a rough harmony of pleasure and function may seem to exist for many people for much of the time, a thoroughgoing harmony is so far from apparent that it seems to be contradicted by any realistic assessment of the facts of human existence (Sidgwick 1874: 191). Nevertheless, the naturalistic brackets leave us no choice. A priori, as it were, the harmony must be there. The task, therefore, is to explain the disparity between theoretical construction and observed fact. This amounts to an explanation of how it is possible for there to be such a thing as mental illness.

PLEASURE, FUNCTION, AND BEHAVIOR

Emotions, feelings, urges, and/or instincts are all very subtle, highly nuanced, and extremely difficult to describe. It is as hard to make appropriate discriminations between them as it is to say what they have in common. Regarding only the positive emotions, it is questionable whether there really is any felt quality that is common to them all (Brandt 1959: 305; Edwards 1975: 273), but from the very beginning of speculation it has been traditional among many philosophers and psychologists (especially those inclined towards naturalism) to claim that they all involve one species or another of pleasure and/or pain. This is, of course, a part of the much criticized thesis of psychological hedonism. One suspects that it is either a tautology (Sidgwick 1874: 44; Brandt 1957: 311), or a misuse of the word *pleasure* that rests on blurring the distinction between sensual, localizable positive feeling (pleasure proper) and all other kinds of satisfaction (self-righteousness, self-respect, aesthetic delight, etc.) (Nowell-Smith 1954: 138–9). Nevertheless, we need some word to designate all positive feeling, i.e., all feeling that inclines us to engage in an activity rather than avoid it. Despite the risk of misunderstanding, we here choose to call it "pleasure."

The words "enjoyment" or even "satisfaction" might be subject to less misunderstanding, but since our overall strategy is to assume the worst and see what follows, and since the hedonistic thesis is generally thought the moral worst case (the psychological counterpart of simple materialism), it is of interest to us to see where it really leads. As will be shown, even if pleasure is interpreted in its narrowest, most sensual sense, it would lead to nothing we need fear, and so even if our generalized use of the word *plea-sure* is misunderstood, no real harm can come of it. Therefore, although we by no means believe that all positive feelings are localizable sensations of pleasure, or even sensations of any sort, we nevertheless follow hedonism and use "pleasure" as the general term for all of them.

In the spirit of naturalism, we then assume a modified form of the essential thesis of psychological hedonism—that these pleasures (or enjoy-ments, or satisfactions) are the motives for all our behavior, or at least for the basic behavior that is required by life and reproduction. The naturalistic brackets then force us to the conclusion that these pleasures are as much formed by natural selection as the behavior they motivate. For we have already concluded that the behavior is so shaped, and obviously this could not be the case unless the motives behind it were fashioned by the same forces.[3] Therefore, a thoroughgoing harmony of pleasure and pain with functional behavior simply must exist. If it did not, health would require us to choose the more painful course, and this, on the whole, is not permitted by natural selection because an organism normally required to choose the more painful course would simply not compete very well.

This harmony of pleasure and pain with behavioral function is the basic theoretical foundation on which any theory of mental health must rest. Given it, mental-health illness can be understood as some sort of dis-ruption of that harmony (discussed more later) in strict analogy to the dis-ruption of the functional harmony of the body by physical illness. But the first problem is to convince oneself that the harmony really does exist.

It is worth noting that the basic idea of the harmony of soul was accepted even by such antitraditionalists as Descartes, who said that it was the natural function of the passions

> to incite the soul to consent and contribute to the actions which serve to maintain the body. . . .[4]

It is also the thesis of all who have attempted to use the theory of natural selection to understand human psychology. Herbert Spencer, for example, put it this way:

> If we substitute for the word Pleasure the equivalent phrase—a feeling which we seek to bring into consciousness and keep there; and if we sub-stitute for the word Pain the equivalent phrase—a feeling that we seek to get out of consciousness and keep out; we see at once that, if the states of consciousness which a creature endeavors to maintain are the correla-tives of injurious actions, and if the states of consciousness that it

endeavors to expel are the correlatives of beneficial actions, it must quickly disappear through the persistence in the injurious and avoidance of the beneficial. In other words, those races of beings can only have survived in which, on the average, agreeable or desired feelings went along with activities conducive to the maintenance of life. . . .[5]

In fact, wherever we find it assumed that life is somehow not supposed to be unduly painful—wherever, that is to say, it is taken for granted that the ordinary tasks of living are supposed to be pleasant, satisfying, or enjoyable, there lies the presupposition of the harmony of the soul, whether or not it is recognized as such. This does not mean, of course, that there might not be circumstances where health requires discipline, i.e., the ability to accept present pain for the sake of long-term pleasure. But it does mean that, if discipline is a form of behavior to which we are adapted, there will be a certain kind of pleasure in it (satisfaction, pride, self-respect, anticipation of future pleasures, etc.), and that generally such severe pleasures will not be required for the most common human behaviors—eating, sleeping, sexuality, socializing, rudimentary learning, speaking, etc.

We must go farther. Certainly, there are two basic motivational mechanisms—the pursuit of pleasure and the relief of pain, and certainly the harmony of motivation and behavior encompasses them both. They are not equal, however. It is of some importance to note that theoretical considerations and rough empirical evidence both show that the pursuit of pleasure has a certain priority over the relief of pain.

The more the normal, life-sustaining behavior of an organism involves the relief of pain rather than the pursuit of pleasure, the more the organism is put into a condition of chronic pain. All other things being equal, such a condition must be less adaptive than one in which the pursuit of pleasure is the primary motivational device, and so the harmony of motivation and behavior must tend to be primarily a harmony of relatively pure pleasures with the behavioral functions.

The empirical evidence is confusing, but it is fairly clear that some such rough harmony does exist at least for the most basic behavioral arenas—for eating, drinking, sleeping, sex, speech, and play, for example. It is only somewhat less clear that the harmony also actually exists for some people in many of the more complicated arenas of behavior. Under certain conditions, for example, productive labor is a source of deep satisfaction for a great number of people. So also are nurturing and all kinds of altruistic acts pleasing to *some* of the people who do them—to *most* parents, for example, and also to those more truly generous people among us, who give, not out of duty, but simply because it feels good to help (a condition found not so much among the young, who, after all, are generally the recipients of generosity, but more commonly among the older, for whom, obviously, care of others [especially the young] is more appropriate; also, it is a condition found, at least according to stereotypes, more often among women than men, and more so among mothers than the childless, all of which makes perfect sense from an evolutionary point of view).[6]

The somewhat surprising fact is that most of the rough empirical facts actually do conform to the conclusions demanded by the naturalistic brackets. But there are a great many complications. Despite the theoretical priority of pure pleasure over pain relief, it is clear that much healthy motivation is often more a matter of pain relief than it is the pursuit of pleasure—as when we snatch ours hands from the fire. This extends to the more subtle, nonlocalizable emotions as well—as when loneliness forces us into social life even if we think we would rather be by ourselves. In general, behavioral functions are pleasant, but sometimes (usually in urgent cases) pain relief is the motivating force (Sidgwick 1874: 46).

Eating seems a good illustration. To eat when one is mildly hungry is very pleasant. The hunger itself is felt as the invigorating, enjoyable state of mind called "appetite," and we wish each other a good appetite as we wish for any other blessing. Simple appetite is not a pain (Sidgwick 1874: 46), despite the fact that Plato, Schopenhauer, and other ascetically inclined philosophers have treated it that way.[7] But if food is not forthcoming, then the pleasant state of mild appetite turns into a genuine pain. If we will not eat for the pleasure of it, nature resorts to the goad of pain relief, and the pain gets worse as the biological need for food becomes more urgent. It is similar with sex. To be sexually aroused is pleasant, and given suitable conditions most people would choose a state of mild sexual arousal over benign indifference, which they would not do if it were really a pain (Ryle 1949: 108). But if the sexual urge is continually frustrated, the whole business becomes more truly painlike, and few would choose that condition over indifference. The same is true for a mild desire for company vs. true loneliness; the simple pleasure of conversation vs. the painful need for it after long travels among those who do not speak one's language; the mere desire for children in one's twenties vs. the fear of permanent childlessness later in life. We are generally motivated toward healthy activity by the pursuit of pleasure, but when the matter is urgent, or when the pursuit of pleasure fails to accomplish its "as if" goal, something worth calling "pain" takes over and all but forces us to be with others, to talk, to work, to rest, to reproduce, as well as to eat, breathe, and sleep, whether or not we believe these are particularly good things to do.

These commonplace facts suggest an important general rule. Since only the more urgent matters are handled through pain relief, it seems to follow that the relief of pain is a stronger motivator than the pursuit of simple pleasure. This does not mean that the relief of any pain will take priority over any simple pleasure, but rather that, given the fact of pain, we will generally sacrifice simple pleasures in order to relieve it. Presumably this is due to the intensity of the felt need to relieve the pain—an unrelenting insistence that is not felt in the pursuit of simple pleasure. This will turn out to be very important later, when we try to understand how it comes about that the harmony of pleasure and natural functioning turns into the lives we actually lead. For now we merely note that while (1) our motivation is generally adapted to natural behavior through the pursuit of pleasure, (2) the avoidance of pain tends to appear on the scene when the matter is urgent, and that (3) the insistent, demanding quality of pain relief causes it to receive priority over the pursuit of simple pleasure.

Pain relief and its relation to simple pleasure complicate the harmony of the soul, but still not nearly enough to account for the difficulties of life as we know it. In general, we undergo a dreary education to prepare for work that is often but a draining means to a dimly perceived end. The work gives us money or honor, but neither seems really to satisfy. The money buys pleasures, but the pleasures often result in pain, or they often have a desperate quality about them that makes them seem as much a burden as a delight. Marriage is difficult, children are a responsibility, social relations are often little more than calculated manipulations, and so on. The phenomena of what is sometimes called "alienation" are endless, and it is wearisome to harp on them. But the fact is that love, work, play, social life—all these perfectly functional behaviors are so infected with emotional contradictions that this talk of a harmony of pleasure and function, however theoretically well-grounded, can seem quite irrelevant to the real circumstances of life.

The naturalistic bracketing of the person forces us to conclude that the complex configuration of behavior and motivation that makes up our daily lives must have arisen out of the relatively simple harmony of the soul. This can happen only if new pleasures and pains arise that disrupt the original harmony. But how can this happen? New pleasures and pains cannot simply arise *ex nihilo*. They must come as some kind of transformation of the preexisting motivations. Even the crudest of such transformations—the threat of punishment—works with the already existing correlations of pain and behavior. It is already painful to be isolated and inactive. We merely create new circumstances in which this pain is artificially associated with the disapproved behavior (as when people used to make children stand in the corner to deter bad manners).

What is needed then is a theory of the transformation of pleasures. More specifically we want to know how the original harmony of the soul is transformed into the emotional complexities (and disharmonies) of empirical life, and then we want to know which of such transformations are properly called "mental illness." The Judaeo-Christian story of the fall, the Platonic story of the transformation of the "city of pigs" into the Republic proper—in which the blame is put on an unexplained desire for luxury[8]—the Rousseauean/Marxist theory of alienation, and the Freudian theory of drive, libido, repression and the unconscious were all theories of this type, and to a severely reformulated version of Freudianism we will have to return. But first we must take a look at the whole business of the transformation of pleasure.

Given the absolute centrality of pleasure in our lives, it is truly remarkable how feeble our vocabulary is for its description. The pleasures of intellect and art, of sex and food, of the wildest lust and the mildest flicker of arousal; the pleasures of a school-yard bully or of Mother Theresa all get lumped together under the almost empty heading "pleasure," and although everyone knows or feels that there are important qualitative differences between them, there is no generally accepted scheme of classification, either in popular speech or among the learned.

In the absence of such distinctions, sensual pleasure tends to be taken as paradigmatic, and so we often end up talking as if the pleasure of generosity vs. the pleasure of miserliness were on a par with the pleasure of chocolate ice cream as opposed to vanilla. All pleasures, in other words, tend to be taken as matters of taste, and this in turn has led to a very popular, very tolerant (and very superficial) brand of moral relativism. Even Kantians tend to take this view of pleasure, but only because they wish to put morality on a nonpsychological foundation, and the absence of qualitative distinctions between pleasures helps make psychology seem irrelevant to moral feeling. Few in philosophy continue to take the matter of pleasure seriously, and this despite the general agreement on an enormous phenomenal qualitative difference between the sweetness of ice cream and the sweetness of revenge.

Because philosophical hedonism does take pleasure seriously, it has often felt the need to bring the concept of pleasure into closer relation to the felt nuances of life. Thus Mill (1863: ch. ii) tried to distinguish between lower and higher pleasures, associating the former with the body, the latter with the pleasures of the mind. The distinction is usually assumed not to work, not so much, unfortunately, because of its semantic inadequacy, but rather because it runs afoul of the utilitarian principle that one pleasure is to be preferred to another only because of its quantitative superiority (Sidgwick 1874: 94; Moore 1903: 80; Quinton 1973: 42). More to the point here, however, is the fact that Mill's distinction would make it appear as if the "low" pleasures, the pleasures of sadism for example, are simply less intellectual than the high pleasure of, say, music appreciation, which simply is not true and reflects the traditional philosophical prejudice in favor of the intellect. (Consider in this regard the fact that sadism need involve no physical contact and is capable of a high degree of refinement and distancing, while music appreciation can be extremely visceral and is always on the edge of breaking into dance, song, humming, or at least the tapping of fingers.)

Francis Hutcheson offered a more subtle and more accurate discrimination among pleasures in his *A System of Moral Philosophy* (1755). There he distinguished between (1) pleasures of the external senses, (2) the pleasures of the imagination . . . and of beauty and harmony and knowledge, i.e., Mill's higher pleasures, (3) the pleasures of sympathy, i.e., pleasure in another's pleasure, and (4) pleasures that arise from the consciousness of good affections and actions, i.e., respect and/or admiration. The higher pleasures are said to be both quantitatively *and* qualitatively superior, and the judgement of qualitative superiority is said to be made by a knowledgeable judge who has personally experienced the relevant pleasures (Strasser 1987).[9] Distinctions of this sort are of value, but the exploration of the psychology of these different kinds of pleasure did not receive much attention, presumably because Hutcheson appealed only to an unexplained "moral sense" to grasp what it was that made the higher pleasures higher.

Generally, the task of making qualitative distinctions between pleasures has been given up, and utilitarians have settled for the merely quantitative distinctions envisioned by Bentham—the better pleasure being quite simply the greater, all things considered and however exactly greatness is to be measured. No more subtle discrimination of pleasures seems to have been generally convincing, and most everyone seems agreed to treat differences in pleasure as differences in taste, even though that would be appropriate only if all were of Hutcheson's lowest sort.

A preference for chocolate over vanilla is quite unlike a taste for the sweetness of revenge. It is a metaphorical extension of the term "taste" and something of a category mistake to view all pleasures in this way. Aristotle knew well that the moral constitution of a person is shown precisely by the constitution of her pleasures. To enjoy the sweetness of revenge or to be oblivious to it says a great deal about the moral worth of a person. Even aesthetic pleasures (a preference for Chopin over Teleman, for hard rock over chamber music, for muted colors, tightly checked shirts and elbow patches over brightly colored, shiny, bold designs) are obviously also matters of character. That, after all, is why taste is important and why we do in fact argue about it. It is simply inaccurate to view such judgments as though they were mere preferences for chocolate. If we cannot make appropriate differentiations between the pleasures of child abuse and the pleasures of love, then how can we seriously expect to understand what is good or bad in human life? Certainly we will not be able to understand mental illness.

THE DISRUPTION OF THE HARMONY
AND THE TRANSFORMATION OF PLEASURES

We presuppose an original harmony of pleasure and behavioral function set by natural selection for human beings in the general conditions of the original natural environment and in the basic structures of hunter-gatherer social forms. When the activities that constitute those functions cease to be pleasant enough to move us to engage in them, or when they actually become painful, then we are at least in the vicinity of mental illness. Presumably there are many ways that this transformation of pleasures could come about. We consider one example in the hope of extracting some general principles.

At sea, in a storm, in order to lighten his sinking ship, a sailor might throw his possessions overboard with a certain desperate fervor, gusto, and "pleasure." To someone who does not understand that life is more important than possessions, that the ship is sinking, that the sailor cannot swim—to a person so ignorant of the sailor's desires and their relation to his circumstances, it might look as if he has lost his pleasure in his possessions (or "lost his mind" as we say). In fact, from the vigor of his actions and the relieved look after he inches the heavy chest over the rail, an insensitive observer might judge that his possessions have even become painful to him and that his pleasure lies in casting them away—a curious kind of frenzied asceticism. One might give the condition a name, dyspropertia, and go on to classify it as a form of masochism.

But what has happened here? The sailor experiences a "pleasure" of some kind when he manages to get the chest over the rail, but obviously it is no simple pleasure. He fears death and he thinks that lightening the load may save him. A very great pain has arisen, the fear of death, and this pain demands relief with such intensity that it overrides and alters the normal configuration of pleasures and pains. What used to be painful (loss of possessions) becomes "pleasant" because it relieves that pain. It is pleasure in a very peculiar sense, not as the relatively simple enjoyment of possessions was pleasant, but as pain relief, an altogether different kind of pleasure.

We noted earlier that the relief of a sufficiently intense pain will take priority over the pursuit of simple pleasure. To this we add another rule, first noted long ago—that the relief of pain is experienced as pleasure.[10] Together these rules provide one explanation (perhaps *the* explanation) of how the required transformation of pleasure can occur. *Whenever a suffi-ciently intense pain appears on the scene, behavior that relieves it will be experienced as pleasure even if that behavior requires the suppression of behavior that would otherwise be experienced as pleasant.* This we take as the basic psychodynamic mechanism through which to understand how the original harmony of the soul gives rise to the discordancies that character-ize our most unharmonious lives.

Thus, there are pleasures and there are pleasures. We broadly divide them into two kinds, the simple or pure pleasures and those that come from the relief of pain. This we take as the basic qualitative distinction between pleasures. If quantity is measured by intensity, then it is interesting to note, as did both Plato and Aristotle, that the quantitatively greatest pleasures would probably be the impure, pain relieving sort. Contrary to the tradi-tion, however, because there is no reason why pain relief cannot lie behind the pleasures of intellect and art, the pure pleasures are not necessarily the same as the so called higher pleasures. Thus, the ultimate usefulness of this qualitative distinction is unclear, but there seems little doubt that it exists, that it was clearly enunciated by both Plato and Aristotle and known to Bentham. Why so little has been made of it in the philosophical tradition is hard to say.[11]

The sailor helps us to understand how the transformation of pleasures comes about, but he is not an example of mental illness. The problem here is not the sailor but the environment, and indeed the most obvious place to look for the pains that alter the original configuration of pleasures is in the environment, not the individual.

The natural environment could change in ways more permanent than the onset of a storm at sea. The temperature could drop, as it did during the ice ages, or game could become rare, causing us to take "pleasure" in uncomfortable clothing, or making hunting more painful than it was "meant" to be, so that we might "prefer" to laze around the fire and eat less wholesome things that are more readily available. This is the fish-out-of-water syndrome. It is surely a very real problem, and it is surely appropri-ate to consider such matters in relation to illness and health. Perhaps the ultimate contribution of the ecology movement will come not in merely cleaning up the environment, but in revealing how and at what cost to the original configuration of pleasures we have come to live in environments other than those to which we were adapted. The sickness here, however, is not so much in the individual as in her relation to the environment and can be cured only by a return to the original environment or a full adaptation to the new one. The return is often impossible, and true adaptation requires the passing of many, many generations, so that a truly satisfactory solution is usually impossible. Since true health is impossible in such circumstances, medical practice must concentrate instead on working out the least debilitating compromise.

Essentially, the same thing can happen when the social environment changes. Moral, penal, economic, or technological changes can make painful the very behavior that constitutes our natural functions. New and unusual behavior can then arise to relieve these pains, and with it come new and unusual pleasures. This can be unintended, as when, no doubt, the invention of agriculture and real estate dislocated the original configuration of pleasure, work, cooperation, possession and land. It can also be deliberate, as when the threat of punishment (i.e., pain) is used to make unpleasant any more or less natural activity—singing and dancing, for example, or various forms of sexuality, or the eating of meat. More subtly, overpopulation and the change in the status of children from economic assets to liabilities have to some extent done this for the basic human urge to procreate. Progressives urge us to adapt to new circumstances and tend to minimize the psychological cost. Conservatives fear the cost and urge us to cling to the old adaptations. Either way, we are fish out of water.

The decision as to how such matters are best handled requires true political wisdom, and we are so far from having such wisdom that we are hardly aware of the need for it. No blanket rule is possible. Given that we are already so far removed from the original conditions of human existence, further technical or social innovations may actually move us closer to natural functioning. Everything depends on the hard-to-discern specifics of each and every case. But if there is a sickness here, it is again not the individual who is sick, it is the society as whole. The individual merely does his best to cope with a social environment for which he was not made.

All of those theories of mental illness that have sought to take the onus off the individual and place it on society instead (Laing 1967, and the entire systems theory approach to mental illness) take off from this particular predicament. There is nothing wrong with this so long as the very possibility of individualized illness is not precluded. There most certainly are distortions of the harmony of the soul that are properly considered social, and much that has been called "alienation" is of this sort. But recognition of this fact does not rule out the possibility that there are also illnesses whose locus is more truly in the individual.

What then makes the individual sick? It is a part of our usage of the word *sick* to mean that the thing designated "sick" is the thing that ought to change in order bring about a return to health. In this regard the locus of the originating cause is less important than the locus of therapy. In the cases already considered, only an alteration of the environment can restore real health, and so the individual should be considered essentially healthy *as long as he would be able to return to normal functioning if returned to the environment to which he was originally suited*. If, however, he is so altered that even with the restoration of the original environment he continues in a dysfunctional condition, then he too must become the object of therapy, and it is he who is ill.

How can it happen that the individual comes to carry the cause of the transformation within himself, as part of himself, even if the first cause of the whole problem was in the environment? In essence, that is the question Freud tried to answer, and it is the question answered by all the depth psychology that is based on his general psychodynamic conceptions. This is presumably not the only possible answer, but it is one that has become so typical of our talk about these matters and is so fruitful for understanding the subtleties of human motivation, that we will give the remainder of our attention to it.

THE ORIGIN OF MENTAL ILLNESS

We know that the sailor is not ill because we understand (1) that he is seeking relief from pain, (2) that pain relief yields "pleasure," (3) that such "pleasure" distorts the normal harmony of pleasure and function, and (4) the sailor is reasonably well aware of all this and knows that, all else being equal, he would prefer to enjoy the normal pleasures. Suppose, however, there were an intense pain that functioned in essentially the same way as the fear of death in our example but was utterly invisible to both the observer and the agent. Suppose that the pain were so deeply internalized that it operated in almost all circumstances and was carried about with one like an infection, regardless of its origin. Such a pain would be particularly insidious, baffling, and intractable, and it would well deserve consideration as the cause of a individualized sort of emotional illness.

Freud's theory of the unconscious makes possible the existence of precisely such a pain. The general name it has been given is "anxiety." To understand why, of all imaginable pains, anxiety is most well-suited to this key role in the theory of mental illness, it must first be rescued from trivialization.

Anxiety is not worry. Worry is the concern one has for impending harm, and so long as it is a more or less rational worry, there is nothing remarkable about it. It is a normal and obviously very functional emotion. Without it we would not provide for the future, and that would be to live less effectively than squirrels. It is true that worry involves a certain sacrifice of immediacy, that it requires living in the future as well as the present, and that this involves a certain amount of tension that could be eliminated by living solely for the moment. Those who really do this, however, are soon dead; and they will not have to wait for starvation in winter. Such a person would not even bother to move out of the way of an oncoming train, since even that simple precaution requires projection into the future. An enormous amount of well-intentioned silliness (and also some far less noble pandering) has been written in popular psychology based on the confusion of anxiety and worry.[12]

It is better to define anxiety as excessive worry—irrational worry, worry that does no good. There is such a thing, and there are timid people (worrywarts) who are said to be anxious in just this sense. The energy spent in this excessive worry is itself sometimes more of a burden than any harm that might reasonably come from the presumed threat. Such worry is pointless, but still is not the kind of thing we want to identify with anxiety. So understood, anxiety would be merely one character trait among many, and not the one emotion that lies at the root of all neurotic behavior (Fingarette 1963: 72). Or as Freud put it

> The problem of anxiety is a nodal point linking up all kinds of most important questions; a riddle, of which the solution must cast a flood of light upon our whole mental life.[13]

There is a third kind of "worry" that is so deep and so omnipresent that to call it worry at all is to trivialize it. This is the thing originally designated "angst" by Kierkegaard and which became so important also for the existentialism of Heidegger and Sartre. In those philosophers it is an emotion definitive of the human condition as such, not something one may or may not feel depending on one's character or circumstances. For them it is all but inescapable—the very thing that makes us human.

Freud's own use of the term seems to blend this anthropo-philosophical use of the word with the common German *angst*, which has all the ambiguities of the English *anxiety*. In any case, there is something like this existential *angst* in the psychodynamic lexicon. Freud spoke of "free-floating" anxiety (1920: 405), by which he meant an objectless fear, a fear that might sometimes seem to attach itself to a particular object (say, business failure or rejection in love), but is actually quite independent of it and is not put to rest when the alleged object is satisfactorily dealt with by objective success. In free-floating anxiety, one is aware of a vague but possibly acute discomfort that seems to alight for a while on a particular object, but soon lands elsewhere in a process that continues *ad infinitum* no matter what objective reassurances might develop.

We will use the word *anxiety* to mean whatever it is that lies at the bottom of this vague, generalized, acute discomfort, this fearful mood in which it is not clear what is feared and is not long relieved by success in dealing with specific worldly threats. While this discomfort may or may not be connected to some forms of worry, it seems clear that it is the phenomenal form of something else that remains more or less obscure. True anxiety does not fear anything in particular. True anxiety is a fear, but its object at first appears too general to be named.

> That in the face of which one is anxious is completely indefinite.[14]

The problem, then, is to understand what it is that anxiety afraid of.

If the existentialists are correct, the matter is ontological and lies in the fear of its own nothingness by a being that is not a thing at all, a no-thing, a free thing, but a no-thing that wants desperately to be a some-thing, the vapor's desire for definition, stability, and structure.

> In anxiety what is environmentally ready-to-hand sinks away, and so, in general, do entities within-the-world. Anxiety thus takes away from Dasein the possibility of understanding itself in terms of the world. . . . Therefore anxiety discloses Dasein as being-possible. . . . Anxiety makes manifest in Dasein its ownmost potentiality for-being—that is, its being-free for the freedom of choosing itself.[15]

For Freud, on the other hand, the matter is moral—resting in the conflict between instinct (id) and morality (super-ego), i.e., in guilt.

> But when the libido is attached to a mental excitation which has undergone repression . . . a bridge is provided by which the conversion of libido into anxiety can be conveniently effected.[16]

Here are two explanations of anxiety that at first seem quite distinct, but they both have one thing in common—the turning of the self against itself. In the one case the self condemns its libidinous energy; in the other it judges its ownmost mode of being, possibility, as unacceptable. But the essence of the matter is the same—the self has judged itself deficient, and so in both cases we have a primordial division of the self against itself, an original "intra-psychic conflict" to use the psychodynamic jargon. And this is the meaning we will give to the word *anxiety*—fear or worry that is rooted not in an objective threat, but in the self's own deep condemnation of itself.

So understood, wherever there is anxiety, there is a scale of values on which the self has judged itself deficient. The specifics of the scale do not seem important so long as the anxiety it gives rise to is general and all but irremediable by specific successful actions in the world. (Were the matter specific and repairable, then some specific, objective act of worldly success could remedy it, and then, in our vocabulary, it would be more a matter of fear or worry than anxiety properly speaking.) The scale could be ontological, moral, or aesthetic. Possibly it is different for different societies and for different people within the same society. But always there is some scale, and on it the self has been condemned. We could call this generally the state of guilt, but to avoid specific connotations of that word we will speak instead of self-condemnation—the sense that one is of little worth on whatever scale of values it is that really matters. Thus the thing feared by anxiety is not anything in the world. It is ourselves. It is, quite simply, the fear that at bottom what we are is just not very good.

There are kinds of self-condemnation that can be alleviated by practice, diligence, competence, confession, restitution, or by securing for oneself a "supportive" environment. It can only be stressed again, despite the trivialization of this concept in popular psychology, that none of this is what is meant. The self-condemnation of what we here call "anxiety" (and that was so called by Freud, Heidegger, and Sartre) is so general that it belongs to a level of selfhood that is prior to most specific activities; it belongs very nearly to an individual's most basic self-consciousness, and to what may be very nearly the basic self-consciousness of the species.

What is here meant by "anxiety" in fact, is so far from the anxiety of pop-psychology that it is more like the Christian doctrine of original sin, and more like the thing meant by the anti-Christian Nietzsche when he defined man as "the red-faced animal." Here is the Christian version:

> In short, man, being both free and bound, both limited and limitless, is anxious. Anxiety is the inevitable concomitant of the paradox of freedom and finiteness in which man is involved. (Niebhur 1941: 182)

And here is basically the same thought in Nietzsche:

> The enlightened man calls man himself: the animal with red cheeks.
> How did this happen to man? Is it not because he has had to be ashamed too often?
> Oh my friends! Thus speaks the enlightened man: 'Shame, shame, shame—that is the history of man.' (Nietzsche 1883: 112)

Both Nietzsche and the theological tradition he rebelled against realized that anyone who escaped the sense of shame would no longer be quite human—he would either be an angel (i.e. saved) or a super-man, but in either case so radically different that from the normal human condition that he would appear to be another species.

Does such intense self-condemnation really exist? One could point to the universality of clothing, the fig leaf, the nominal loincloth or penis sheath worn by even the most natural peoples. We could ask why among the animals this one alone feels a need to hide or alter its body? One could point to the restless human spirit, its infinite capacity for discontent, and ask why it is so impossible for this creature to be a peace with itself. One could point to its ancient hunger for eternity, from which springs all religion and all science (Eliade, 1949), as well as to its modern need to alter its conditions, to have a history, to make progress, to improve. We have always been the restless creature. How could this be unless we have judged ourselves and found ourselves deficient?

Such considerations are suggestive, but not, of course, decisive. Instead of attempting to prove the existence of this self-condemnation, we approach it through the back door and ask instead about its intensity and its modality. Later we will ask about its consequences.

THE INTENSITY OF ANXIETY

How great is the pain of self-condemnation? How does it compare to more familiar types of pain? It seems fair to approach this question by asking how much self-condemnation we can bear, and whether we bear it more or less well than we bear other forms of pain.

Self-condemnation is the negative correlate of self-respect. Its painfulness is presumably then in direct proportion to our need for self-respect. How great is that need?

It is clear that for *some* people self-respect is the greatest need. These are the people who will sacrifice wealth, position, or friendship if so required by their sense of duty. They are the natural Kantians, and if self-righteousness is their greatest vice, a lonely self-respect is their greatest consolation.

Most of us do not at first seem like this. We are less principled, as we say — and more willing to work out an accommodation between principle and practice, implying perhaps that we would sacrifice some principle (and hence some self-respect) for other kinds of gain.

This view of the more accommodating person presupposes that he is a more or less self-conscious and deliberate hypocrite, i.e., that he has clearly acknowledged moral, political, or aesthetic principles, knows that his behavior violates them, and nevertheless chooses to do so. But while characters of this type appear in fiction, they are seldom encountered in real life. The human need for self-justification is just too strong, and our capacity to live lives that much out of joint with our thought is simply not very great. The fact is that in almost all cases the accommodating person believes, or says she believes, that her course of action is the correct one. She is an Aristotelian, believes in moderation, and thinks it unreasonable to be required by morality to sacrifice so much. That kind of "morality" strikes her as excessive, and she may even accuse its practitioners of a kind of fanatical zeal.

This is a kind of moral/intellectual opportunism, to be sure, but the point is that it is overwhelmingly common and that opportunists almost never believe that is what they are. They believe they are making reasonable adjustments to circumstances, and when they do acknowledge that they are doing wrong, we generally note the absence of real guilt in their voices and the worldly smile that tells us they think themselves wrong only by conventional standards, not by the standards of real life. Sometimes, rarely, someone will say that he is doing wrong and sound as if he means it. The rest of the time it is denied or at least mitigated by a ready adaptation of principle to conduct. In the concentration camps, the principled ones died first. The rest were seldom self-conscious hypocrites. They merely adopted an ethic of survival.

The fact is that we need to believe, or to believe that we believe, in the rightness of what we are doing. True cold-blooded hypocrisy is as difficult as it is rare. It should even be counted a left-handed sort of virtue because it requires one to maintain the integrity of one's moral cognition in the face of one's own moral corruption. Thus, hypocrisy has been called "the homage that vice pays to virtue." But the fact is that most people cannot indulge in it.

This, in turn, has a very important consequence. It means that, contrary to first impressions, self-respect is of greater worth to us than might at first appear. We almost never sacrifice it for a greater good. Rather, when we must choose between it and something else, we simply adjust our scale of values to do away with the contradiction that diminishes our self-respect. The criminal makes criminality his value. By and large when the ambitions of a businessperson, politician, scholar, and artist bring them into conflict with ordinary morality, all do essentially the same thing. For everyone, the need to justify seems paramount.

Certainly, there is self-deception in this intellectual opportunism, and it may well be far from praiseworthy. But just as certainly it is a tribute to our need for self-respect. It does not seem wrong then to conclude that self-respect may be our greatest need, or at least that we have few needs that are more pressing. While this conclusion may at first seem to mix moral hopes with empirical facts, there is no need to persuade anyone who has actually seen or experienced the collapse of life and ego that comes with the true loss of self-regard. It is as terrifying as it is rare, and little is more feared than an honest confrontation with one's own self-condemnation. We would not be far wrong to conclude that anxiety is the greatest of pains.

THE MODALITY OF ANXIETY

How much pain can a human being bear? Beyond a certain point the tortured body simply faints, which is a way of saying that when the pain passes the threshold of what can be borne, the body seeks refuge in a self-imposed anaesthesia. That is for what we call "physical" pain. Are there not emotional pains in the face of which we faint?

Freud began the psychoanalytic theory of motivation when he named the unconscious and attempted to sketch its workings. In his terms it comes to this. There is a pain called "guilt" (the foundation of anxiety), which for some reason and for at least some people is too great to bear. By a process called "repression" this pain is then pushed into the unconscious (which is spoken of sometimes as a storehouse of knowledge, sometimes as source of agency that resides "inside" the conscious mind). Although the pain is thus avoided so far as the conscious mind goes, the painful thought continues to influence behavior through the mechanisms of projection, symbolization, denial, dissociation, defensiveness, etc. This behavior constitutes the symptoms of mental illness. It can be very specific bits of bizarre behavior (like washing the doorknob before touching it, or walking around the bed three times before going to sleep) or it can be the more general styles of general behavior that make up entire character types (oral, anal, etc.).

There is much of Freud that we need not accept. Specifically, we can remain silent about Freud's particular conception of the contents of the unconscious (the death instinct, the Oedipus complex, penis envy, the exaggerated role of sex, and so on). And we must certainly not take literally the metaphorical language he used to describe the unconscious (as another person within, a demon almost, in relation to whom we are the passive victims). In general, however, we simply cannot do without the unconscious, an idea that was once fashionably overworked, but is now somewhat shunned with the fading of Freud's deification. The unconscious is another much-abused idea. Like anxiety, it needs purgation, simplification and resurrection, a task attempted in more detail by the next section of this chapter. For the moment, we take its existence for granted and note, as have almost all the great novelists, that the complexities of human character simply cannot be grasped without it.

We need not accept from Freud the particular way he chose to populate the unconscious. We do not have to hypothesize repressed sexual desire behind every eccentricity. We do not have to accept a death instinct, a desire to return to the womb, penis envy or any of the more spectacular items that came to be associated the Freudian unconscious, and that, more than anything else, made it appear a phantasmagorical construction without empirical foundation. Nor need we accept anyone else's vision of the particular contents of the unconscious—Jung's collective unconscious, for example, or the Nietzchean/Adlerian idea of a will to power. About such hypotheses we can remain undecided, while clinging to the simple, commonsensical idea that if such a thing as repression exists at all, then the unconscious will contain (indeed, must contain) whatever we are most ashamed of. This may be sexual desire; it may be the will to dominate; it may also be the desire to cry, to love, or to pray; it may be anything at all, and it may change from individual to individual, from culture to culture and from time to time depending on the scale of values that guides one's sense of shame. But whatever it is that is repressed, it will always include whatever we are most ashamed of, and the goal of such repression will always be to avoid the pain of self-condemnation and the loss of self-respect. Indeed, it is hard to imagine what other reason there might conceivably be for hiding from one's own beliefs.

Given our understanding of anxiety, it is then clear why its modality is so different from other sorts of pain. If fear of the loss of self-respect is the prime motivator of unconscious beliefs, and if anxiety is understood as self-condemnation, then it is clear that anxiety will almost always be unconscious. We may be aware of an acute discomfort, and we may call this "anxiety," but the heart of the matter remains hidden, and from this comes the peculiar objectlessness that defines the specifically anxious state.

Certainly this much is true: if we are motivated to repress any of our beliefs, then surely we will repress our self-condemnation. That some people might with relative ease manage a bare intellectual acknowledgement of self-condemnation does not contradict this. What is at issue is the entire complex of belief, idea and emotion. To bring a judgement to full, clear consciousness is to feel its emotional impact, and the only proof of such feeling is the overt behavior that goes with it—tears, contrition, lamentation, the gnashing of teeth, and the beating of breasts. It is to avoid all this that we anaesthetize ourselves to begin with, which thought makes clear enough the urgency of our need to keep it that way.

THE UNCONSCIOUS AS SELF-DECEPTION

While we need the unconscious, we do not need to take literally Freud's metaphor for it—the notion of the unconscious as a separate person or agency within us. Freud spoke of the unconscious sometimes as a mere repository for knowledge of which we are very dimly aware, and sometimes as a demon-like, alien power that resides "within" us, manipulating the conscious mind, and thereby rendering it the passive puppet of invisible machinations. There is no really pressing reason to object to the first notion of the unconscious. In that usage unconscious knowledge is rather like knowledge that one has forgotten (but might yet recall) or like inarticulate thoughts (that might yet be well expressed), and from Plato to Leibnitz and Collingwood this idea has had a respected place in the philosophical tradition. But there are many good and pressing reasons for recoiling from the unconscious as a source of agency when that agent is understood as a person other than the conscious mind itself. First of all, it is counter-factual—in the sense that (1) there is no possible direct empirical verification of it, and (2) (for reasons to be explained) it results in a falsification of those genuine experiences that might, on some other interpretation, be reasonably described as experiences of unconscious motivation. Secondly, quite aside from empirical considerations, the very concept of this demonic unconscious has serious conceptual difficulties. And worse still, this sort of talk has gone a long way towards undermining the legitimate sense of moral responsibility for one's actions.

The demonic unconscious is a psychological echo of the reductionist, deterministic swagger of nineteenth-century scientific materialism, and Freud's understanding of his own discovery was sometimes biased by this sort of reductionism. But the unconscious can also be understood phenomenologically. Not only is it the sole explanation for a wide range of commonplace experiences, but it is itself a commonplace phenomenon. It can be understood as nothing more than the familiar but puzzling mental state called "self-deception."

The conceptual problem concerning the demonic unconscious grows out of the problem of how the self-same mind can willfully maintain two contradictory attitudes towards or beliefs about the same state of affairs. Ever since Plato (*Republic* 437a ff., 439 ff.) it has been customary to handle such logical contradictions by sacrificing the unity of the self. The contradiction is eliminated by dividing the self into two or more parts (reason and desire in Plato, or spirit and flesh in Christianity) each of which may then be said to have a different opinion about the same object.

Confronted with the reasonably hard fact of the willfully contradictory character of consciousness (and also for other reasons), Freud adopted this traditional solution. He divided the self into parts, one of which he called "the unconscious," the other "the conscious mind," and he spoke of relations between them as if they were relations between two different people who happened to inhabit the same person. Thus he sometimes spoke as if the deceptions of repression, projection, etc., were performed by the unconscious (conceived as agent) upon the conscious mind, thereby making the conscious mind passive and not responsible for any actions that might result from the deception.

This notion of the unconscious (and indeed the whole metaphor of the self as composed of parts each of which is a center of independent agency) has received a great deal of philosophical criticism. When the metaphor is taken literally, it is forgotten that the parts of the self are precisely parts of a single, identical self and that whatever is "done" by any of them is done by that unitary self. If my desires "want" something but my reason does not, it is not someone other than myself who wants it, even if it is also true that it is I who think it a bad thing to do. It is fair to say that in such circumstances I am confused, at variance with myself, uncertain, etc.; but it is simply wrong to say that it is someone else inside me (my desire) who wants it, while I, understood as reason, do not.

And so it is with the conscious and unconscious mind. There are good empirical reasons to speak of the unconscious, and it is sometimes a useful (but dangerous) metaphor to speak of it as a center of agency. But the unconscious is not something inside me other than myself. It is my unconscious, after all, and what it does is done by no one other than me.

If one attempts seriously to construe the matter otherwise, then one is driven to conceive the act of repression as something done by the unconscious to the conscious mind. The unconscious thus becomes an agent that hides from the conscious mind certain alleged truths that are particularly distressing to the conscious mind. Obviously, these presumed truths are not so distressing to the unconscious mind or another act of repression would be needed whereby the unconscious mind hid those "truths" from itself, and so on ad infinitum. The unconscious does not deceive itself. It deceives only the conscious mind, operating rather like an overprotective parent who, with no selfish motive whatsoever, and without sharing the child's values, hides from the child whatever "truths" the child would find especially distressing.

All of this is very convenient for the conscious mind! It gets all the benefits of self-willed and self-serving ignorance, while remaining entirely innocent of the slightest intent to deceive! Its ignorance is utterly sincere, and yet it never has to face its own deep fears. It is as if whenever I very much wished for (but would not perform) a certain species of immoral action, someone else were to (1) read my mind, (2) perform the deed, (3) do it without my having the slightest knowledge that the deed had been done, (4) without my knowing that he had the power to read my mind, or indeed (5) without my knowledge of even his bare existence. And what is more, (6) he does the wicked thing not out of any desire of his own to do it, but simply to spare me pain!

What is to be said of such a notion? It is not a self-contradiction. Such a thing appears logically possible, but surely it is a rather preposterous Rube Goldberg construction to explain what is far more simply and satisfactorily explained by the commonplace notion that it is no one other than I myself who deceives myself about alleged truths that I do not wish to acknowledge. In short, it is I who lie to myself by rendering some of my knowledge unconscious and that I am, therefore, responsible for it.

Thus we arrive at the notion of self-deception as the commonplace and empirically verifiable meaning of the notion of unconscious agency. The fact is that there is direct experience of this less spectacular kind of unconscious and that common speech handles the matter in a way that is perhaps not less paradoxical, but is truer to the facts (Gardiner 1968). Many have noted that the clearest and most common examples of the workings of the unconscious are referred to in ordinary speech as self-deception (Fingarette 1969). It comes to simply this: we do not wish to know something and so we blind ourselves to it, as, for example, when I do not wish to be reminded of my unpaid bills and so "forget" about them and manage to direct my glance elsewhere when I pass in their vicinity. This is a most ordinary and undeniable experience, but it is not for that reason less remarkable. I know the bills are there, on that table, where I always stack them, but I manage to keep my eyes away from that spot in order to spare myself the unpleasant feeling that would come from clearly acknowledging that I have not yet tended to them or haven't got the money to pay for what I have already consumed. The effort not to look presupposes the knowledge of what is there, an effort that must be maintained every time I pass in the vicinity and manage to keep my attention from falling on the threatening objects. I am both aware of the bills and not aware of them. To deceive myself I have to know precisely the thing I want to keep myself in ignorance of. From a purely logical point of view the whole business may seem quite impossible, but the plain fact is that we most certainly do it.[17]

Moreover, it is manifestly we who do it. This is made empirically clear by our own behavior when such self-deceptions are acknowledged. They are more or less severe and are acknowledged (i.e. brought to full, clear consciousness) with corresponding degrees of difficulty. But when we acknowledge even the mildest of them, it is with a certain wry, sheepish embarrassment, and when we acknowledge the deeper ones it is often with great remorse, proving in both cases that the conscious mind accepts responsibility for its own deception. Thus, the empirically accessible, real phenomena of self-deception speak loudly against the idea that it is something done to us by the unconscious conceived as an alien source of agency. To the contrary, we accept without question that it was we ourselves who did the deceiving, and that is surely why common speech had the good sense to call it *self*-deception.

No division of the self into two, one of whom fools the other, can account for the spontaneously sheepish smile that greets an acknowledged self-deception, and there is no significant gain from turning the paradox of self-deception into the question of how (or why) the unconscious mind can (or should) do the bidding of the conscious mind without the conscious mind's knowing anything about it. The simpler way of speaking is, therefore better, and so we take the notion of repression (understood as the principle activity of the unconscious) as but self-deception in fancy dress. When we speak of the unconscious hereafter that is all we will mean.[18] This is not at all meant to deny (or to affirm) the possibility of another kind of unconscious mental life, especially if the unconscious is understood only as a repository for certain kinds of very deep and rather unusual kinds of knowledge. It is meant only to show that we need not involve ourselves in it in order to understand the most basic examples of mental illness.

NEUROTIC PLEASURE

Given this understanding of the unconscious, we return to the effects of anxiety on the constitution of our pleasures. Because anxiety is essentially self-condemnation, because self-condemnation is nearly the greatest of pains, and because we will most certainly deceive ourselves about whatever thoughts cause us the most pain, it follows that in anxiety the heart of the matter is almost always unconscious in the sense that we have successfully deceived ourselves about its existence. But it does not, therefore, cease to motivate us. Here we follow the Freudian theory—a repressed desire remains a source of motivation even if it does not do so by becoming a demonic agent. This happens through the mechanisms of pleasure transformation previously described. Unconscious self-condemnation, like any other pain, forces us to seek relief. And just as all pain relief is experienced as "pleasure," so is the relief of unconscious self-condemnation. But there is a great difference. Ordinary pain relief is generally recognized as such. Few confuse it with simple pleasure and few would choose it over the simpler pleasures that would have been available had the pain not come along to begin with. The sailor knows, as we say, that he does not really want to throw his belongings overboard.

With unconscious pain it is different. The relief of unconscious pain is not recognized as such, and so its "pleasure" seems to be a simple pleasure. If the unconscious pain is self-condemnation, a very great pain, then the "pleasure" of its relief will be correspondingly great. Thus, the "pleasures" associated with the relief of unconscious self-condemnation will appear to be relatively simple pleasures and also pleasures of the greatest importance. The idea of being "cured" of them will seem absurd. In fact, one's entire self-esteem will be bound up with them, and so one will fight desperately to maintain them despite the fact that they are not really wanted.

The pleasures of anxiety-relief are not ordinary pleasures. Since the pain relieved is self-loathing, the pleasures of anxiety-relief are the pleasures derived from doing well and thereby demonstrating one's excellence. This presupposes a scale of values of some sort and a certain amount of proficiency as measured by that scale. Given that proficiency, there comes the "pleasure" that relieves the self-condemnation—the peculiar type of reassurance that comes from thinking well of oneself, or from being successful. Such self-respect is not a relaxed assurance of one's worth, but rather a more or less nervous reassurance gained from the successful effort to measure up. It is a very problematic kind of self-respect. When a moral scale of values is chosen it is called "self-righteousness"; and when it is aesthetic, it is a large part of what is called "snobbery." But whatever the scale of values, "pride" is the commonplace name for the pleasures to which it gives rise (Horney 1950).[19]

It would not seem to matter what values we pick. Any will do so far as the relief of anxiety is achieved. One could pick the Christian values of love and self-sacrifice, or one could play the cruel warrior for essentially the same reasons. One could take pride in business prowess, or be an artist, a thinker, a revolutionary. One can be traditional or individualistic, aggressive or meek, creative or conformist. There is presumably infinite variety in the behavior from which the "pleasure" of reassurance can be gained. But when motivated in this way, all such behavior involves the unconscious pain of an original self-condemnation and the creation thereby of another self that is manifested in the "pleasure" of what has been called "neurotic pride" (Horney 1950).

As the "pleasure" of anxious pain relief overrides simple pleasure, so the self that was constituted by the original harmony of pleasure and function is replaced by a new one. The transformation of the harmony of the soul is also a transformation of self and, properly speaking, a distortion of it. The new self relates to the old self as the new "pleasure" relates to the old. Its falseness is indexed by the quotation marks around "pleasure." And, of course, we do not know that the transformation has occurred. In fact, we are forced to believe that the new self is the true one because it was to convince us of this untruth that the new self arose to begin with. Were we to disbelieve, the entire point of the self-deception would be undone and the tears would have to be faced. Hence, the Freudian concept of resistance. Self-condemnation thus not only dooms us to live in ignorance of who we are and what we really want, it supplies us with a false self to believe in and a motive for clinging to it with utter desperation.

Because self-condemnation is individualized, unconscious, and intense, it creates a wide variety of eccentric pleasures that override ordinary pleasure and can cause an entire personality to shift to what it would never have been had the self-condemnation not been operative. Since the original self performed in a more or less pleasant way the activities to which we are naturally adapted (our natural functions), self-condemnation will tend to (but need not always) take us away from those common healthy functions into others that are dysfunctional and more highly individualized. It is a virus carried about within the psychological body and wedded to it by the bond of pride. It disrupts the original harmony of the soul by creating the eccentric pleasures of pain relief and doing so in a way that systematically blinds us to the entire process. This is mental illness. All behavior motivated by the relief of self-condemnation we will call "neurotic." So deep is this self-condemnation, however, that it is nearly true to call humankind the neurotic animal. The neuroses arise, says Freud, when

> the ego . . . enters into opposition with itself. . . . Such a dissociation, perhaps, exists only in man, so that, all in all, his superiority over the other animals may come down to his capacity for neurosis.[20]

Part III
The Good

4
The Paradox of Human Nature

THE DUPLICITY OF HUMAN NATURE

Up to this point we have spoken of human nature as if it consisted of a univocal set of perfectly harmonious dispositions. That was a simplification required for the elaboration of one side of a significantly more complicated truth. No great thinker from Plato on has ever really thought human nature so straightforwardly harmonious, and now that we have come to the subject of anxiety, conflict, and illness, we are forced to consider the complications they introduce into the question of our nature.

That there is a certain duplicity about human nature is a thoroughly recognized fact that often seems the defining characteristic of the contemporary viewpoint. Heidegger, for example (1927: 32, 67), defines humankind as the being whose being is an issue for it, meaning by this that our being lies not in what we already are (as it does for all mere things), but in what we are not yet, in our "to-be," in which futurity replaces the solidity of presence as the fundamental modality of being. Sartre (1946) made this notion into the defining formula of existentialism—that for humankind existence precedes essence—and concluded that there is, therefore, no given human nature other than the task of freely creating a temporary self-definition. In both of these formulations we see a hostility to the notion of a fixed human nature that is typical of the contemporary educated sensibility. It is widespread in the literature of the twentieth century, and it is presumably reflected also in the reluctance of empirical anthropology to discuss anything so restrictive as human nature in general and to focus instead on cataloging the wide variety of differences in human culture.

It is not so often realized, however, that a very significant portion of the most traditional philosophical anthropology also shows a deep appreciation for the equivocal character of human nature. Aristotle, for example, who has a minimal tolerance for paradox, not only asserts humankind to have a fixed nature, but also recognizes that it is the peculiar nature of this being to negate that fixed nature, and that therefore, in a sense, humankind becomes itself only in the paradoxical attempt to negate itself. For him the fixed side of human nature is represented by the traditional definition—the rational animal. Since Aristotle rather clearly states that happiness is to be understood as the fulfillment of essential nature, we would expect human happiness, for him, to lie in a judicious blending of our animal (or earthly) elements with the divine spark that (for Aristotle) is represented by reason. And indeed Aristotle does grant to this "mixed life" a certain second-class happiness (*N.E.*, X, 1178a8–23). But he denies it the highest status and says rather that

> we must not follow those who advise us, being men, to think of human
> things, and being mortal, of mortal things, but must, so far as we can,
> make ourselves immortal and strain every nerve to live in accordance
> with the best thing in us . . . for reason more than anything else *is* man.
> This life is therefore also the happiest. (*N.E.* X, 1177b31ff)

Aristotle struggles here with what is for him an uncomfortably paradoxical anthropology in which the truest fulfillment of human nature comes not from the fulfillment of what is merely human, but from the attempt to negate our essential humanness—to be as God. This means that it would be the peculiarity of human nature that it must at least try to negate itself in order to become that which it most truly is.

It is important to note that Aristotle is not alone in this. His notions here are almost certainly derived from the Platonic anthropology of the *Symposium*, wherein (203–4) the human essence (or at least the essence of philosophy, the most essentially human activity) is understood to consist of eros, which is the desire for that which is lacking in a defective form of being, and which, if ever completely fulfilled, would drive that lower form of being into a state of nonerotic contentment that is appropriate only to God. For Plato, the essentially human (or philosophical) mode of being is that of lack combined with the dim knowledge of what is lacking—poverty combined with resource. This is eros, the continual effort to achieve self-transcendence through the achievement of a godlike satiety.

In a primitive way, the same notion of self-transcendence towards the gods is suggested by the moral sensibility of the *Iliad*, whose heroes self-consciously struggle to be godlike and immortal, and it presumably appears in the implied anthropology of the fall when Eve is tempted by the promise that if she eats the forbidden fruit she will become like God. Indeed, according to Eliade (1954: 34) this attitude also is typical of the self-conception of all archaic peoples.

> the man of a traditional culture sees himself as real only to the extent that he ceases to be himself . . . and is satisfied with imitating and repeating the gestures of another. In other words he sees himself as real, i.e., as truly himself, only and precisely insofar as he ceases to be so.

This means that the duplicity of human nature has been long recognized and that, therefore, it is almost a foregone conclusion that there will always be at least two meanings for the notion of human nature. On the one hand, there is humankind as the negator of himself—a fluid, dynamic character who in his modern form takes a fixed shape only to slip ironically away into some new projection of himself, and who, in his ancient form, is the tragic striver, forever struggling nobly against himself to be that "best" that it is impossible for him to be. But in either case there must already be something there to be negated. The rebel cannot rebel against a vapor. She must find in herself some form of fixed being to begin with, and even if she chooses to struggle against it, it may yet be true that it is to that fixed being that she in the end returns. In any case, while it is certainly true that the nature of human nature must include the distinctively human, self-negating, fluid and divergent aspect of human existence, so also must the word *nature* refer to some distinctively human, relatively simple, fixed human nature (whatever in particular that may be conceived to be—the rational animal, the toolmaker, the laughing animal, the featherless biped, etc.). Any truly satisfying anthropology simply must take account of both aspects of our being.

THE ORIGIN OF ANXIETY AND SELF-NEGATION

The relatively fixed side of human nature is rooted in the body, in its monotonous stability from culture to culture, generation after generation. But this solidity is not limited to the body. Because it is rooted in the body through the laws of genetics and evolution, the harmony of the soul must be approximately as stable as the body itself. Its configuration of pleasures is the body-in-consciousness, just as hunger and sexuality are the motivational organs of the digestive and reproductive systems.

Whatever exactly the harmony of the soul is, it is our fixed human nature, and it is set for us by nature. So far as we are constituted by it, we are passive and "thing-like," at least to the extent that it is right to characterize *any* animal as thing-like. Its elaboration has been the aim of all anthropology that has sought the natural, original, unalienated, or unspoiled, human essence, and while our "doubleness" certainly makes it more difficult to chart this aspect of our nature than that of the other animals, it is not fundamentally incapable of scientific or rational apprehension.

Insofar as we are, like all other things, things that simply have a nature, that nature, is defined by the original configuration of pleasures. But we are also the anxious animal, the animal divided against itself and, therefore, continually rejecting and recreating itself, godlike, "a self-propelled wheel" to quote Nietzsche, and so also, it is our nature to negate this harmony for the sake of novelty, for transcendence, for power, for progress, or simply to relieve our sense of inadequacy. Our restlessness is an empirical fact. For the naturalistic brackets the question is only how nature itself could produce a creature whose nature (in part) lies in the negation of its own nature.

If humankind is seen as nature plus something else (the supernatural, a spark of God, the Platonic memory of transcendence) then there is no problem about human doubleness. On that understanding humankind is simply the union of two opposed principles (flesh and spirit, perhaps, or mind and body), and from this stems our paradoxical nature. But from within the naturalistic brackets there is only one source, and so the question arises why, in our case alone, nature should produce this chameleon of a species. Biologically, the question is simply why this species came to have such a remarkable adaptability.

Put this way, the answer seems clear. From within the naturalistic brackets the divine spark is merely one more mechanism in the struggle for reproductive success. Every other animal is content to be itself and lives in the simplicity of a nature that is entirely fixed. We are the anxious animal, born to self-condemnation, self-negation, and self-recreation. We are also the adaptable animal, the imaginative animal; and we are the dominant animal. The answer immediately suggests itself. Is not our domination rooted in our adaptability and our rational imagination? Is it not clear that a creature that is especially dissatisfied with itself will have a special incentive to adapt itself to new circumstances and even to invent or seek out the circumstances to which it must adapt?

In general pain is a functional disadvantage. The squirrel who enjoys collecting nuts will replace the one who needs the goad of pain, all else being equal, and so, generally, pain will be selected against. But if there were a pain that enhanced domination, then that pain, once it made its appearance, would be selected in the short run, even if the price of that domination were a species of unhappiness.

Such apparently is self-condemnation. It is a pain that is relieved through achievement on a scale of values. As such it is a pain that can transform the harmony of the original pleasures in a wide variety of ways and thereby make the human being adjustable to a far wider variety of circumstances (social and environmental) than was possible within the original harmony. From this would stem an enormous reproductive advantage, an advantage that is surely great enough to account for our domination as a species.

Further, there is the matter of the specific values chosen by the effort to negate the original self. If we look at the early history of western civilization, we see that the values chosen enhanced domination of the environment in quite obvious ways. We see that while the neurotic self at first claims contempt for the pragmatic or reproductive ends that constitute the original harmony of the soul, in fact the values through which it defines itself could not have been better chosen for those most mundane goals.

To judge from the *Iliad* (IX, 410–20) the first negation of selfhood chooses the values of the warrior-hero who manifests his doubleness by despising all that is purely human (a long life spent in a peaceful occupation close to family and home) and pursues instead immortal glory in the field of horrible combat.

> For my mother Thetis the goddess of the silver feet tells me
> I carry two sorts of destiny toward the day of of my death. Either,
> If I stay here and fight beside the city of the Trojans,
> My return home is gone, but my glory shall be everlasting;
> But if I return home to the beloved land of my fathers,
> The excellence of my glory is gone, but there will be a long life
> Left for me, and my end in death will not come quickly.

This heroic, neurotic self rejects plain humanness, symbolized as domesticity and long life, and chooses instead the "godlike" values of warfare, courage, strength, and competition. His "pleasure" becomes "the pride of his great strength." But from a hard-boiled evolutionary point of view, nothing could be clearer than that these warrior values confer an obvious reproductive differential upon their possessor. At the crudest level they are simply the values of the dominant male, destroying other males and carrying off their women. So long as the violent, inherently antisocial character of these values does not completely rend the social fabric that makes them possible, they serve the ends of reproductive advantage. It is of more than just passing interest, therefore, that the conflict between Achilles' social character (his relations to his friends, and allies) and his glory (his relation to the Trojans) is one of the *Iliad*'s most basic themes. It is also important to remember that the original quarrel between Achilles and Agamemmnon is over a woman, i.e., over the bearer of the hero's seed. But the most critical point is that however horrible their work, and however infantile these virtues may seem to us, to Homer they make the hero nothing less than godlike, i.e., beyond the limits of mere human nature.

Achilles is intellectualized by thoughtful Odysseus, who is echoed by the clever, mystery-solving Oedipus, who is in turn replaced by Socrates, Plato, and Aristotle. In the course of Greek history a revalorization occurs, at least among the intellectuals, in which humankind is no longer deemed godlike by virtue of its physical strength or skill or courage, but by reason of its reason. Henceforth, we are the rational animal, and this rationality is, of course, projected onto God so that in pursuing the new value we remain as fully godlike as Achilles.[1] To us who are the heirs of this tradition, Socrates does indeed seem more truly godlike and heroic than the crude and savagely splendid Achilles. But at a deeper level they are the same. Socrates's contempt for the domestic, the mortal, the feminine, and the naturally human, is, if anything, still greater than Achilles's.

> When we went inside we found Socrates just released from his chains, and Xanthippe—you know her—sitting by him with the little boy on her knee. As soon as Xanthippe saw us she broke out in the sort of remark you would expect from a woman. 'Oh, Socrates, this is the last time you and your friends will be able to talk together.'
>
> Socrates looked at Crito. 'Crito,' he said, 'someone had better take her home.'
>
> Some of Crito's servants led her away crying hysterically. Socrates sat up on the bed and drew up his leg and massaged it, saying as he did so, 'What a queer thing it is, my friends, this sensation which is popularly called pleasure.'

For his wife and children he cares nothing. Because it serves the mundane end of physical reproduction, heterosexual love is inferior to love between men (*Symposium* 208eff.), which at its best is a kind of moral/intellectual comradeship-in-arms. The body is a mere burden, and life is a battlefield, like the Trojan plain, in which to work out the longing for ontological glory, which longing is consummated in philosophy, itself a kind of dialectical warfare and (also like warfare) a continual practicing for death (Phaedo 64–66).

But no matter how sublimely conceived the ultimate goal of reason may be, this extravagant cultivation of rationality inevitably serves the end of mundane power. It is true that the great Greek philosophers did not think of reason as primarily technological (though clearly the sophists did). Still the worldly benefits of even the purest intellectual prowess are always available to the society as a whole. If Plato and Aristotle were above them, others were not. The undisputable fact is that the hunger for self-transcendence again chose values that were of the greatest biological service for the reproductive success of the species. In fact, compared to the opportunities for power, control and domination unleashed by the works of intellect (in time, the entire technological prowess of western civilization) the brute power of an Achilles is but the strutting of a child.

It is unsettling, of course, to associate the longings of philosophy with self-condemnation, anxiety and illness, and it may seem too easy to assert this in an age that is quite familiar with such claims as applied to the arts. There are presumably motives for engaging in philosophy other than those emphasized by Plato (or by the Greeks, one could say, since Aristotle and at least some of the pre-Socratics show similar attitudes). Therefore, it is important to point out that for the ancients too there was something deeply wrong with their heroic figures, be they warriors of words or flesh and blood. Indeed, that sense of the ineluctable wrongness of their heroes is the seed from which tragedy grew. Achilles is a splendid monster and is known to be such by Homer. The cleverness of Oedipus saves the city, but his admirably rational efforts to use knowledge for the sake of good also bring upon the city sickness, pollution and plague and lead finally to his own ironic blindness. And most of all there is the fact that Plato never tired of hinting at the problematic nature of Socrates, who, in close relation to his erotic quest for transcendence, said of himself (*Phaedrus* 230a) that he did not know whether he was a tame and gentle animal [*sic*] or a monster, implying that the simple, domestic life pictured in the *Republic's* pig-city, which he himself declared to be the "true and healthy life," is somehow less than fully human, and that a full-fledged human being, if such is illustrated by the life of Socrates, is somehow inherently monstrous, sick, or unnatural (Griswold 1986: 39–41, 94–5).[2] Philosophy, for Plato, was itself one of the luxuries associated with intemperance. Undoubtedly, Plato hoped that philosophy would amount to a cure for intemperance, but he apparently thought also that the seeking of cures is a sign of illness.

In any case it is clearly true that the values chosen by early western literature are rooted in a fundamental condemnation of the biological (and metaphysical) condition of humankind and that those values are such that they served mightily to make humankind the dominant species on earth. Thus it is not simply because we are rational that we dominate the earth, nor because of our courage, inventiveness or skill. Rationality, imagination and courage are mere tools. Everything depends on the ends toward which they are used, and those ends in turn depend on the emotions that drive us. It simply must be true that, in part at least, we dominate the earth because we are discontented with ourselves, because that discontent can most easily be assuaged by achievement, and because achievement for us is, at first, measured by domination, whether it is the petty domination of the warrior or the spectacular attempt of the thinker to grasp all being in a net of words.

HEALTH AND NATURE RECONSIDERED

There is then a straightforward evolutionary reason for our self-condemnation. Anxiety has contributed to our domination of the biosphere. Nature has given us both the fixed and distinctively human harmony of the soul, and also our (equally) distinctive tendency to transcend, negate or destroy that harmony in the effort to make ourselves into something we are not. In one sense, therefore, both the harmony and its negation are quite natural, and therefore the question arises of how one can claim that the harmonious condition of the soul is more natural or healthy than its neurotic variations. One could push the matter still farther, in fact, claiming that since anxiety is natural, anyone who did not negate herself, anyone who resided solely and simply in the original harmony, would not be fully human.[3]

I would suggest that the key to this problem, which constitutes, of course, the most typical objection to all matural teleology, lies in the fact that our human nature is radically equivocal, and in the consequent fact that the word *nature,* when applied to creatures as paradoxical as ourselves, is also radically equivocal. Biologically speaking, we are rather like devices that were expertly, intricately and harmoniously designed over a long period of time to do quite well in an original environment, who were already fully defined and teleologically complete (i.e., distinctively human) by virtue of that design, and who were then given just one more trick, anxiety, which caused us to reproduce still better in a wider variety of environments, but did so at the price of our condemnation of our own already-human nature—at the price of a partial distortion of that intricate, original self. The advent of anxiety did not create a new species, but it did make it our nature to alter what was already our truly human nature. For us therefore "nature" must always have two meanings. Depending on which is meant, we will come to different conclusions about the naturalness of an instinctive life or a life of high achievement and sophistication that rests on a neurotic distortion of the original selfhood.

It does not follow from our paradoxicality that there is no real human nature. If that were true, we would be utterly flexible. That is manifestly counterfactual. There are limits to our elasticity. At a minimum we must say that human nature is constituted by *both* those limits and the effort to transcend them, by *both* the original harmony and the supervening anxiety that transforms it.

Now if no more than this were said, human nature would be merely the sum of the two poles of paradox that define it. But the truth seems to be something rather more subtle than that. It is not just that the human being is composed of two things, instinct and self-condemnation, just as one might say it is composed of animality plus rationality. Rather, we must see that human instinctual life (which, it must be remembered, certainly includes speech) is and was sufficient by itself to define an acceptably human mode of being (the rational animal), and so also is the negation and transformation of those instincts through the operations of anxiety (the neurotic animal, the animal that is ashamed of itself).

A word that has two distinct sets of criteria sufficient to identify its proper usage is an equivocal term, and so the term *nature* in the phrase "human nature" is equivocal. Depending on which meaning is intended, a relatively simple instinctual life (which would include a measure of uncomplicated rationality), or a neurotically complicated life may be properly called "natural."

Obviously, when the notion of nature was used to define mental health in chapter 1, it was with the former meaning in mind. There is, however, no question that in one sense or another of the word *nature, both* the harmony of the soul *and* its neurotic transformation are natural.

The truth then appears to be that in one sense of the word both sickness and health are natural. At the same time, teleology has always insisted that the true nature of an organism is not shown by whatever condition it might be "naturally" found in, but rather by what is generally called its "most excellent condition." In an analogous way, there are certain very clear asymmetries that confer a priority on what we might call "harmony-nature" over "anxiety-nature."

The first and most significant asymmetry concerns the psychodynamics of desire that make the harmony of the soul more persistent than any and all of its transformations. Indeed, the word *transformation* is misleading here. In anxiety's transformation of the original psychological material, that material is not simply destroyed, as when a tree is transformed into a house or the grass is assimilated by the cow. Anxiety can effect only a relatively superficial alteration of pleasures through the mechanism of unconscious pain relief. But the moment the pain ceases, the original constellation of pleasures returns, just as the sailor rediscovers the pleasure of his possessions (and the pain of their loss) the moment the storm is over. The original self is not so much destroyed in the process of transformation, as it is buried, and it remains there, as it were, awaiting the circumstances in which it can reappear. Perhaps the appropriate metaphor is the relationship of a balloon to a force that distorts its shape. The presence of pain renders the psyche elastic, but it always can and sometimes actually does return to something like its original configuration. This critical asymmetry between the two notions of human nature gives to the original harmony a far greater right to be constitutive of human nature.

Second, it should be noted that there is a certain logic that corresponds to the asymmetry between the two human natures, a logic that is reflected in points made by both Plato and Aristotle about the relation of pain relief to the notions of true and false pleasure and desire. In essence they both claim that only the pleasures of the harmonious soul can be called "true pleasures," a point that is empirically confirmed when the sailor (or the recipient of successful therapy) says of her eccentric pleasures that she "never *really* enjoyed them" anyway. To the extent that only the desires of the harmonious soul are "true" desires, so the harmonious nature is our truest nature. This illuminates the priority of the harmonious nature from yet another angle, an angle that is more fully explored in chapter 6. See also Veatch's comments (1992) on the good as constitutive of desire in the teleological account of psychology.

Third, it is important to notice that the logical and dynamic priority of the harmonious nature is the reflection of a straightforward temporal priority that is very nearly decisive on its own account. The harmony of the soul contains all that ties us to the rest of animate nature. It is thus far older than anxiety and presumably contains the totality of our instinctive life except for the anxiety-motivation itself.[4] Age, it must be remembered, is a very important criterion for the establishment of legitimacy from an evolutionary point of view. What we call "nature" is conservative and tradition-loving. Pollution, i.e., the destruction of the "natural" environment and its replacement by an "artificial" one, is a time-bound concept. Given enough time, the natural order would adjust to the pollutants of industry. Artifice is eventually incorporated into a remade nature and a system of new natures is created, as happened after the advent of oxygen. In the short run, however, these pollutants wreck havoc on what is then commonly and properly called the "natural environment," i.e., the environment into which the dynamic and structural features of the organism have evolved with great intricacy and internal harmony over an unimaginably long sequence of biological ages.

Finally, there is the matter of sheer quantity. We have already noted that the harmony of the soul contains all the instinctual elements of our most ancient past and almost all of the uniquely human motivations of our more recent past. Over and against all this the neurotic self has only one motivation. Our capacity for anxiety, although it gives rise to a quite marvelous variety, is itself still but a single source of motivation.

The harmonious self is thus the ever-persisting source from which the neurotic self emerges. It is more correct to say that it is cloaked or distorted rather than destroyed by its neurotic transformation, and so, over time, these transformations presumably circle around it (so that it is their approximate vector sum), or, better perhaps, they may be said to radiate from it like trips from home. But in any case, the harmonious self reemerges as soon as the disturbing force relents; it is much older than the neurotic self and it is immeasurably bigger. Nothing can deny the neurotic self's claim to be natural in its own carefully limited sense of the word *nature,* but these broader considerations amount to a set of very pressing reasons for granting that to be a very minimal sense of the word.

One last and extremely suggestive point can be made in this regard. It gives to the original meaning of human nature a certain priority, but it is a quite different kind of point and may be said to absorb or incorporate the late-coming meaning without attempting to assign it a secondary status. Even if we take human nature as the mere sum of two opposed but equal natures, we would still be logically forced to grant a certain important kind of priority to the original harmony.

Suppose that human nature is the paradox here described. It is then our nature to negate our already existing nature. For such a creature there is no possibility of avoiding self-negation. Either we allow our (natural) capacity for self-negation to negate our original self, or (in a still more sophisticated but presumably still natural use of self-negation) we attempt to negate the self-negating aspect of ourselves. In other words, we may attempt to turn self-negation on itself and thereby try self-consciously to return ourselves to as much as possible of our original selfhood. This is, of course, to maximize our original nature. Although it is indeed to negate the self-negating part of ourselves, it is also a use that very self-negating self, and so it is a preservation of it. The negation of self-negation, therefore, maximizes what it is our nature to be, in every sense of the word. Such activity, therefore, has much to recommend it as the most nature-fulfilling activity that it is possible for a human being to engage in.

This reflexive self-negation, as we might call it, is not merely a verbal construct. It is a very real, very sophisticated, and very important human activity. Insofar as self-negation is always artifice vis-à-vis the original self, the negation of self-negation may also be said to belong to the realm of art and artifice. It is, however, art in the service of nature, the art that, in Aristotle's words, perfects nature. In our modern language it is therapy. In it the urge to dominate the world or one's rivals (so far as that urge has a neurotic motivation) is converted into the urge to dominate oneself (one's neurotic self). The control of the other is converted into self-control, which self-control is also the liberation and discovery of the nonneurotic self. It is in many ways the dawn of a truly moral consciousness. It is at least the dawn of self-knowledge, and possibly of moderation.

Because the negation of self-negation fulfills both our harmonious and self-negating natures, there is good reason to call it the most human nature of all. In the unlikely or impossible case of its perfect completion, there would, of course, be a kind of return to the original harmony in which would remain only the barest vestige of the self-negating self. But this would be a return that was at the same time an unquestionable advance, or, to use Hegelian language, it would be an absorption of the original thesis into a higher synthesis—the innocence of the saint rather than the innocence of naiveté. But the task, of course, is never complete. The return is always a process of partial reappropriation and not the kind of wholesale appropriation of the past that is associated with romanticism. Thus the fullest and truest human nature does not reside solely in the evolutionary past. The truest human nature, the human nature that most encompasses both senses of the word nature, resides in the partial and ongoing negation of self-negation—in the continual process of self-discovery. It is, in part, a rational, sophisticated, and artful projection of the past into a future, a projection that determines a present that negates the self as a dead fact that is simply happened upon (the neurotic self) and seeks instead to recreate it by a process of discovering what it is that one has always really been. It is *both* nature as the primitive past *and* nature as the highest attainable perfection.

5
Human Nature/Human Goodness

THE FIXED SIDE OF HUMAN NATURE

The self from which we are driven remains our truest self, the object of a profound human nostalgia that gives rise to innumerable stories of the fall and recurs on the modern scene in the romantic longing for natural man. This longing can be part of a political eruption, as in the anarcho/communist ideal of an unalienated human nature. But it can also be religious, psychological or even academic, as in the anthropologist's former search for the primitive or "untouched" human condition. It can also be a popular mixture of all these modalities, as during the 1960s when an entire generation seemed to reject civilization, reason, age, authority, and tradition. But one way or the other, this nostalgia for an original harmony of the soul remains a perennial facet of human existence.

It is not, in itself, a foolish thing. For the reasons given, the idea of a species-wide truer self beneath the apparent one is not absurd. The original configuration of pleasures simply must be there as the original psychological material out of which is elaborated the complex, phenomenal self and to which we might yet return at the moment of release from tension.

But what is that deeper self? This question used to be asked by wondering whether human nature is good or bad. It comes to this: whether our natural functions, the things we would do if we lived in the original configuration of pleasure and behavior, are gentle or violent, social or so lacking in care for others that the natural human being would live in isolation even when he lived with others.

Beginning with Hobbes, early modern philosophical anthropology tried to answer this question by seeking the pre-social human being. It was simply presupposed that society was not a natural thing and that the true human nature would show forth if we could strip away in thought the artificialities of socialization.[1] Now, though, it is generally agreed that this was a conceptually misguided approach. There are no more people apart from society, than there are turtles apart from their shells. Social life *is* our shell—our protective claws (technology) and our intelligence (speech and education). It makes no more sense to think of the pre-social human as the natural human than to think of the pre-shell turtle as the truest turtle.

Social man is natural man. This simple fact, though clearly recognized by the tradition from Plato to Thomas Aquinas, was denied by a great deal of early modern philosophy, and the tendency of existentialism to identify the social self with inauthenticity has kept something like the early modern attitude alive right up to the end of the twentieth century. Analytic philosophy has not discussed the matter much; Marxism has defended the traditional point of view, but as a means to its political agenda; and empirical anthropology, partly out of a (perhaps misguided) intellectual humility and partly from fear of the imperialist uses to which the notion of human nature has been put, prefers to speak of the diversity of cultures. There are peoples as gentle as the forest pygmies or the Tasaday, we are told, as depressed as the Ik, as cruel as the Kwakiutl and warlike as the Sioux. Instead of the human essence, we are given the nonjudgmental elaboration of human differences, a tendency that was virtually built into the recent meaning of anthropology. Consider, for example, the very first sentence of Ruth Benedict's *Patterns of Culture* (1934: 1).

> Anthropology is the science of human beings as creatures of society. It fastens its attention upon those physical characteristics and industrial techniques, those conventions and values, which distinguish one community from all others that belong to a different tradition.[2]

What is common to us all is human nature. Benedict's attitude makes it clear enough that, with due allowance for the exceptions,[3] much of recent anthropology has not only not been looking for such a nature, but, if there is such a thing, it has probably studied human beings in such a way as to obscure it.

Conceived solely as the study of differences, anthropology cannot help us. It can hurt us, however, if we believe that in some straightforward way the remarkable diversity it has found disproves the existence of a normative human nature. That would be a form of moral empiricism, the error of which was long ago pointed out when Thomas Aquinas said that any genuinely universal natural law would still have to be adapted by the human law to the circumstances of time and place and so would have to show a certain degree of variation, a point that continues to be made in recent philosophical critiques of "sociological relativism.⁴ To this must now be added all that has been said about anxiety and the "natural" distortion of human "nature," so that we most certainly should not expect the fixed side of human nature to show itself unequivocally in any society— not even in the most primitive—and even less should we expect it to be merely the lowest common denominator of conduct, some minimal residue of behavior that happens to turn up in all societies. Any detailed teasing out of the human essence from the wealth of empirical material would be a task that requires not only the widest factual knowledge, but also the most subtle interpretive abilities, guided, in part, by a theory of psychological transformation. That is hardly to be attempted here, but a few very broad considerations do seem sufficient to outline the most likely answers to our most pressing moral questions.

The fact that social life is the human shell, the immaterial but no-less-biological organ without which we would be the weakest of animals points to the basic truth about human nature, which, even if it is not the whole truth, must surely be the truest simplification. If we cannot exist without society, if society is the condition for the possibility of our most basic means of biological survival (education, speech and reason), then to deny that we are at least reasonably well adapted to social life would be like saying that dogs are not well adapted to barking and biting or cows to grazing. Certainly, it is possible to imagine circumstances in which so ill-constructed an organism might come to pass, but the general likelihood is overwhelmingly against it, and this a priori likelihood seems to be confirmed by the growing weight of empirical evidence.⁵

But if we are reasonably well adapted to social life, then there must then have been an original harmony of pleasure with social needs. In some rough way, then, all the behavior that is a necessary condition for the existence of society must be behavior to which our original harmony of the soul inclines us. Since a great deal of moralizing concerns precisely the conditions for social life, a great deal of morality must stand within the original configuration of pleasure and behavior. In some rough way, therefore, we simply must be naturally good.

This is hardly a new point. As argued in the introduction, the view that human goodness is founded in nature is the oldest ethical viewpoint, far older than Aristotle, but it received from him its earliest explicit formulation in the claim that we are by nature political and that the function of the political life is to perfect the virtues to which nature has already inclined us.⁶ It was codified by St. Thomas in his conception of natural law.

> there is in man an inclination to good, according to the nature of his rea-
> son, which nature is proper to him: thus man has a natural inclination . . .
> to live in society; and in this respect, whatever pertains to this inclination
> belongs to the natural law; for instance, . . . , to avoid offending those
> among whom one has to live, and other such things . . . [7]

Rousseau represented one attempt to revive part of this idea in modern
times, and parts of the doctrine of alienation in early Marxism represent
another. The fact is that this point of view is so commonsensical, so subject
to day-to-day confirmation, and so plausible a priori that almost no one in
the philosophical pantheon has denied it except for some of the philosophers of emergent capitalism. Even Hobbes, the most famous of these,
somehow has to pay allegiance to an idea that seems so obviously true.

It is instructive to see how he does this. Like Aquinas, he has his laws
of nature that he conceives to include the necessary conditions for social
life. Foremost among these he puts the desire for peace, but included also
are prohibitions against ingratitude, arrogance, pride, iniquity, and, in
short, all that would be proscribed by a consistent application of the golden
rule (1651: I,15), which would surely include a good deal of the behavior
that is called "moral." Thus, even for Hobbes morality is included within
the laws of nature.

But having said this much, and despite the label "laws of nature"
Hobbes must go on to minimize the true naturalness of this natural law or he
would undercut his entire conception of war as the natural human condition.
He does this by claiming that the natural law is merely a discovery of reason
rather than a description of the natural inclinations of the human soul, which
means that we ought to desire that they hold in fact, but not that our desires
are actually formed by them (and even less that we are obligated actually to
act on them prior to the establishment of the social contract (1651: I,15).

This last point is very important. In Thomas Aquinas there are two
ways for the natural law to inhere in a creature, either by reason or through
the creature's nonrational inclinations (Q. XCI, A.2, esp Reply Obj. 3). It is
true that the former is what he is usually speaking of when he speaks of its
inherence in human beings, and it is also true that the dual or fallen nature
of human nature forces him to be very careful, if not equivocal, about the
question of whether human passion is in conformity with the laws of
nature. But to whatever extent the Edenic, biological inclinations of man
have survived in the fallen condition, so also, for him, is the natural law
still present in our passions.

> in the first state. . . . Adam had no passion with evil as its object. . . . For
> our sensual appetite, wherein the passions reside, is not entirely subject to

reason, and hence at times our passions forestall and hinder reason's judgement, and at other times they follow after reason's judgement, according as the sensual appetite obeys reason to some extent. But in the state of innocence . . . the passions of the soul existed only as consequent upon the judgement of reason.[8]

Thus for Thomas the locus of natural law was both reason and the natural inclination of the passions, with due allowance made for the fallen condition of the species. Hobbes, however, places it only in reason, thereby changing the meaning of "natural law" in ethics and separating it from *all* anthropological considerations. Because, for Hobbes, the passions ought to conform to natural law but utterly do not, human psychology, or at least the behavior it gives rise to, must be radically and fundamentally restructured by reason so as to make society possible and give any real force to the natural law. This makes the application of the so-called natural law into what is, in Aristotle's terms, an act of violence wherein form is simply imposed on a material reality (human emotion) that has no inherent tendency in that direction. It is art, but only nominally is it the art that perfects nature. In fact, it is art that simply reshapes nature in accordance with art's own wishes, the art of the carpenter rather than the gardener, of the tyrant rather than the parent or king.

This hedging on the meaning of "natural" reflects the fact that even such a conventionalist as Hobbes saw that the bulk of traditional morality was in fact a precondition for the possibility of social life and that, therefore, it too had to be natural in some sense of the word. In effect, he altered the meaning of the word *natural* in order to allow for this possibility while still insisting that the natural condition of humankind was one of rampant amorality. But if we avoid this verbal shilly-shallying and grant the plain biological fact that social life is a part of real, material human nature, then so must be the rough outlines of morality. And what that would mean is that the rough outlines of morality must be included within the basic harmony of the soul.

Thou shalt not kill; thou shalt not steal; thou shalt not lie—these basic moral rules, though far from complete or unambiguous, and whatever else they may also be, are at a minimum the basic preconditions for the existence of human beings together in a common space. If we have to worry continually about being killed by our neighbors; if we expect them to be constantly changing the rules of property (whatever they may be) so as to satisfy their greed at our expense; if we expect each other to lie and so are unable ever to trust one another, then either living together becomes literally impossible or the "society" so constituted becomes sufficiently dysfunctional that it would not fare well in the process of natural selection. Indeed, such a society would be rather more like Hobbes's state of civil war than a civil society. It would presumably collapse of its own weight in fairly short order, especially under archaic conditions of life when the band can be dissolved and reconstituted by the decision of a single family to simply walk away. Wherever there is a reasonably stable society, then, behavior must in one way or another more or less conform to these moral rules. Even the proverbial band of robbers must treat each other with a minimum of decency if they are to work together (*Republic*, I,352b–e).

While this does mean that a certain peacefulness and honesty is almost certainly a part of human nature, it does not mean that it is always clear who or what cannot be killed, stolen from, or lied to. The standard criticism of the viewpoint advocated is that it does not give rise to very specific moral injunctions, and there is a certain truth to this. Cows, dogs, members of other tribes, wandering strangers, caravans, enemies of God, soldiers of other countries, etc., may or may not be killed in different stable, enduring societies. The injunction against murder is absolute (in the sense that all societies must have it) but it is also subject to wide varieties of interpretation. So also does the specific nature of property vary from one society to another, and the point at which a white lie becomes a serious lie, etc. Social life can survive under numerous interpretations of the basic prohibitions. But it could not survive if we utterly disregarded them in relation to those closest to home. Within the group of those who live together and must cooperate with each other (i.e., among neighbors), there must be certain rules of the game, however exactly specified, and those rules must more or less prohibit many of the things that have been traditionally considered immoral. Even such apparently small matters as politeness, courtesy, and respect for elders are probably quite necessary for social functioning, and, therefore, "natural," even though their exact contents at any given time or place is presumably subject to the widest variation.

On the other hand, there are almost surely many points of morality, especially our morality, which would not be included within the primitive harmony. The foremost discrepancy stems from the parochialism of the primitive moral sphere. The configuration of pleasure in the original harmony of the soul need apply moral treatment only to those in one's own immediate community, so that the idea of universal human rights, as we understand it, need not be included (which corresponds to the fact that in many archaic languages the word for "human being" and the name of the tribe are said to be the same).[9] Second, since the harmony of the soul would have to include only the necessary conditions for the possibility of society, it need not include such moral "luxuries" as equality of opportunity, rights of privacy, freedom of speech, religion and so on, many of which are so important to the modern democratic sensibility (and few, if any of which exist among primitive people). Certainly, society can exist without the recognition of these rights, and so there is no reason to think they have the biological status of the basic moral rules.

These are presumed defects in the morality of the original harmony of the soul, and these defects ought not be denied. Indeed, the whole idea of natural morality becomes rather comic when it is put through a series of logical gymnastics to make it coextensive with all that is appropriate to our particular form of social organization, as if our democratic ideals were a priori not only in all respects the best form of society, but also the most natural. Without denying these defects, therefore, it is still useful to think about their source and the extent to which there might be some natural remedy for them.

Hobbes is correct, I think, in claiming that the basic preconditions of society can be at least partly summed up in the golden rule (which is presumably the reason why the golden rule is an almost universally acknowledged moral principle). The golden rule, however, begins with one's own subjectivity, one's own desires, and if, as has usually been the case among humankind, one does not want freedom, privacy, or certain forms of equality, it will not incline one to give it. But since no one can tolerate life-threatening neighbors, being stolen from by them, or generally lied to by them, we can derive from the golden rule rough and rather parochial prohibitions against these gross forms of misbehavior. But finer moral discriminations are not likely to be forthcoming on a species-wide basis.

This defect stems from our taking the golden rule as a principle of reason that is applied to a presumably indifferent emotional material. The probability, however, is that the golden rule is psychologically effective (i.e., affective) not as a rational principle (like Hobbes's natural law) but as emotion itself, i.e., as a part of the original configuration of pleasures. It is presumably a codification of the feeling of compassion, which compassion is presumably a part of the original harmony of pleasure with the needs of social life. If so, the parochialism of the original harmony is considerably mitigated.

Compassion is not simply kindness toward others. We take it as exactly what its etymology indicates—the tendency to feel what another feels, or what we sometimes now call "empathy." It is operative when the sight of a human being in pain causes us to wince, or in the tendency to smile back when another person smiles at us. Though it can certainly be unlearned, the basic stuff of compassion does not seem to be learned in any very important sense of the word. The youngest infants smile when they are smiled at, young children cry at the sight of other children crying, and unsophisticated adults can become so empathetically involved with even movie actors that they forget they are watching a performance. Far from being learned, it is likely that if we did not first have this natural compassion we would never have been able to develop a common vocabulary for the description of emotional life, and it hardly seems a very great assumption to believe that adult human beings have as much untutored compassion as do children, dogs, and chimpanzees.

In any case, a natural inclination towards compassion (sometimes called "sympathy," "benevolence," "humanity," or "altruism") has formed a good part of most moral psychology. It is to be found in Hutcheson (1728), Hume (1736: V), (1751: appendix II), and Smith (1759). It is the foundation of Rousseau's theory of the natural goodness of man (1755: 223ff); and in the form of altruism and kin selection, a place has been found for something like it by contemporary sociobiology (Wilson 1979: 148). We assume then that we are put together in such a way as to feel the feelings of others. While this does not mean that we cannot also be jealous, petty and cruel, it does mean that to one degree or another compassion is always there to act as a brake on our own more aggressive emotions.

It is not clear how this natural compassion works, and so it is not clear how far it extends. What seems to be the case is that the more the other looks like us, or, as we say, the more we can identify with the other, the more compassion we feel. If the other is not of our tribe, we may hardly recognize him as a person, and our capacity for sympathy will presumably be less than our compassion for those who look and talk like us. Monkeys receive less compassion than people (even people of another tribe), but still more than dogs. Cows get less than dogs, fish less than that, insects get still less, and vegetables almost nothing at all. The potentiality for compassion extends as far as we can imagine the experience of pain or pleasure, and how far that goes depends on how much like ourselves the other seems to be. But compassion is always there to some degree, more so, perhaps, among less-sophisticated peoples. Some archaic peoples ask forgiveness of the game they kill, and some far-from-unsophisticated Hindus believe that (bad) human souls can be reincarnated as insects. Descartes, however, was able to convince himself that the sentience of animals was a matter for serious philosophical debate.

Compassion is there, and it is quite universal, but it hardly turns us into saints. It does, however cause us to extend kindly treatment beyond our immediate neighbors. Consequently it extends the list of prohibitions beyond the bare minimum required for social life, thereby mitigating to some uncertain degree the parochialism of natural morality.

Compassion is only one factor among others. Its existence does not preclude the existence of aggressive instincts. It is rather that whatever our aggressive tendencies might be (and there is no need here to deny them), compassion acts as a brake and holds them within certain limits. We will hurt others, especially if we cannot identify with them, but generally no more than we think we have to, just as primitive people kill animals, and almost all animals kill animals, but only to get what they need. As Rousseau put it (1755: 227), the maxim that expresses the effect of compassion on the totality of human behavior is "Do good for yourself with a minimum of harm to others." While this certainly does not define a life of *pure* compassion, and while it is possible to imagine higher moral ideals, such a life is not a bad one. Moreover, it does seem to be how most animals and most archaic people actually work. There is a great deal of barking and shouting but a near minimum of actual bloodshed. Housecats and humans with attenuated moral sensibilities are the only exceptions.

While we can be reasonably well assured of a rough decency in the basic harmony of the soul, the exact contents of this primitive virtue will probably never be known. The emotional ground of the prohibition against incest is almost certainly there, but, in addition to the matters already mentioned, one wants to know about other sexual taboos, about monogamy, slavery, abortion, the whole tangle of matters connected with religion and innumerable other issues that cause us so much trouble. In some cases, empirical research combined with philosophical, psychological, and ethical sophistication may yield real answers, but in many cases we will probably never have clear knowledge about either the basic harmony or its application to circumstances for which it was not intended.

This does not show, however, that primitive decency is unimportant. It does show that it is significantly incomplete when viewed from the standpoint of contemporary moral problems and that it cannot simply replace what we now call "morality." It remains true, however, that the most fundamental tenets of morality merely duplicate in verbal formulae the emotional configuration of primitive decency. To a considerable extent morality merely converts emotions into rules that may then be forced on a psychology that has, for one reason or another, become reluctant (Wilson 1975b).

Is the natural human being then good or bad? Neither, given all that we may mean by these terms, but we are naturally decent, and what this decency lacks in scope and refinement is compensated for by the spontaneity that motivates it. It is from the heart, it is innocent, and it has a ready smile.

What then would we be if we did not try to recreate ourselves in the image of our aesthetic, moral, or political imaginations? Not the best thing we can imagine, but social and compassionate by nature, and also probably somewhat selfish, parochial, and aggressive, all of it blended in a more or less amiable hodgepodge of logically inconsistent behavior. And this decency is still there at the center of our being; it is our nature. For most of us this is good news. We are better than we thought, even if we are not as good as we might like to be.

If, as seems probable, we add to this basic decency a tendency to respect the customs and traditions of one's own people, then there opens up the possibility of a relatively painless enhancement of rough virtue into the full virtue of a civilized human being through education, imitation, and what is called "socialization." As long as the basic harmony of feeling and function is not much upset by this education, it is presumably all to the good. We end up not only decent, but fully acculturated members of our tribe, i.e., Iroquois or Englishmen. But the basic social forms do not in this process have to be forced on some recalcitrant or indifferent material. We are already disposed that way. It is just a question of keeping out the weeds—a little pruning here and there, a bit of decoration.

THE MEDICAL AND THE MORAL

If the original configuration of pleasure and behavior is the ground of human decency, then random or unplanned deviations from it are quite likely to make us less decent or positively bad, just as such deviations from any highly evolved structure are not likely to make the organism do better the very thing it had evolved to do. Since mental illness is a distortion of that configuration, it must come close to being vice. This means that the medical and the moral are inseparable, and that, in turn, opens an entirely new (and also very old) perspective onto the meaning of moral life.

This critical point should not be exaggerated. The medical and the moral overlap throughout the most important arenas of human behavior, but they are not identical. Not all deviations from common decency are matters of psychological illness (ignorance and/or adaptation to hostile circumstance, for example, can also cause the behavior that deviates from decency), and not all mental illness is immoral since some anxiety-relief may be harmless eccentricity and some of it may actually conform to or mimic the behavior that is associated with the highest moral standards (as masochism and hostility can masquerade as self-sacrifice). But the likelihood is that anxiety-relief, because it is a distortion of a basically decent configuration of emotion and conduct, will generally result in less-than-decent behavior. The medical and moral are not identical, but it just so happens that the bulk of their denotations is common to them both.

The precise importance of this commonality is not immediately clear, but it becomes more so if we take note of a certain general structure that would seem to be common to nearly all unhealthy behavior. It is unlikely that the "pleasures" of anxiety-relief would cause us to engage in totally new forms of behavior, i.e, forms of behavior to which we are not already in some manner disposed and for which there is some already-existing word. The throwing of things overboard, after all, was not something the sailor did for the first time when the ship began to sink. He had, no doubt, thrown refuse over the rail, as well as anchors and life jackets, long before the storm came up. The general activity of throwing things overboard was not something new. What happened was that his fear caused him to engage in that particular species of behavior *in a way* that he had never done before. In the storm, he threw over *more* things and *a greater variety* of things than he had done before, and presumably he did it with an *intensity* we had not hitherto seen in regard to this activity. If we tried to describe the change in his behavior with the language available when it first emerged, we would surely say simply that he threw things overboard much more than he had done before or that he did it to a greater *degree* than before. And if we did not appreciate the quite sensible motivation that gave rise to the behavior, we would certainly think that he was engaging in it *too much*.

At the same time, viewed from the perspective of a different arena of behavior, we could say that this same activity amounted to doing *too little*. For example, in regard to care for his property (or that of others) he seems to have become quite deficient.

Presumably it is fair to generalize from this example. If so, we get the conclusion that neurotic activity is generally a variation on some arena of linguistically identifiable, healthy behavior that can be roughly character-ized as being too much or too little of it. Thus, neurotic behavior is gener-ally an excess or a deficiency when measured by the norm of health, as for example, frigidity is a deficiency of behavior in the sexual arena and neu-rotic bullying is an excess of pleasure in domination. This is confirmed by the fact that in virtually all the definitions of mental illness provided by DSM III, the words *excessive, reasonable,* or *appropriate* play a crucial role.[10]

This is a terribly important fact. It shows that there is not only a great commonality in the substance of health and decency, but also that the gen-eral structure of mental health and illness conforms to the general structure of virtue and vice as understood by Aristotle.

Neurotic deviation from health thus has three basic characteristics: (1) it is likely to be a violation of common decency, (2) it is characterized by excess and deficiency when compared to decency and/or health, and (3) it is "pleasant" to the person who engages in it. This means that in the tradi-tional language of morality, deviations from psychological health are gen-erally vices. This, in turn, means that health encompasses some rough form of virtue.

That health is nearly virtue and that illness comes close to being vice is a surprising thing to say. But, as argued in the Introduction, while it is surprising to us now, it is actually the oldest of moral views, beginning, no doubt, in the most ancient connection between healing and religion and holding sway until the decline of teleological thinking. From modern times on, morality and medicine went their separate ways (among the intellectuals, at least). Ideas such as the health of the soul became unfashionable with all but the untutored and those attracted to eccentric religious thinking (Christian Science, for example, or the current "spiritualization" of health in the so-called alternative or new-age culture). But until the rise of the mechanical world-view, virtually everyone believed that the medical was imbued with the authority of the moral. Thus, in the ancient world disease was almost always experienced as pollution or punishment, and even now there remains a very strong tendency, even among the most sophisticated, to feel, if not to think, that illness is something to be ashamed of. And surely this conceptual blending forms at least a part of the great (but fading) moral prestige of the medical profession.

To better appreciate this point it is important to remember that the idea of ethics as mere obedience to a set of morally authoritative rules is a relatively modern notion. In the Greek notion of virtue at least, virtue was manifested in a certain fullness of the person (or excellence, as it is sometimes translated), a living-up-to-one's-own-human-nature, and this, in turn, was often explicitly understood to require that the virtuous person actually enjoy his virtues.[11]

Hobbes, Locke, Rousseau (in *The Social Contract*), Kant, Mill— almost all the great modern moral thinkers and the entire philosophical tradition that has been based on them (and which has been so rightly criticized by MacIntyre, Veatch, and others) do not think in terms of virtue. Instead, they understand morality as a matter of whether one's behavior conforms to the appropriate rules (however these might be conceived). The pleasure that the agent may take in such behavior (i.e., the specific psychological configuration of his pleasures, his character) is of no great importance to them. With morality so understood, its connection to health was inevitably obscured, and thus there simply had to grow up the hostility that has existed since Freud between mental-health therapy and much of modern moral thought (Fromm 1947: 18).

Properly speaking, we probably ought not even to say that health and morality were once the same. It is virtue and health that have the intimate connection, and it was virtue that was the ancient "moral" ideal. "Morality" is perhaps best thought of as the name for the normative ideal that replaced virtue after the decline of teleological thinking. Virtue does not concern rules of behavior but rather the subtleties of character and hence the configuration of our pleasures and pains. To have the virtue of generosity is not merely to give to others. It is to be a generous person, and that means being the sort of person who enjoys giving and who takes pleasure in the pleasure of others. The theory of virtue is thus inevitably a moral psychology.

Morality focuses instead on propriety, on the rules to which behavior must conform if it is to be judged acceptable. Morality is legalistic rather than psychological. It tends to find psychology irrelevant, and when it speaks of character it tends to understand it as mere will power, the ability to force morally correct behavior on emotions that would pull the self in other ways.

If health and primitive virtue are one, then the ancient view turns out to have been justified and we have one more reason to conclude that ethical thinking need no longer be stuck in the moral mode. Morality will remain important, of course. As previously emphasized, it is needed for all sorts of matters for which virtue gives no clear guideline, and it is certainly needed for people whose configuration of pleasures is distorted enough to make virtue painful. It is needed for political life, so that we can live together with such people and bring them up to a minimal level of socially acceptable behavior. It is needed wherever great precision is required (as in contract law, for example, or in any precise enumeration of rights and duties). By no means can we do away with morality. But it should not be conceived as the heart of ethics, and it certainly should not be taken as the highest ethical ideal. In these respects, it may be replaced by virtue, where virtue is understood as precisely that union of pleasure, spontaneity and decency that constitutes emotional health.

THE POSSIBILITY OF HAPPINESS

If we could be rid of anxiety and the behavior that arises to relieve it, then, ignoring other factors for the moment, primitive virtue would surface of its own accord. Combined with the blessings of tradition and convention, this would make a most remarkable, most truly excellent person in whom spontaneity and goodness formed a seamless whole—the union of freedom and goodness dreamt of in the anarchists' ideal. Given the way that such notions have been abused in the political and popular psychological attitudes that followed the 1960s, however, a strong note of caution needs to be sounded.

Any thoroughgoing union of pleasure and goodness, freedom and responsibility, selfishness and friendship, is an extraordinarily rare thing. While all people know some of it (depending on their character), to know it all would be to have a disposition that is essentially saintly. This is nothing that is to be had merely by fleeing the corrupting influences of civilization, by destroying the forces of political oppression, by tinkering with the economy, by resolving to think well of oneself, or by surrounding ourselves with support groups designed to tell us that whatever we are is fine.

The desire to be ignorant of one's own self-condemnation is as strong as any human desire, and it is much stronger than the desire to be free of anxiety (see pages 84–87). In a certain limited way, it seems in many people to be stronger than even the desire for real happiness (though it does, of course, represent the desire of the neurotic self to pursue happiness as it conceives it). Thus, the most conscious effort to effect healing by bringing self-condemnation to the surface does not succeed anymore than does an effort to commit suicide by consciously resolving not to breathe.

But there are times in life when the self-deception becomes unraveled—when the fabric of a life collapses, for example, or at exactly the right clinical moment, in love affairs, in the confrontation with death, and in certain kinds of religious experiences. At these unplanned and unpredictable "moments of truth" that so fill the world's literature, it becomes possible to reclaim some part of the original self. But in these cases the self-discovery seems not so much an achievement as an event—an involuntary and enormously painful loss of self and a simultaneous and altogether surprising discovery of it, usually so dramatic as to considered a form of death and rebirth. Until such moments, attempts to return to nature, to let go, to know that one is all right, etc., generally get caught up in the mechanics of anxiety relief and become part of the problem. They tend to accomplish only a suspension of the moral rules, which in turn merely throws us more overtly into our neurotic tendencies. Presumably there is therapeutic value in this, but for normal living it is hell.

Although no quick fix follows from the decency of the original self, there does follow the possibility, however small, of genuine healing, and that is a very great thing indeed. It entails nothing less than the possibility of happiness.

Aristotle understood happiness as activity in accordance with function and virtue, and he understood such activity to be pleasant for the virtuous person (see chapter 6). Since natural human functioning includes rough decency and so has every right to be called "virtue," and since such activity is generally pleasant (see chapter 1), we can rework the Aristotelian definition and understand it as the union of spontaneity and basic decency, of pleasure and the goodness that it is our nature to be. To the extent that we can achieve this union, we can be at peace with ourselves and our society (if it is not radically unjust), and we can satisfy as many of our desires as intelligence, circumstance, and education allow.

On the other hand, if, as Freud and Hobbes maintained, the requirements of social life contradict the demands of human nature, then the benefits of civilization can be purchased only by a large quantity of self-condemnation, guilt, and repression. Such a life is in conflict with itself, one pleasure bought with the denial of another, and so it could not be considered truly pleasing even were its "pleasures" lasting. In fact, however, the pleasures of pain relief, though intense, are notoriously short-lived, with the result that neurotic success never satisfies for long.

Healing could take many forms—as many as there are ways of being brought face-to-face with one's self-deceptions. Whatever crushes our pretensions will do it. It is rare, and presumably it is always partial, but it does happen, and when it does, it brings about a reunion of pleasure and function that is strictly analogous to the return of healthy functioning to a sick body. It is thus health, and it is virtue. It is also a very plausible way to think of happiness.

6
Virtue and Morality

True happiness is the union of spontaneity and goodness. Its only alternatives are pleasure without social cohesion and society at the cost of fundamental repression. The vast bulk of the eastern and western philosophical tradition believed this union possible (at least for some), but Hobbes, Rousseau, Freud, Nietzsche and Heidegger did not, and it is their "realistic" and romantic attitudes that represent the general thrust of modern thought.

A large part of the distinctively moral attitude (as opposed to the attitude of virtue) can be thought of as the attempt to understand ethics through goodness alone, to understand it, that is to say, through mere conformity to right rule without sensitivity to the nuances of character. Its achievement is propriety. Its failure lies in its tendency towards self-righteousness and inflexibility, and in its inability to explain the relationship of pleasure to ethical life.

On the other hand, the attitude of spontaneity has its most obvious contemporary expression (and trivialization) in semi-popular psychology. Its lure is freedom and gratification; it is well-suited to a consumer society. Its gross failure lies in its contempt for interpersonal standards and in the vacuousness of the amiable nihilism that seems to have become our cultural common coin.

Logically, the solution seems simple. Let us have the virtues of both, a moral order that springs from the purest spontaneity. This optimistic possibility rests on an empirical question—whether there exists in the human psyche a basic harmony of pleasure and (at a minimum) rough decency. Indeed, the union of spontaneity and goodness is the real meaning of the harmony of the soul. We have argued that the naturalistic brackets require such a harmony, that there is a psychodynamic explanation for its distortion, and that a return to it is at least partially possible. This does not seem a wildly optimistic thing to say. To deny it, in fact, seems excessively pessimistic, since it forces us to believe that we are emotionally less well constituted than any other animal. To deny it is essentially to deny our animal past—a vestige of the exaggerated sense of the uniqueness of our species.

Nevertheless, outside the existentialist adumbration of authenticity, there has not been much discussion of spontaneity in the contemporary philosophical literature of ethics, not even in the recent literature on virtue ethics, which, quite properly, redirects attention away from moral rules to questions of character, feeling, emotion, and pleasure.

> Virtues are dispositions not only to act in particular ways, but also to feel in particular ways. To act virtuously is not, as Kant was later to think, to act against an inclination; it is to act from inclination formed by the cultivation of the virtues. Moral education is an 'education sentimentale'.[1]

But there is little speculation on the psychology of the 'education sentimentale', and little discussion of whether one set of feelings (i.e., pleasures) might be more or less spontaneous or natural than another. Presumably this is because it is taken for granted that the "inclinations" can be adjusted through social engineering or personal effort to whatever conception of virtue might be adopted.

In contemporary academic philosophy, the kind of psychological speculation here called for (which used to be called "moral psychology") has been shunned as an intrusion of philosophy into the empirical, while in the empirical science of psychology, moral considerations have been considered so poisonously unscientific that only recently has anyone dared to suggest an overlap between moral values and psychological health, and then more in the literature of popular and humanistic psychology than in mainline psychology.[2] The result is that the possibility of a harmony of the soul has remained invisible, both in the sciences and in philosophy, despite its overwhelming common-sensicalness, despite the fact that it is a relatively easy deduction from the most general features of Freudian psychodynamics and Darwinian evolution, and despite its overwhelming presence at the very foundation of the western tradition in the philosophy of Plato and Aristotle.

The historical point is important. The fact is that the harmony of the soul was probably the central teaching of western ethics as long as the classical ideal of virtue remained the basic concept for the elaboration of ethical feeling. Since the beginnings of the modern era, however (or since the Enlightenment, according to MacIntyre), virtue has been a dead idea, absorbed into and misunderstood by what has come to be called "morality." To understand why the harmony of the soul became a philosophical non-topic, we need to understand better the difference between morality and virtue. That done, it will be clear that the harmony of the soul is the central doctrine of Greek ethics. Hopefully, it will also be clear that what is happening in the mental-health movement may be nothing less than a rediscovery of the classical ethical ideals, however unlikely that may at first sound.

The difference between virtue and morality cannot be overstressed.[3] We speak of the original harmony of pleasure and decency as "rough virtue." Where it holds sway, behavior is spontaneous *and* decent, with minimal guidance from rules. Morality represents, in part, the intellectualization of this rough virtue. It is partly the attempt to make virtue more precise so that everyone, no matter what her emotions, can know exactly what is expected of her and exactly what to expect from others. It is also partly the attempt to extend the basic outlines of the virtuous psychology into important spheres of action that it does not specify. But whatever the goal, morality involves a translation of living virtue into clear rules—of the spirit of the law into its letter, to use the Christian phraseology—or, as we should prefer to put it, of matters of character into matters of law. Once the need for this intellectualization of virtue is accepted, the task can become so engrossing that the fact of translation gets forgotten. One can get caught up in the logical niceties of one way of stating the rule vs. another, in the precise relation of the rules to each other, and in the question of whether there might be higher order rules (laws) from which the lower order rules can be deduced. Indeed, the greatest moral questions can come to seem whether there might not be one supreme moral law from which all the subordinate rules follow and what the epistemic justification of such a law might be. At that point the original notion of virtue is lost, and we have become comfortable with morality as a discipline akin to mathematics on the one hand, and law on the other. Ever greater precision and systematization can be demanded. Soon one wants a science of ethics, empirical (Mill) or a priori (Kant), and when these fail us, the nihilistic or relativistic conclusion begins to seem inevitable (Nietzsche, Ayer).

In all this, it is forgotten that virtue was grounded in psychology and anthropology (i.e., moral psychology) not logic. This has caused us often to misread the history of ethics, looking for answers to distinctively *moral* questions in the works of Plato and Aristotle and thereby missing their distinctive ethical vision. In what follows, we will focus on the *Nicomachean Ethics* in order to show that Aristotle's virtue, despite a tendency of his own towards the intellectualization of virtue, nevertheless clearly understands it as a union of spontaneity and goodness—a harmony of affect and behavior that elaborates what we have called "rough decency." This is important to understand, partly for the purely historical point, and also to show that the harmony of the soul was not an idea attractive only to dreamy romantics.

THE SPONTANEITY OF GOODNESS IN ARISTOTLE

> We must be content then, in speaking of such subjects [ethics] . . . to indicate the truth roughly and in outline, and in speaking about things that are only for the most part true and with premises of the same kind to reach conclusions that are no better. . . . For it is the mark of an educated man to look for precision in each class of things just so far as the nature of the subject admits. (*N.E.* I, 1094b22–30)

Rules, laws and systems have their uses, but the life of virtue is no more tailored to satisfy the scruples of philosophers than is any other form of practical life. Ethics is a doing, a praxis. Its business is to get the job done, not to serve as an object of discussion. In general, doings are proceeded by the doer's having gotten the knack of something—the knack of how to hold the saw, for example, how much to tighten the bolt, how hard to push the needle into the patient's flesh, etc. Students are given rules to help them learn these matters: push firmly but gently; tighten until a solid contact is made; hold the saw at a comfortable angle. As most everyone knows, such rules are useful as springboards to actual experience, but the experience itself is the real teacher. The person who knows *only* the rules (who has book knowledge) knows little indeed. If one tried to learn such matters by intellectual effort alone, the teacher would have to anticipate every exception to the rough generalizations she offers, to write rules that would adapt the generalizations to each class of exceptional cases, which new rules would in turn need still more subtle adaptation by still more refined rules, and so on, *ad infinitum*. All of which may have a certain use, but cannot be what really goes on in practical learning. Matters of praxis are learned rather by breaking out of the entire circle of talk into the realm of deeds, and there in engaged silence the thing is really learned.

That much is clear for skills. We would all laugh at the intellectual who refused to pick up the hammer because he did not yet know how to use it. (But what if the nail gets knocked off the vertical? How can I bang it sideways without knocking it over? By hitting it softly, you say? But how softly is that?) We would also be amused if, from our inability to supply him with rules of sufficient clarity, he concluded that carpentry was relative to the carpenter or had no cognitive content.

For Aristotle, ethics, too, is praxis, and the rules of ethical life are no clearer and no more specific than the rules of any other kind of practical action.

> the whole account of matters of conduct must be given in outline and not precisely . . . questions of what is good for us have no fixity, any more than matters of health. *The general account being of this nature, the account of particular cases is yet more lacking in exactness; for they do not fall under any art or precept, but the agents themselves must in each case consider what is appropriate to the occasion, as happens also in the art of medicine or navigation. (N.E.* II, 1104a4–10)[4]

It has been noted again and again that the available ethical rules have to be applied carefully and sensitively to particular circumstances. Indeed, this was the germ of truth in the "situation ethics" that was so popular two decades ago (Fletcher 1966). "Thou shalt not lie" is the rule, but only a moral fanatic would feel obligated to tell the Nazi at the door about the Jew he is hiding in the basement. The rule turns out to be just a rough guide for those who have not yet got the moral "knack."

It has also been understood, though not so universally, that interpretation of this sort cannot be carried out by following still more specific rules. In ethics as in carpentry, the intellect operates syllogistically, subsuming particular cases under universal rules, and the real problem is usually whether or not an unusual particular case (the Nazi at the door, a burl in the wood) is really an example of what is intended by the rule. Another rule can, of course, be written to clarify the original rule. ("'Lying' does not mean telling a deliberate untruth to illegitimately constituted authority, when that action will result in unjust harm to another person.") Then that rule will itself need interpretation. (What is harm? What is illegitimate authority? And so on.) In any complex life situation, we will at some point have to judge without unambiguous guidance from rules, and that is precisely the point at which sensitivity, judgement, or knack is irreplaceable. To that extent ethics and skill are quite alike.

They differ however in this: One does not get the feel of when to lie and when to tell the truth merely by lying and telling the truth—as one learns how hard to push the needle into the flesh by pushing it. This is because it is not as clear in ethics as it is in nursing what constitutes successful performance of the act. In skills, success and failure are pretty much recognized by all concerned; in ethics the matter is enormously more complicated. Since we do make concrete decisions, something must fill the gap between abstract rules and the particular circumstances of real-life situations. What we want to understand is Aristotle's conception of what that is.

Sometimes Aristotle speaks of a special, nonscientific, but still rational cognitive faculty called "practical wisdom." It is this he says, that gives us the knowledge of right and wrong in particular circumstances.

> practical wisdom is . . . concerned with the ultimate particular fact, since the thing to be done is of this nature. (*N.E.* VI, 1142a23)

Like Plato, Aristotle thinks of the particular as part of the world of becoming. This makes it not quite fully knowable for him.

> Therefore, since scientific knowledge involves demonstration, but there is no demonstration of things whose first principles are variable, . . . practical wisdom cannot be scientific knowledge . . . because that which can be done is capable of being otherwise. (*N.E.* VI, 1140a33–38)

Practical wisdom is thus essentially the mediator between what Plato would have called "Being" (the realm of clear and fixed rules) and "Becoming." It is that which recognizes the invariant, but recognizes it in the flux of particular circumstances. Indeed, so close is it to the flux, that practical wisdom is possibly more like sense perception than it is like thought.

> Practical wisdom is concerned with the ultimate particular, which is the object not of scientific knowledge but of perception—not the perception of qualities peculiar to one sense, but a perception akin to that by which we perceive that the particular figure before us is a triangle. (*N.E.* VI, 1142a23)

Apparently then Aristotle seeks a mediator between intellect and sense perception, a faculty that will supply the minor premise of the practical syllogism, but aside from giving this faculty the name "practical reason" he really has no account of it to give. Nor could he have done so, since in the terms of Greek metaphysics his problem involves the intersection of being and becoming (i.e., the mystery of participation) and language can grasp only one side of that relationship (Timaeus 49a, 52b). In the contemporary idiom, we would probably say that Aristotle is bumping up against the problem made famous by Wittgenstein, the question of how rules are to be applied when their key concepts signify only a net of family resemblances rather than a univocal idea. Not knowing what to say about the matter, he simply gives the name practical reason to whatever deals with the matter, and this he understands as a sort of perceptually sensitive intellect or an intellectual form of sense perception. This so puzzles him that the full context of the previous quotation makes it appear that he has thrown up his hands and declared that practical wisdom is simply the capacity to act rightly (however actually brought about) so long as one has, in some unspecified way and to an unspecified degree, thought about the matter.

> Therefore, since scientific knowledge involves demonstration, but there is no demonstration of things whose first principles are variable, . . . practical wisdom cannot be scientific knowledge nor art. Not science because that which can be done is capable of being otherwise, not art because action and making are different kinds of things. The remaining alternative is that it is a *true and reasoned capacity to act* with regard to the things that are good or bad for man. (*N.E.* VI 1140a34)

Despite the unanswered questions raised by these passages, in them Aristotle does seem to want to understand the thing that mediates between rules and situations as some kind of cognition. But a few pages earlier he puts the matter somewhat differently:

> The origin of action is choice, and that of choice is desire and reason with a view to an end. This is why choice cannot exist without reason and intellect *or without a moral state; for good action cannot exist without a combination of intellect and character.* . . . *Hence choice is either desiderative reason or ratiocinative desire.* (*N.E.* VI, 1139a32–b5)

And more simply still:

> therefore both the reasoning must be true and the desire right, if the choice is to be good. (*N.E.* VI, 1139a24)

Choice is deliberation and deliberation about right and wrong is the activity of practical wisdom. The previous passages, therefore, make it clear that for Aristotle the successful employment of practical reason requires more than sound cognitive faculties. It requires appropriate desires, the right affective structure of the soul in which the intellect is 'embodied'. So much is this so, for him, that he does not know whether proper choice is a species of reasoning informed by moral desire ("desiderative reason") or a kind of desire that is informed by reason ("ratiocinative desire"). In either case, even the most powerful of theoretical intellects will not be able to make correct moral choices unless it belongs to a good character. A good character is not simply one that acts properly. It is also one whose desires are in harmony with right action.

> Lovers of what is noble find pleasant the things that are by nature pleas-
> ant, and virtuous actions are such, so that these are pleasant for such men
> as well as in their own nature. (*N.E.* I, 1099a13–15)

For Aristotle, virtue quite simply requires that the virtuous person take
pleasure in virtue. That is to say, Aristotle's virtue requires what we have
called "the harmony of the soul."

It has been said (Burnyeat 1980: 70) that a "one-sided preoccupation
with reason and reasoning" is a "perennial failing in moral philosophy with
which Aristotle was familiar in the form of the Socratic doctrine that virtue
is knowledge." Aristotle's answer was, in part, his doctrine of habit.

> In makes no small difference, then, whether we form habits of one kind
> or another from our very youth; it makes a very great difference, or rather
> *all* the difference. (*N.E.* II, 1103b25)

This habituation is by no means merely the mechanical formation of
behavior. Rather it is the formation of the affect that underlies it. It is the
"education sentimental" referred to by MacIntyre.

> We must take as a sign of states of character the pleasure or pain that ensues
> on acts; for the man who abstains from bodily pleasures and delights in this
> very fact is temperate. . . . For moral excellence is concerned with plea-
> sures and pains. . . . Hence we ought to have been brought up in a particular
> way from our very youth, as Plato says, so as both to delight in and to be
> pained by the things that we ought. (*N.E.* II, 1104B4–13)[5]

These passages are not isolated instances of the harmony of pleasure
and virtue in Aristotle. Kosman (1980: 104) has pointed out that throughout his discussion of the moral virtues, "Aristotle makes it clear that the
activities for which virtues are dispositions are of two sorts, actions and
feelings, praxeis kai pathe."[6] Here are Aristotle's words on the relation of
pleasure, pain, and virtue.

> By passions I mean . . . the feelings that are accompanied by pleasure and
> pain; . . . by states of character [I mean] the things in virtue of which we
> stand well or badly with reference to the passions. (*N.E.* II, 1105b20)

> To feel both fear and confidence and appetite and anger and pity *and in*
> *general pleasure and pain* may be felt both too much and too little . . .
> but to feel them at the right time, with reference to the right things,
> toward the right people, with the right motive and in the right way is what
> is both intermediate and best, and this is characteristic of virtue. (*N.E.* II,
> 1106b17–22)

[The life of the virtuous person] has no farther need of pleasure as a sort of adventitious charm. For the man who does not rejoice in noble actions is not even good, since no one would call a man just who did not enjoy acting justly. . . . If this is so, virtuous actions must be in themselves pleasant. (*N.E.*, I, 1099a15)

Despite the undeniable fact that Aristotle often urges us against following our pleasures and pains (presumably our *uncultivated* pleasures and pains), and despite the fact that virtues are clearly for him not simply passions, he nevertheless just as clearly expects virtue to be pleasant to the virtuous man and understands that education for virtue is, in part, an education of one's pleasures and pains.[7] Moral education, for him, is precisely the cultivation of the harmony of the soul.

Since it is habit, for Aristotle, that produces this harmony, and since it is habit that is the prerequisite to moral (but not theoretical) reason, it is clear that Aristotle was at least close to thinking of cultivated affect as the thing that bridges the gap between general rules and concrete situations. When he speaks of "desiderative reason" or "ratiocinative desire" he may be intending to break down the sharp distinction between cognition and affect, as suggested by both Burnyeat (1980: 73) and Annas (1980). In that case, the peculiar form of perception involved in practical reason may be nothing more than educated sentiment, the moral "instincts" of a well-bred person. Though startling from the intellectualist point of view, this would not be an outrageous thing to say, and it is certainly close enough to the way people actually behave. In any case, it is clear that for Aristotle a good character, i.e., a virtuous configuration of pleasure and behavior, either replaces or supplements or is a part of the moral reasoning from which ethical knowledge proceeds.

Presumably, this is why Aristotle is not bothered by the alleged "vacuousness" of his doctrine of the mean. For him all moral rules come down to the tautological Delphic inscription, "nothing in excess," or, in his own words, "not too much and not too little." With only the most minimal attempt to supply determinate interpretations of this quintessentially vague doctrine, he assures us that whoever follows it will possess every virtue. From the viewpoint of the theoretical intellect this is a terrible deficiency, and reams have been written about whether or not Aristotle can break out of the circular reasoning with which he makes a minimal gesture at greater specificity. Almost all agree that he fails to do this, but this does not constitute a fault in Aristotle's theory, as assumed by the intellectualist critics. Rather the whole point is that the intellect alone is not sufficient for the achievement of virtue. First, one must *be* a virtuous person—one must have the right pleasures and pains—and then one will know how to interpret the rules.

HABIT AND NATURAL PLEASURE

We have spoken as if it were habit and habit alone that creates the harmony of pleasure and behavior that is essential to virtue. Indeed, Aristotle does put tremendous emphasis on the importance of habituation in moral education. This sounds like his version of what we would call "socialization," and thus there is a tendency to assume that the harmony Aristotle refers to is a human creation, a product of art, convention and/or a contrivance of reason rather than something that exists by nature. In that case, though he unquestionably believes in the harmony of the soul, it should not be for him a natural thing, but rather a product of human art.

For Aristotle, however, the relation between art and nature is subtle, and it is even more subtle in the case of virtue. In general, art, for Aristotle, is not a creative force. His doctrine is that art imitates nature, and he generally speaks as if this imitation is not a slavish copying but a "perfecting" of the dispositions that already exist "by nature." (The usual example is the "perfecting" of a wild plant by allowing it to grow with proper moisture and drainage, unmolested by predators, etc.)

Virtue is more complicated. Regarding it, he says:

> Neither then by nature nor contrary to nature do the virtues arise in us; *rather we are adapted by nature to receive them and are made perfect by habit.* (*N.E.* II, 1103a25)

The passage can be variously interpreted. One can take it to mean, with Ross,[8] that the inherited basic human dispositions are morally indifferent and that reason simply imposes "right rule" on them, as the carpenter imposes order on the architecturally indifferent wood. But this does not seem to give a strong enough sense to the idea of "natural adaptation" or to take seriously the idea of perfection. Moreover, it would make nonsense of the basic claim of Aristotle's ethics—that virtue is fulfillment of human nature (I,7). It is not the nature or function of the wood, as wood, to become a house; the wood is not perfected by being made into a house. That could be said only if the wood had of its own accord an imperfect tendency to become a house (as the seed becomes the plant). Moreover, to be adapted to something means, at a minimum, to have some special fitness for it, and the wood is no more specially fit to be a house than it is to be a mailbox, a fire, or a piece of paper.

What Aristotle seems to want is to characterize the relationship between a human being and his virtue as less close (i.e., natural) than that between a seed and the mature plant, but closer than that between the wood and the house. This would be an eminently commonsense thing for him to try to do. Few think that people become virtuous merely by being allowed to grow up, and few believe that virtue is an out and out imposition. The problem is to find a way to characterize this middle ground.

However that is done, the material out of which a virtuous life is made is the concatenation of pleasures we are born with. If these pleasures are "naturally adapted" to virtue, and if they are "perfected" by it, then there must then be in them some tendency toward virtue. In the language of the previous chapter, this can only mean that for Aristotle there must exist some sort of natural harmony of the soul.

Just as clearly, however, there must be some strong, interfering factor that requires the relatively strong hand of habituation to bring that tendency to its full realization. What is this interfering factor, and why is there so strong a need for habituation that Aristotle flirts with denying the naturalness of virtue? Although he desperately needs to understand this in order to complete his theory of virtue as fulfillment of human nature, Aristotle makes only the faintest gestures at answering these questions. All he really knows is that despite our adaptation to virtue things can and usually do go wrong (especially in badly managed societies). He knows only that all of us need to learn what comes without effort to the animals—to live in accordance with one's nature. He does not know about anxiety, and has no doctrine of the unconscious, but he desperately needs a theory of the transformation of pleasure.

Because both Plato and Aristotle thought teleologically, they both believed that happiness and pleasure must coincide with virtue. Consequently, both had a priori reasons for believing in an original harmony of pleasure and function.[9] Consequently, also, both were rather puzzled by the undeniable empirical fact that virtue is often painful and vice pleasant. These unhappy truths are, in fact, the most cogent evidence against the teleological outlook, and they involve issues that touch on nothing less than the justification of the ways of God to man.[10] Although neither Aristotle nor his teacher knew how to handle the problem, it never caused them to loose faith in the basic harmony of the human psyche. That faith is seen most clearly in their efforts to explain the pleasure of vice so as to preserve their basic teleological vision.

Contrary to what he suggests elsewhere, in the *Republic* Plato does not drive a very strong wedge between pleasure and happiness. To do so would have made happiness too unworldly. To the contrary, he insists that the philosophical life is the most pleasant of lives (583a, 586d). But not to distinguish pleasure and happiness would have resulted in an unacceptable hedonism, however deferred its pleasures may be. Plato's middle ground was to distinguish between true and false pleasures, and to identify happiness with only the true ones (583bff). The basic harmony of the soul could be preserved if it could be shown that the pleasures of vice were the false ones (584c) and the pleasures of virtue the true ones. The "original" harmony of the soul would then consist of a harmony of only the true pleasures with virtuous behavior. False pleasures would be the pleasures that motivated vice, and it would be these false pleasures that made it appear that vicious people could be happy. True happiness, virtue and (true) pleasure would thus all coincide, appearances to the contrary notwithstanding.

This is no small matter for Plato. It must be remembered that dramatically speaking the entire point of the *Republic* is to prove that the just man is happy. This is the burden taken on by Socrates in Book II, and it is the logical motivation for all the complex metaphysical, epistemological, political and psychological structures of the dialogue. Indeed, the supreme claim of the *Republic* is that the cosmos is ordered by the idea of the good. This cannot be true if the virtuous man is unhappy. Thus the hypothesis of false pleasures functions for moral psychology precisely as did the epicycle for Greek astronomy. It explains away the apparent irregularities of the world, and makes it possible to have a rational faith in the efficacy of the good. If this hypothesis, or something like it is not true, Plato's entire world-view must fail.

With an eye toward these overwhelmingly important ends, Plato either invented or borrowed from current medical theory the distinction between simple and pain-relieving pleasures. The simple pleasures were to be the true ones and the pain relieving ones were called "false," "apparent," or "illusory." He failed, however, to make a convincing case for the correspondence of these types of pleasure to the pleasures of virtue and vice— and this, mostly because he was unfortunately wedded to the idea that the body corresponded to vice. His misguided anti-corporalism led him to identify the pain-relieving pleasures with the pleasures of the body (eating, sex, scratching an itch). In the same vein, he seems to have wanted intellectual/aesthetic pleasures (the pleasures of the mind, of high culture and of the mythical ruling class) to correspond to pure pleasure and to virtue, as if art or philosophy could not serve the end of pain relief, and as if smelling a flower (his own example of a pure pleasure) were not a bodily pleasure.

This way of working out the distinction between true and false pleasures is very wrong. Art, philosophy, or indeed, any element of high culture can and unfortunately often does serve the ends of neurotic pain relief. That is why there is so little real happiness in snobbery. Nor does it seem right to call the pleasures of eating "pain relief," even though the extreme forms of hunger are painful. In general there is no simple correspondence between pain relief and any specific behavioral arena (sex, art, philosophical discussion, food). Certainly any life activity can be used to relieve pain, and in all probability there are pure (or nearly pure) pleasures connected with them all.

In any case, even if eating, drinking, and sex, were mere pain relief, they are certainly not vice since the they are unquestionably a part of our biological functioning—a part of what we might call "animal virtue," and this must be a part of any reasonable account of human virtue.

Plato's project miscarried badly, and that is probably why the subject of true and false pleasures has received so little attention in subsequent philosophical literature. The Platonic anthropology was too transcendentally biased, and his (mis)association of the vice with the body was just too strong for the inherent power of his distinction between true and false pleasures to be seen. This did not, however, prevent Aristotle from adopting it wholesale. He too wonders why vice is pleasant, and interestingly enough he uses the notion of illness to explain it.

> The same things do not appear sweet to a man in a fever and a healthy man. . . . But in all such matters that which appears to the good man is thought to be really so. [Therefore] those also will be pleasures that appear so to him. . . . If the things he finds tiresome seem pleasant to someone, that is nothing surprising, for men may be ruined and spoiled in many ways . . . those [pleasures] which are admittedly disgraceful plainly should not be said to be pleasures, except to a perverted taste. (*N.E.* X, 1176a8–20)

These disgraceful pleasures ("sick" pleasures, as they are popularly called) presumably constitute at least a large part of the pleasures of vice. For Aristotle they are not even real pleasures,

> In reply to those who bring forth the disgraceful pleasures, one may say that they they are not really pleasant. (*N.E.* X, 1173b20)

Nor are they "natural."

> Now for most men their pleasures are in conflict with each other because they are not *by nature* pleasant, but the lovers of what is noble find pleasant the things that are by nature pleasant, and virtuous actions are such, so that these are pleasant for such men as well as in their own nature. (*N.E.* I, 1099a12–20)

Where does Aristotle think these allegedly sick, unnatural or unreal pleasures come from? Whatever that is, that simply must be the interfering factor that prevents the human tendency toward virtue from reaching fruition on its own.

Owing to the excess of pain that men experience, they pursue excessive and in general bodily pleasures as being a cure for the pain . . . which is the reason why they are pursued—because they show up against the contrary pain. (*N.E.* VII, 1154a 28–32)

Here is Aristotle's psychodynamic explanation for the pursuit of excessive pleasure, and it turns out to be nothing other than Plato's theory of pain relief. Excessive pleasure is rooted in excessive pain. Since excessive pleasure can be seen as the cause of all vice, this passage amounts to a general explanation of the pleasure of vice in terms of pain relief. This is made even clearer by the following:

The pleasures that do not involve pain do not admit of excess; and these are the things pleasant by nature and not incidently. (*N.E.* VII, 1154b 15)

Where there is no pain relief, then, there is no excess, and where there is no excess, we already know, there is only moderation. Vice, for Aristotle, is some kind of pain relief.[11]

That Aristotle has gotten this from Plato seems clear enough. The pleasures of vice are simply the false pleasures of the *Republic* and *Philebus*. It is unfortunate, however, that Aristotle has no more to say about he psychodynamics of vice than did his teacher. He does not tell us what the relevant pain is, nor does he ask why some people feel it and others do not. He has advanced Plato's psychology only by tacking onto it his theory of the mean. The misleading association of pain relief with the body persists, and if anything, Aristotle is less sensitive to the unconscious than Plato. But this does show that Aristotle was thinking in terms of a basic set of pleasures that constitute virtue (the ones that are pleasant by nature). These are the pure pleasures, and they are there "first." A pain of some sort supervenes upon them, and the pleasure that comes from the relief of that pain causes an immoderate, excessive pleasure which distorts various life activities and so gives rise to the different sorts of vice. Vices then are distortions of the personality that push one into (or pull one away from) an arena of behavior more than would otherwise have been the case. All excess and deficiency (and hence all vice) is thus a modification of the original or natural harmony of pleasure and virtue.

For Aristotle, wisdom in human affairs involves, at least in part, the ability to read the complexities of human motivation beneath the apparent simplicities of human behavior crudely described. To an insensitive observer, the qualitative motivational difference between pain relief and simple pleasure (and hence between the psychodynamics of vice and virtue) appears as a merely quantitative behavioral difference between too much or too little. The critical difference is hidden, invisible to those who cannot read motives from actions.[12]

Aristotle may even have been able to countenance the thought that the pain-relieving quality of vice is invisible to the person who feels it. At least he points out that people generally think their own behavior moderate and judge excess and defect in others on the basis of that assumption.

> The brave man is called rash by the coward, and coward by the rash man, and correspondingly in the other cases. (*N.E.* II, 1108b24)

Proceeding in this self-centered way, we are not likely to admit that our own behavior rests on the relief of a pain that we would rather never have experienced in the first place. Here is the hint that leads to the unconscious. If Aristotle had seriously pursued it, we might not have had to wait for Freud.

That is to speculate, but there can be no doubt that the primitive harmony of pleasure and virtue does exist in Aristotle. It corresponds precisely to his realm of "natural" pleasures (and these in turn correspond more or less precisely to the original or pure pleasures of the *Republic*[13] and *Philebus*). If the idea of a coincidence of spontaneous pleasure and virtuous behavior is a romantic dream, then it is a dream that Aristotle is almost as guilty of as any eighteenth-century poet. Indeed, it is a dream that must be dreamt by anyone who takes seriously the idea of virtue as something distinct from morality.

We come then to a surprising, almost astonishing congruence of the modern idea of mental health and the classical ideal of virtue. For both there is an original harmony of pleasure and function, and for both of them this harmony is disrupted by a pain, the relief of which produces a distorting pleasure. Because contemporary mental-health practice has often associated itself with a misguided sense of what is scientific, and because of the contemporary prejudice against value judgement, medicine has not wanted to admit that it encompasses the ethical. Because the ancients knew nothing of anxiety and the unconscious, because of their overestimate of reason and their prejudice against the body, we do not associate them with the ideals of psychotherapy. But these associations notwithstanding, health and virtue are very nearly the same thing. We may call the goal of therapy "self-realization," the "true self," "the unconscious made conscious," "the ability to love and work," or even "social adjustment," and all of these definitions are true when properly understood. But the goal of therapy is also virtue. This should be acknowledged. Sometimes pushing forward brings the past into clearer focus, while at the same time ancient insight can help to broaden the tunnel vision of the moment.

7
Consequences

From the very beginning there has been tension between the scientific and moral conceptions of the human condition, but since Freud that tension has often focused on the conflict between therapeutic concern and traditional moral attitudes. It bears on such specific issues as sexual freedom, abortion and divorce, on which the therapeutic community has tended toward one pole and the tradition another, but it bears also on such fundamental moral concepts as responsibility and conscience. The naturalization of motivation that is inherent in the scientific outlook has always tended towards reductionism, thereby casting doubt on the free, responsible agent of traditional morality. The Freudian "reductionism" of the unconscious seemed to continue that drift, and so also the Freudian theories of socialization and drive that converted the traditional notion of conscience into the internalized voice of semi-tyrannical paternal authority.

In addition to these problems, there is the entire matter of the nature of ethical knowledge. The scientific age brought with it the redefinition of *knowledge* that is inherent in the honorific title "science," i.e., the notion that only a certain strictly defined methodology—the thing now called "scientific method"—could achieve something worth calling knowledge (in Latin, *scientia*). The exclusive appropriation of the word for knowledge by this particular method entailed the conclusion that traditional moral knowledge, which even in its own terms was too vague to be considered knowledge according to the new standards, was not knowledge (*scientia*) at all. This led ultimately to the utilitarian and Kantian attempts to produce a "scientific" morality, and the now-often-acknowledged limitations or failure of these schools has led to a general acceptance of relativism and/or nihilism.

Thus the question of whether or not the traditional conception of ethical knowledge was really worth calling "knowledge" is more than just one important question among many. It may in fact be the key question that requires resolution if virtue is again to be taken seriously.

It goes without saying that a thorough discussion of these matters is impossible in the final chapter of this or any other book. But what has already been said about the reunion of health and virtue has certain consequences that bear upon these questions in interesting ways and point to possible resolutions. At the same time the promise of light shed on these problems adds cogency to the ideas already advanced. For this reason is seems worthwhile to point out certain benefits that flow from the reunion of health and virtue. First of all there comes a notion of freedom that allows us to sidestep the entire debate about determinism and gives even "negative" freedom a good measure of positive ethical substance. Second, the reunion gives rise to a notion of conscience that is remarkably like the traditional one. Third, we get from it a clear and cogent explanation of why, as the tradition knew but could not explain, practically useful ethical knowledge cannot be rendered demonstrable by any impersonal methodology, an explanation that at the same time explains why this fact ought not be taken to disprove the genuinely interpersonal validity of ethical truth.

It is hoped that these three consequences might diminish some of the familiar hostility that has grown up between psychotherapy and ethics. When ideas usually taken to be antagonistic are suddenly seen to be similar, each throws the other into a new and fruitful light. Each can then be separated from its particular historical associations and used to deepen the other. Psychoanalytic theory goes a long way toward explaining the psychodynamics of pleasure and pain, which were ultimately unintelligible for Plato and Aristotle. Without anxiety, the unconscious, and the acceptance of the body (which is perhaps our era's greatest achievement in ethics), the Greek theories of virtue are sadly defective. But without the reaffirmation of values that comes with the resurrection of virtue, therapy remains an amoral technology, its professed goal a mere metaphor, and quite possibly a dishonest one at that.

The psychodynamic deepening and the democratization of virtue on the one hand, and the detechnoligization of therapy on the other are the great benefits that follow from the reunion of health and virtue. Reunited, ethics and psychology would even hint at the possibility of an integrated vision of life—at something worth calling "wisdom." But here we attend only to certain minor theoretical benefits to be gained from this reunion—the recasting of three problems that were made pressing, presumably, by of the transformation of virtue into morality,[1] and which, therefore, can be at least partly resolved by the reunion of health and virtue. The problems of freedom, conscience and moral knowledge have each of them been a battleground in the war between science and morality. The effort here is to make peace by suggesting that with the reunion of health and virtue we can do justice to both sides of the argument.

FREEDOM

Freedom is unquestionably the leading moral and political idea of our times. It is thus shocking to learn that before the modern era it did not have this status (Berlin, 1958: 13). Plato and Aristotle, for example, were perfectly capable of understanding both political and moral freedom as they are currently understood, but neither took much interest in it, and they do not use the word *freedom* with the full set of honorific connotations to which we are accustomed. For Plato, in fact, the term seems sometimes to have had a negative connotation (*Republic* 557b), and although Aristotle mentions that freedom is cited as a justification for democratic rule, he never takes up the issue and tends to understand democracy as the rule of the poor rather than the reign of freedom.

The modern emphasis on freedom and its apparent unimportance in traditional theory has helped make the notion of virtue seem irrelevant to the modern sensibility. And yet there is a notion of freedom inherent in the traditional theory of virtue that, interestingly enough, in its most important features is identical to the notion of freedom that is found in psychoanalysis. This is not freedom from nature—the Kantian autonomy of the will or the existential ideal of nonreified selfhood. Rather, it is a kind of freedom that exists comfortably within nature (a naturalistic sort of freedom) and consists in the understanding of that nature rather than the transcendence of it. It is a bit difficult to recognize in the classical texts because the Greeks tended to call it "wisdom" instead of "freedom." But this wisdom is the wisdom of self-knowledge (the knowledge of one's true pleasures, true desires and hence of one's true good) and so we can recognize in it freedom as it is understood in the biblical claim that "you shall know the truth and the truth shall make you free."

Such a notion of freedom offers the possibility of sidestepping the entire tedious debate about free will and determinism. If there is a significant and ethically satisfying notion of freedom that exists within nature (however determined that nature may be), then obviously there is no pressing need to worry about the extent of determinacy within nature or about whether there can be acts of volition that can initiate new chains of causality within the natural order.

To be done with the debate over determinism would be a great benefit to be derived from the updating of the Greek notion of wisdom. But there is perhaps an even more tantalizing prize. The most pressing problem about freedom concerns not the notion of freedom as transcendence over nature, but what is sometimes called "liberty," "political freedom," or "negative freedom," and which is, roughly speaking, freedom understood as simply the absence of restraint (wherein that restraint is usually understood as some sort of external force). This is freedom as it is popularly understood, and so conceived it is the object of nearly universal praise in contemporary democratic societies. It is, in fact, so frequently and so highly praised that it comes to appear to many not as simply one good thing among others, but as the ultimate good, or the only good that ought to command *everyone's* allegiance.

Now while this political freedom is certainly a good, it fails us badly when it is given this ultimate status. As is so often said, by itself it is a purely formal notion—freedom from interference, but not freedom *for* anything in particular, except perhaps the toleration of other people's freedom and the (presumably minimal) restraints on my own behavior that this entails. But shall I smile at my neighbor or be unpleasant? Shall I drink heavily or use drugs? Shall I seek as much money, fame or honor as the law allows? Negative freedom gives me the right to do as I choose in these presumably personal matters, but it gives me no guidance about which alternative to pick, and it is with these "personal" matters that the real substance of ethics, character and virtue lies.

The problem of course is not that there is anything wrong with negative or political freedom. It is clearly a good thing, and the right amount of it is unquestionably a part of a just and good society. But just as clearly it needs to be supplemented by something that has positive ethical content. If that something is itself a further development of the very root idea that makes political freedom attractive to begin with (the general notion of the absence of restraint), then it can be said not just to supplement negative freedom, but to complete it, and that is all to the good in a society so oriented to the praise of freedom.

Such in fact is the freedom of self-knowledge—the species of freedom that goes with both virtue and health. The root idea out of which negative freedom grows is the absence of restraint. When the self is understood as a simple, univocal thing, that restraint is necessarily thought of as an outer force, sometimes natural (a harsh climate, for example), but usually political (a government hostile to one's interests) or social (the absence of economic opportunities). Both the traditional and the psychoanalytic notions of freedom, however, grow from the notion that the self is not univocal—that it has complex internal relationships with itself and that *to a certain extent* political metaphors are well suited to understanding them. Thus, there are inner restraints that are just as real as the external ones, and self-deception is foremost among them (Young 1986: 53). Self-knowledge, therefore, becomes a necessary condition for the realization of the true goal of political freedom, or, otherwise put, even negative freedom (the absence of restraint) cannot be had by purely political means and requires a deep form of self-knowledge.

Negative freedom is thus completed by the freedom of self-knowledge. But if the self is what it has here been argued to be, then self-knowledge entails also rough virtue, and so freedom turns out to be no longer a merely negative concept at all, but a concept with all the positive moral content of virtue itself. The mere absence of restraint turns out to entail a good measure of moral content. Thus even Kantians who insist that there is no real freedom apart from moral truth may find some degree of satisfaction in the way that the synthesis of health and virtue bears on the question of freedom.

To make these points in more detail, we must first be more specific about the traditional notion of freedom. This is found most clearly in Plato's *Gorgias,* where we find an extensive analysis of the meaning of power (dynamis). There Socrates has to refute a politically ambitious young man who thinks that power (as we normally understand it) is what he and everybody else really wants. To him this seems obvious, since power is nothing but the ability to change things as one wishes them changed, and like most people he sees no great problem about knowing what it is one wishes (466b–467b, 468e). Everyone, he assumes, knows what she wants, and power adds to this only the ability to get it.

Socrates refutes Polus by pointing out that the apparent good is not always the true good, and that the ability to change things without knowing how to guide them towards one's own betterment is not true power anymore than an infant with a gun could be said to be truly powerful merely because he is capable of killing people (466d). Desire is among the hardest of things to understand (presumably, for Plato, because of the way goodness, pleasure and pain get mixed together). Consequently, few of us really know what it is that we want. Since power is the ability to get what we want, self-knowledge is its precondition. Thus, the philosopher (idealized as the one who understands the true object of desire) is far closer to freedom than the politician (who has only the technical knowledge of how to manipulate people, called "rhetoric" by the Greeks).[2]

We call the freedom consequent upon knowledge of the true object of desire "aretaic" freedom in order to distinguish it not only from freedom as political liberty (Mill), and also from freedom as spontaneity, rational or not (Kant, Sartre), but also from freedom as the acceptance of sheer necessity (the stoics, Hegel, the later Marx). This aretaic freedom is a matter of the relation of the self to itself in which the masquerade of the not-self (false desire) is exposed. Aretaic freedom is thus not harmed by the interference of that which is clearly other (external political or natural forces) in the self's pursuit of its own goals, but by the masquerade of an inner other as the self (the masquerade of false desire as real). What it requires, therefore, is self-knowledge rather than power over the external world, which self-knowledge can be viewed as a kind of power over oneself, or self-mastery, although that paradoxical metaphor is not to be taken literally (Cf. *The Charmides*) and points to the thorny issue of self-deception (see page 000).

At this point it should come as no great surprise to announce that this same kind of freedom exists in Freud. Indeed, Freud constitutes a most excellent example of freedom within nature because he came upon his own notion of freedom while denying utterly the notion of transcendent freedom. Indeed, freedom, properly understood, is the entire goal of psychotherapy, but at the same time Freud's entire work rests on thoroughgoing determinism in the interpretation of mental life.

On the one hand he is a typical nineteenth-century deterministic reductionist. According to Gay

> [Freud] followed his deterministic course of thinking without uneasiness, with no sense of its obscurities, its problematic nature. He understood it to mean, quite straightforwardly, that just as there is no event in the physical universe without its cause . . . , so there is no mental event, or mental state, without its causes.[3]

On the other hand, Freud's entire goal was precisely to make the unconscious conscious. "Sigmund Freud was a determinist," says Gay, "but his psychology is a psychology of freedom." The formula "Where id was there shall ego be" expressed the entire goal of psychoanalysis (1933: xxii, 80), and this amounts to nothing but learning what one's desires really are in order to make a clear, rational and free choice among them. "Analysis," says Freud, "sets out to give the patient's ego freedom to choose one way or the other" (1923: xix, 50n.).[4]

Neurosis for Freud is "a form of slavery" from which we can be freed.

> as long as mental forces that significantly affect human decisions—wishes, anxieties, conflicts—are unconscious, they act as determinants that the person making the decision cannot take into account. (Gay 1978: 54)

In this sense, then, therapy for Freud produces freedom. Clearly, this is freedom of self-knowledge (the knowledge of one's own desires, of the way one has repressed them and of the compromise pleasures that one has unconsciously settled for). This self-knowledge does not require us to somehow slip through the web of natural determinism. The desires revealed by therapy are for Freud just as much determined by nature as they were before (he tended to call them "instincts" or "drives"), and whatever degree of determinism exists in nature controls us just as much as it ever did. The therapeutic conception of freedom is thus not the freedom of creative or transcendent spontaneity. It is aretaic freedom, the same freedom-as-self-knowledge that was pursued by Plato and Aristotle, though it is here sought by different means.

One might think that even if this is true, the Freudian theory of neurosis, because it makes neurosis depend on the operations of the unconscious, relieves us thereby of responsibility for our neurotic behavior. And if neurosis is largely vice, one could conclude that we are free of moral responsibility for the portion of our vicious behavior that stems from neurosis.

Here, the danger comes from the metaphor of the demonic unconscious. Repression, however, as previously argued (see page 89) is *willed* ignorance, and willed ignorance is not simple ignorance. In fact, it requires one to know the very thing one does not know. "I know that which I do not know," is the basic tenet of both the Platonic myth of recollection and the Freudian theory of the unconscious. In this context, it means that my unconscious machinations are still mine. If I succeed in not being aware of them, it is I who have deceived me, not someone else called "my unconscious." In denying to myself my own reality, I have alienated myself from myself by setting up a pseudo-self to desire the things that pain me. This is strange behavior, but it is not something that is done *to* me. Rather it is I who create the unconscious by the act of self-deception. Therefore, I am responsible for it and no one else. Therapy consists in learning precisely this, and it is only when the responsibility for the repression is accepted that its damage can be undone.

Once the original self-deception is in place, it does make a certain amount of sense to think of us as its passive pawns. But for the original deception we can blame only our own unwillingness to face a painful (supposed) truth. In this respect, neurotic behavior can be compared to that of the drunk. Once intoxicated, he is out of control and not responsible for what he does. But it was he who chose to get drunk in the first place, and therefore it is he who is responsible, to a certain appropriate degree, for all that ensues from his choice to spend a few hours freed from the painfulness of sobriety.

Thus the therapeutic attitude toward freedom has had to be twofold—to forgive and render blameless insofar as the self was deceived (the favored strategy among therapists, since is in there it less danger of driving the repression deeper), but also to encourage the acceptance of responsibility at the right clinical moment (when the defenses are down but there is enough ego-strength to resist retreat into denial when, that is to say, the guilt can be productive). We need not understand how the paradoxes of the self are possible as long as we preserve its inherently ironic nature. If we savor the full irony inherent in the idea of willed ignorance, we will be comfortable with both our active and passive roles in relation to our virtues and vices.

The question then is the extent to which the naturalistic or aretaic notion of freedom can satisfy the contemporary need for an ethics of freedom. Immediately, it must be said that aretaic freedom cannot substitute for political freedom. If one is actively hindered by social or political forces from pursing one's own goals, then one is in a genuinely unfree situation that cannot be rectified by increased self-knowledge.

By the same token, however, it is also true that unless one has self-knowledge, all the political freedom in the world cannot by itself create a genuinely free situation. If freedom is generally understood as the absence of hinderance to the achievement of one's desires, then it requires *both* self-knowledge *and* appropriate external circumstances. Aretaic freedom and political freedom complement each other and together make up a full account of even negative freedom.

What is more, it has been shown that the freedom of self-knowledge entails rough virtue. What this means is that negative freedom entails positive freedom—freedom from is also freedom for—and that the substance of this positive freedom includes rough virtue. There is no real freedom at all, therefore, not even full negative freedom, without ethical content. And so we may say that aretaic freedom deepens political freedom and gives it day-to-day ethical substance, while political freedom gives to aretaic freedom practical effectiveness in the field of real social activity.

On the other hand, there remains the notion of freedom as freedom from nature (the moral freedom of Kant or the existential freedom of Sartre). It is obvious that these kinds of freedom are not compatible with aretaic freedom. They are both transcendent forms of freedom because each of them presupposes a self that is capable of constituting itself independently of the constitution of nature. For the purposes of this book, such a self was ruled out by methodological fiat in the use of the naturalistic brackets. Our question has been what we would be if we were no more than nature, and our goal has been to show that the answer is nothing that we need fear—that nature alone would have made us quite good enough to satisfy a reasonable ethical sensibility. But inevitably it will be objected that even if health and illness are exactly as here argued, all that has been proven is that we are essentially decent animals, not moral animals, because the truly moral element of human life lies in choice and freedom rather than in the constitution of our desires. Unless we somehow choose our desires and our character, it might be said, rather than having them merely thrust upon us by nature, we remain unfree and less than truly moral.

There are two means of dealing with this point. The first is to grant that we must indeed be free to be truly human, but to insist that the requisite notion of freedom is supplied by aretaic freedom. Aretaic freedom, which is won by self-knowledge, is first of all something distinctively human because (1) no other animal either seeks it, needs to seek it, nor would be capable of seeking it, and (2) when humans seek it they are compelled to use (but not to use exclusively) their distinctively rational faculties. Moreover, (3) it requires great effort to do this—effort that entails the kind of commitment, resolution and choice that evoke moral admiration and are also distinctively human. None of this requires any transcendence of the laws of nature, but surely it is enough to satisfy our sense of human dignity.

The second point is negative and deserves more extensive elaboration. It argues that the requisite notion of freedom is not supplied by the notion of a supra-causal spontaneity, and that hence, even if such spontaneity does exist, it would not be recognized by us as constituting the ground of moral responsibility. This has been the approach taken by a long line of empirical and/or analytic philosophers who have advocated a doctrine of freedom within nature, even if nature is understood in the most causally restricted ways.

The tradition of arguing that there is no incompatibility between freedom and a firmly fixed, regular, predictable and entirely natural character structure seems to have begun with Hume. He argued that the idea of freedom as the spontaneous, unpredictable, or irregular was a chimera because we did not in fact experience any such thing, and also that it was useless because it was not required for the morally significant sense the word *freedom*. Worse, it was actually antithetical to the qualities of character that we do in fact find morally praiseworthy (1748: VIII; 1739: II, iii, 1&2). There has been a long sequence of modern defenders of essentially the same viewpoint, beginning with Hobart (1934), and going on through Nowell–Smith (1948), Ayer (1954), Hampshire (1959), and others, all of whom make the basic point that spontaneous behavior, far from being the kind of thing that enables us to hold people responsible for their actions, is really simply erratic behavior and, therefore, is closer to madness than to morality.

> when a man's actions seem to us quite unpredictable, when, as we say, there is no knowing what he will do, we do not look upon him as a moral agent. We look upon him rather as a lunatic. (Ayer 1954: 275)

The determinist argument depends on seeing one's desires as determined by the laws of nature and the self as determined by its desires. But the idea of the self's being determined by its desires (in the important sense of "determined") is a bit like speaking of the car as enslaved to its engine, or the computer to its circuits. It is a category mistake in which a very large part of what I am is treated as an alien thing that makes me into something I would not be on my own, as if I were the clay and my desires were the potter. As Philippa Foot puts it:

> On the whole it is wise to be suspicious of expression such as "determined by desire" unless they have been given a clear sense, and this is particularly true of the phrase "determined by the agent's character." Philosophers often talk about actions being determined by a man's character, but it is not certain that anybody else does, or that the words are given any definite sense. One might suppose that an action was so determined if it was *in* character, for instance the generous act of a generous man; but if this is so we will not have the kind of determination traditionally supposed to raise difficulties for a doctrine of free will.[5]

In ordinary speech the word *responsible* tends to be used more than the word *free* to designate morally praiseworthy behavior. While "free" may suggest to some an independence of natural causality, "responsible" surely does not. To be responsible is not to be free of one's desires (not even if those desires are set by a causally determined natural forces). To be responsible is simply to have the desire, to know that one has it, to weigh it against other desires and then, all things considered, to do the deed. As Hampshire puts it:

> A man becomes more and more a free and responsible agent the more he at all times knows what he is doing, in every sense of this phrase, and the more he acts with a definite and clearly formed intention. . . . It is not by itself a threat to the reality of human freedom that some close observers are able to predict, accurately and with confidence, that which a man is going to do before he does it. The threat arises when his own evidently sincere declarations of intention turn out to be comparatively worthless as a basis for the prediction of his actions.[6]

If in this quotation we read "desire" for "intention," then it comes down to this: to be free is to know one's desires and act in accord with them. To this we add the suspicion (with which Hampshire agrees) that failure to act in accord with one's desires is often a failure to know them. Freedom thus again comes down to self-knowledge (along with other things) and has little to do with the transcendence of the laws of nature by spontaneity, rational or otherwise.

We have no real experience of people behaving in ways that are "free" of the laws of nature and ordinary language does not record the modern philosopher's worry about the consequences of the mechanical conception of nature. Interestingly, neither does the literature of pre-philosophical people. The same sense of the compatibility of freedom and determination is dramatically illustrated in the *Iliad* in which favored heroes are given supernatural aid to ensure a predetermined end. Without the slightest sense of incongruity, Homer heaps praise and glory on the successful warrior. Things are determined, but the heroes remain as fully heroic as if they are in every important way the authors of their deeds.

Surely this has much to do with the fact that in Homer the gods never intervene so as to make the heroes act out of character. In fact, in the *Iliad* the aid of the gods can easily be seen as a sort of magnifying glass through which the true character of the hero is brought out. How differently we would feel if Hera tricked Achilles into becoming a vegetarian or got him to take part in a peace demonstration![7]

The suggestion then is that for pre-philosophical literature, for classical Greek philosophy, for common experience and for ordinary language, freedom has little to do with spontaneity as independence from nature. People are now and always have been held responsible for their characters whether or not they are in some way "set by an external force." The whole issue of freedom vs. nature is a peculiarly modern philosophical problem and almost certainly a category mistake of one sort or another. Surely, that is reason enough to believe that aretaic freedom is more worthy of the honorific connotations of "freedom" than is spontaneity, rational or otherwise.

The switch from morality to virtue thus puts the question of freedom and responsibility on a footing that is both very old and very new. The questions of freedom from nature and the need to protect the self to save it from reification, are replaced by the problem of self-knowledge. Surely, this is a more useful way to look at it. It diverts us from sterile debate and directs us toward a genuinely moral struggle. It steers us away from nihilism and preserves our sense of human dignity. Moreover, it shows us how we are free enough to justify our sense of guilt, which ought to satisfy the moralists, but at the same time it clarifies the respect in which we ought to be forgiving, which should satisfy therapists and those who do not wish to judge.

CONSCIENCE

There is a notion of conscience that seems to lead to relativism and/or paradox, and there is a traditional notion that does not. Something very much like this traditional notion follows logically from the proposed reunion of health and virtue and to that extent justifies it. Moreover, the reunion of health and virtue improves the traditional notion in that it explains why the "still, small voice" of conscience is so hard to hear.

For lack of a better term, we may speak of the "modern" notion of conscience. In it, conscience is equated with the sense of guilt and/or duty, from whatever source derived. So understood, the conscientious behavior of different individuals can be quite contradictory. If this notion of conscience is then combined with the common idea that personal conscience must be the individual's final moral authority (Garnett 1969), a certain dilemma results. Since a given individual's conscience might lead him to do things I consider immoral (Nowell–Smith 1954: 247, Bennet 1974), and since I grant the moral authority of that individual's conscience, it appears I am forced to accept a species of paradoxical relativism wherein I am forced to admit that he ought to do something that I think he ought not do.

On the other hand, there is the traditional notion of conscience. This is the notion of conscience as an innate "still, small voice" that for unclear reasons urges us toward certain common modes of conduct. In part, it does this through a sense of guilt, but it is not coextensive with *all* feelings of guilt and is, therefore, harder to discern than its modern analogue. Moreover, this "voice" is assumed to urge roughly the same course of action on all people.

These points are related. It is very important for the traditional notion of conscience that it not be easily heard—that is, that it be easily misunderstood or not recognized for what it is. For it is a foregone conclusion that the attempts of different people to consult it will sometimes yield different results. Therefore, only if the attempt to consult conscience is fallible can the content of conscience even possibly be thought the same for all. Given the world as we know it, the infallibility of conscience (based perhaps on a Cartesian notion of a person's privileged access to the contents of his own moral consciousness) is a guarantee of its relativity. By the same token, the fallibility of conscience (the very feebleness of its voice) is a condition for the possibility of its interpersonal validity.

Another characteristic of the traditional notion of conscience is that its voice is generally assumed to be in some sense deeper than the voice with which we most frequently express our beliefs about right and wrong. That is to say, the traditional conscience is thought to be constituted by (or to constitute) those beliefs about right and wrong that are most truly ours, but which we may not in ordinary discourse acknowledge to be ours at all. This obviously presupposes that (contrary to the Cartesian picture previously drawn) our best opinion at any given moment about the nature of our moral beliefs may not be correct. Thus Raskolnikov, at the outset of *Crime and Punish-*

ment, thinks he possesses certain very unconventional beliefs, but finds out by the end of the novel that he had a deeper and in some sense more authentic level of selfhood that held more or less traditional moral beliefs to which he had been untrue (perhaps because of reading too much Nietzsche). So also Alcibiades in Plato's *Symposium*, who, despite his ordinary, sober and presumably superficial opinion of himself, feels shame when (and only when) he is in the presence of Socrates (*Symposium* 216b-c).

One form or another of this traditional conscience is found in Plato's theories of eros and recollection, in St. Paul, Plotinus, Augustine, Aquinas, Shaftesbury, Hutcheson and Butler (1726). Butler is also sometimes said to be source of conscience as a source of infallible knowledge (Anscombe 1958: 2, Fuss 1964: 112), which infallibility, as pointed out, is not a part of the traditional notion of conscience and would seem to fit better with the modern one.

This traditional notion of conscience has the advantage that it does not lead to the relativistic and paradoxical conclusion. Sundry unexamined feelings of guilt and/or duty are not for it the authentic voice of conscience, and it is only this authentic voice that has final authority. The authentic voice is assumed to speak univocally. So, neither the paradox nor the relativism follow from its authority. This traditional attitude is quite compatible with the view of Nowell–Smith (1958: 248) that in some circumstances we ought *not* to act in accord with conscience, if conscience is meant in the modern sense of the word. For it makes sense to say that we ought not obey any and all feelings of guilt that we might have, but it does not make sense to say that we ought not obey our most legitimate mode of access to moral truth (Garnett 1969: 83, Szabados 1976: 467).

Of course there is a certain sense in which even the traditionalist must agree that one ought to do something that he believes is wrong. It goes without saying that one ought to do the best one can to determine the right course of action and act on that determination, so that doing the best one can to determine the moral truth must be each person's final authority. It is also true that even after doing the best one can, one can fail to determine the truth correctly. In that case, it would follow that one ought to act in accord with moral error (or at least that I must recommend for you action that I believe to be wrong). And if one means by "conscience" merely "doing the best one can to determine the moral truth," then indeed the final authority of conscience may seem to entail the original paradox.

But this seems clearly a sophism of some sort—a hedging on the notion of final authority, perhaps, in which the final authority for the determination of truth itself is confused with the final authority for the determination of a particular person's course of action at a particular time. But in any case, it is not a problem peculiar to moral knowledge. It would apply to any attempt to understand anything at all. The student of arithmetic, for example, ought to do the best she can to determine the correct answer and then she ought to answer boldly. She might, of course, make a mistake in this matter, and so it seems to follow that she ought to speak out the incorrect answer.

There is obviously a sense in which she ought to speak only the correct answer and also a sense in which she should say whatever she thinks is true, but whatever the precisely correct expression of the equivocation is, it is not a problem that concerns the specifics of conscientious behavior. Rather, it applies to the entire concept of doing the best one can in any area of knowledge, or in any endeavor at all. Presumably one must always do "the best one can," and for it one deserves a certain kind of praise. It is still unfortunately true that in a wide variety of ways the best one can do may not be good enough.

What we see from this is that the traditional notion of conscience does not lead to the relativistic conclusion (a) because it is not itself inherently relativistic, and (b) because the attempt to drive it in that direction by importing the notion of doing the best one can is not successful. But if we think more deeply about the notion of doing one's best we will be led to the real heart of the problem of conscience and to the intimate connection that exists between it and aretaic freedom.

The notion of conscience as doing the best one can has about it a certain difficulty that makes it unclear that the relativistic paradox would follow even if allowance were not made for equivocation. It is essential to the generation of the paradox that one be sincere in one's effort's to determine the moral truth, for no one would say that an insincere conscientiousness (if there can be such a thing) had done the best it could or that it has final authority. This casts doubt on the relativistic conclusion. Was Himmler sincere in his assertion that he thought it his sad duty to exterminate six million Jews and that he had to struggle hard against the temptations of pity (Bennet 1974)? While it is possible to claim that he was sincere, and hard to prove conclusively that he was not, such a claim does not sit well with most people, and certainly not with those who are concerned with the vagaries of human self-knowledge. Instead of a sincere but eccentric consciousness, most people would see here a consciousness divided against itself—a consciousness that does not know that it is lying, but which also has every possible motive for lying, and which, therefore, in some other sense of the word *know,* probably knows very well that it is lying. The problem of sincerity thus turns into the problem of self-deception, and it is of great interest that Butler, who certainly had no psychoanalytic axe to grind, identified self-deception as the great corrupter of conscientious knowledge (Szabados 1976).

But if there be any such thing in mankind as putting half-deceits upon themselves, which there plainly is, either by avoiding reflection or (if they do reflect) by religious equivocation, subterfuges, and palliating matters to themselves; by these means conscience may be laid to sleep, and they go in a course of wickedness with less disturbance. All the various turns, doubles, and intricacies in a dishonest heart, cannot be unfolded or laid open; but that there is somewhat of that kind is manifest, be it called self-deceit or by any other name.[8]

It seems quite clear that Himmler's "conscientiousness" rests on his capacity to render himself ignorant of (a) his own murderous and/or tyrannical desires, (b) the self-serving character of his sense of justice, and (c) whatever deeper feelings of humiliation, betrayal, resentment and/or inferiority that may have given rise to his surface personality. If sincerity means saying what one really believes, and if Himmler has deceived himself about what he believes, then his protestations are insincere and are not the manifestations of any form of conscientiousness at all, and certainly not of one that would be acknowledged to have final authority. Even if one means by "conscience" no more than "doing the best one can to ascertain the moral truth," it is not at all clear that Himmler has done this, even though he seems to think he has. Most certainly, we are not going to take his word for it.[9]

The appearance of sincerity and self-deception in the discussion of conscience makes it clear that the idea of the unconscious bears critically on the notion of conscientiousness. Just as the notion of knowing one's own desires turns out to constitute a large part of the meaning of freedom, so does it constitute a large part of conscientiousness, at least if conscientiousness must be sincere and if sincerity implies the absence of self-deception. The very personal qualities that make aretaic freedom possible are also the conditions for conscientious living.

Herein lies the sense of depth that is associated with the traditional voice of conscience. Conscience speaks from the most fundamental level of selfhood and is blocked in those who are inauthentic or self-deceived. That much has been pointed out by existentialism from Nietzsche to Heidegger, and need come as no surprise. But if we add this to the synthesis of health and virtue herein proposed, we end up with a notion of conscience that is in all important respects identical to the traditional notion of conscience in which the concept of self-deception functions exactly as it did for Butler.

Generally, one does not expect anything like the traditional notion of conscience to be associated with Freudian psychology because the Freudian superego seems to be precisely what was previously called the "modern" notion of conscience, and because the deepest layer of the self in Freud, the id, is frequently assumed to be a reservoir of (at best) amoral urges. Now, the Freudian superego most certainly is an example of the modern notion of conscience, but its bare existence does not preclude the existence of other, deeper kinds of guilt that might be more like the traditional notion of conscience. Indeed, everyone must acknowledge that there is a kind of guilt that stems from childhood subservience to authority, but there is no danger to the traditional theory in the reification of the superego as the locus of that particular species of guilt. The problem lies in the second point (the amorality of instinct), and it quickly vanishes if one merely replaces the (entirely unempirical) Freudian theory of instinct with the one advocated here. Then instinct has sufficient moral content to constitute the ground of the traditional voice of conscience, and also sufficient ambivalence and vagueness to explain the obscurity of that voice. The voice of conscience is so weak, not because its quietness is an ad hoc device for explaining away the contradictory evidence, but precisely because it calls from the depths of the unconscious wherein it has been "imprisoned" by the workings of self-deception. Like all unconscious desires, these instincts are forced to exert themselves in a variety of disguises—disguises that make their voice seem especially weak, obscure, and inaudible to the consciousness that has repressed them (however clear the matter may be to others). Now, however, instead of seeing them as the disguises through which amoral urges seek covert satisfaction, we can see them as the attempt of decency to make itself felt on a consciousness that, through neurotic pride, has misidentified its welfare and its selfhood.

The possibility of this re-interpretation of Freud was recognized and seized upon by Erich Fromm as long ago as 1947 in his distinction between the authoritarian and humanistic conscience. The former he called the "internalized voice of authority" (1947: 148), and it is identical to the Freudian superego. The latter he describes as "the voice of our true selves, which summons us back to ourselves, to live productively [i.e., to work], to develop fully and harmoniously [i.e., to love]—that is to become what we potentially are. . . . [It represents] not only the expression of our true selves; it contains also the essence of our moral experiences in life." (1947: 163). Clearly what Fromm calls "humanistic conscience" is what in our language might be called "aretaic" conscience, and it is clear that it embodies many of the concepts we have used to elaborate the notion of mental health (true self, work, love, harmony, and, most importantly, "the essence of our moral experiences" or what we have called "rough virtue").

This notion of aretaic conscience is troublesome, in part, because it de-emphasizes the role of intellect. One notion of conscience, after all, is that it is a kind of confused intellectual apprehension of moral truth, and in comparison to this notion the emphasis here on emotion, instinct, urge and repression may seem degrading or even reductionist. It is, therefore, important to see that the intellectualist interpretation of conscience is not a necessary or even dominant part of the traditional notion. In the two principle sources of that tradition, conscience is largely nonintellectual. In St. Paul, for example, conscience (suneidesis) is said to be the effect of the moral law's being written "in the hearts" (kardiae) of the gentiles, not in their minds (Romans 2: 14–16.). In Plato, where the myth of recollection serves as a sort of semi-mystical intellectual support for the notion of conscience, it is also true that the theory of eros as a kind of blind emotional attachment to ethical truth (the beautiful) is found in close association with the myth of recollection and supplies to this known-but-forgotten knowledge its affective force. It is thus quite within the spirit of Plato to interpret eros as instinct, to see it as aimed at the essential human good, and to find therein the ground of conscience.

The close connection here suggested between sexuality, conscience and the unconscious may also appear troublesome, but it is at least equally tantalizing. The fact is that both Plato and Freud tended to use "sexuality" or "eros" as the general term for instinctual life (the death instinct in Freud excepted). Moreover, both of them had doctrines of "false" desire that entailed that a good measure of this sexuality was unconscious, in Plato because the object of desire was known but forgotten (i.e., unconsciously known), in Freud because it was actively repressed (i.e., conveniently forgotten). In both of them the "forgotten" object of desire continues to attract, as Alcibiades is attracted to Socrates, despite Socrates's superficial ugliness, in ways that Alcibiades can admit to only when drunk (i.e., when his defenses are down), and as, in the more familiar Freudian scenario, the repressed sexuality continues to urge us into relationships and activities the attractiveness of which we do not understand. In this regard, the only really critical difference between Freud and Plato is that for no pressing reason at all Freud chose to include in his conception of instinctual life the desire for activity that was essentially self-destructive, ugly, senseless, excessive, wicked, and/or fundamentally asocial. It should, therefore, come as no surprise that when we alter his theories on this point the remaining doctrine is essentially in accord with the most traditional ethical ideas.

THE PROBLEM OF ETHICAL KNOWLEDGE

It is often said that the principle problem of philosophical ethics is to provide a rational justification for ethical truths. If the operative conception of reason is broad enough, that is a view that fits in well with what has here been said. On the other hand, if one's notion of reason is demanding and narrow, then it is just as true to say that philosophy's goal is to explain the unavailability of such justification without falling into relativism. For it goes almost without saying that even if the truths of ethics are in some sense of the word *rational,* a rational demonstration of usefully specific ethical truths that is convincing to all normally well-educated people of the same culture is not a real possibility. The problem thus is to explain the unavailability of this demonstration while not undermining the sense of rationality that enables us to maintain the interpersonal and intercultural validity of ethical truth.

Such was the task of Plato. He wanted to save ethics from the conventionalism of the sophists by making it a part of rational knowledge, but at the same time, he took care to provide an explanation of why that rationality is not factually available to "the many." Platonic metaphysics has the dual function of making a rational account of ethics possible in principle, but also of providing an epistemic escape clause, as it were, that guarantees the *de facto* unavailability of that account to most people because of the nearly universal human tendency to take one's orientation from the truth value of sense perception.

This is also true in Aristotle where the rationality of moderation is strenuously insisted upon, but where the mode of its apprehension (practical reason) is incapable of purely logical (or "scientific") elaboration.

In Judaeo-Christian philosophy the notion of the fallen condition of man was readily accepted as sufficient reason for the unavailability of a generally convincing form of moral rationality, and so the lack of a science of ethics was not taken to threaten the essential idea of moral reason. But in the atmosphere of the enlightenment, when religious notions came to be considered obfuscations, and where the faith in human reason and the continual improvement of the human condition was unrestrained, there grew up a desire for a more straightforwardly rational morality, something that would give morality a ground nearly as clear as logic itself. It was this spirit that gave rise to the three great modern forms of ethical theory— social contract theory, utilitarianism and Kantian deontology.

In Hobbes, the reconstruction of political philosophy was a part of the general reconstruction of science proposed by Descartes. In it the social contract was to function as a kind of *cogitio* for the generation of moral truth, and by virtue of it all moral uncertainty was to be eliminated. (Hobbes's almost paranoid fear that the slightest bit of legal and/or moral undecideability would lead rapidly to a state of civil war can be understood as a translation of Cartesian doubt into the political sphere.)

Kant too sought a science of ethics, but thought that it would fall into uncertainty and parochialism if it were allowed to rest on empirical grounds. The foundation of morality thus had to lie in *pure* practical reason. From this concern stems the categorical imperative, which is, under most interpretations, little more than the law of noncontradiction applied to a moral subject matter.

Utilitarianism too wished to make ethics as certain as logic itself.

> There is, or rather ought to be, a *logic* of the *will*, as well as of the *understanding*: the operations of the faculty, are neither less susceptible, nor less worthy, than those of the latter, of being delineated by rules. Of these two branches of that recondite art, Aristotle saw only the latter. . . . (Bentham (1789, xxxi)

It is now generally accepted that reason will always fail, both in principle and in fact, to provide this logically convincing justification of moral truth. The presumption is that utilitarianism and Kantianism went as far as possible in that direction, and because we have no general epistemology (like Plato's) within which to interpret their failure and because, in the spirit of the enlightenment, we still reject any such religious notion as the fall, the conventionalist conclusion has been frequently drawn—that is, that the indemonstrability of ethical truth shows, or at least strongly suggests, that in the most important way these are not "rational" truths but rather conventions, constructions of one sort or another, that are rooted in the will are not transculturally (or perhaps even transpersonally) binding.

Through the likely story told herein, the reunion of health and virtue does provide a certain kind of rational ground for ethical truths, a ground that even allows, to a certain extent, for the elaboration and discovery of these truths by the social sciences. But it does not, however, provide the rationalization of ethical truth desired by the enlightenment. Indeed, it disparages the very idea of such a justification, suspecting that it stems from a misguided quest for certainty, precision, clarity, and/or specificity. From the viewpoint of virtue ethics (at least as enunciated by Aristotle and foreshadowed by Plato) the problem of ethical knowledge is solved, not by providing the required justification, but by understanding why such a justification is impossible and why this does not entail any radical contextualization of ethical truth. From the traditional viewpoint, the problem of ethical knowledge is not so much a problem to be solved as it is an ineluctable part of the human condition. It is something to be explained (but not remedied) by a full-scale theory of virtue. So understood, the desire for its solution simply vanishes.

Aristotle's understanding of the unavailability of clear ethical knowledge comes out in a series of apparently innocent remarks that are often passed over by philosophers who assume that he sought the same sort of knowledge that they do. Aristotle, for example, did not think it proper for certain types of people to hear lectures on ethics because their inexperience makes it impossible for them to understand, and their strong emotions make it impossible for them to follow, whatever ethical truth there might actually be.

> Hence a young man is not a proper hearer of lectures on political science; for he is inexperienced in the actions that occur in life, but its discussions start from these and are about these; and further, since he tends to follow his passions, his study will be vain and unprofitable, because the end aimed at is not knowledge but action. And it makes no difference whether he is young in years or youthful in character; the defect does not depend on time, but on his living and pursuing each successive object as passion directs. (*N.E.* I, 1095a2–9)

The passage strongly suggests an intimate connection between the cognition of moral truth and the character of the knower—a connection that becomes clearer in the already-cited passages on the importance of habit.

> It makes no small difference then whether we form habits of one kind or of another from our very youth; it makes a very great difference, or rather *all* the difference. (*N.E.* II, 1103b24–26)

Here Aristotle insists that intellectual excellence is insufficient to alter the moral condition of a habitually vice-ridden person, suggesting again that the vicious cannot know moral truth, a point that is finally made without ambiguity in Book VI.

> This eye of the soul [practical wisdom] acquires its formed state not without the aid of virtue, as has been said and is plain; for the syllogisms which deal with acts to be done are things which involve a starting point, . . . ; and this is not evident except to the good man; for wickedness perverts us and causes us to be deceived about the starting points of action. Therefore it is evident that it is impossible to be practically wise without being good. (*N.E.* VI, 1144a30–37)

> It is clear then that it is not possible to be good in the strict sense without practical wisdom, nor practically wise without moral virtue. (*N.E.* VI, 1144b30)

Thus, for Aristotle, ethical truth is systematically distorted by an intellect that is embodied in a bad character. Bad people cannot know the good, in which profoundly commonplace observation lies the key, for Aristotle, to the whole problem of ethical knowledge—that in ethics the ability to know cannot transcend the selfhood of the knower. To know the good one must first live it, and this means that good and bad are known with something other than (more than or less than, depending on your point of view) the intellect alone.

We refer to this entire matter as "the corruptibility of intellect" and mean by it the inseparability of cognition and character. We note that it applies only to moral reasoning. In mathematics, chess, or physics there is presumably no intimate connection between the person thinking and thing thought. In these disciplines, the emotional constitution of the thinker has no bearing on the criteria of truth, and so the most undeveloped, extreme, and unhappy people may think the truest and most brilliant thoughts. Thus in these areas we get child prodigies. And thus we get a familiar intellectual type whose every ounce of energy is focused into intellectual achievement, while his personal life remains an utter and largely unconsidered mess. Such people can excel in many areas of intellectual work, including many aspects of philosophy, but they cannot understand the nuanced details of ethical truth. There are no child prodigies of practical wisdom.[10]

For Aristotle the corruptibility of the intellect is a salient fact of ethical life, and from it follows a certain kind of relativism.

> For the brave man appears rash relatively to the coward, and cowardly relative to the rash man. . . . Hence the people at the extremes push the intermediate man each over to the other and the brave man is called rash by the coward. (*N.E.* 1108b19–25)

Even without the corruptibility of the intellect, there would be tendency for this to be true. Human beings simply prefer to believe that they are virtuous, and so there is a strong tendency to judge the character of others from that point of view. But that alone is not the problem Aristotle is getting at. When this tendency is combined with he corruptibility of the intellect, it becomes more than a mere tendency. It becomes a necessary part of the epistemology of vice. Vice systematically hides what Aristotle calls the "starting points of action" (whatever he means by that) and so makes moral reasoning relatively useless to the vicious. The possessors of a vice cannot in all honesty really understand that a vice is what they have. They can understand certain externals of their vicious behavior (that they drink more than others, for example, and that, therefore, as judged by the prevailing norm, they are excessive). They can understand that others disapprove of them, and they can even decide prudentially to knuckle under to this pressure. It is not impossible that they might conclude that their behavior violates the social contract, the categorical imperative or that it is injurious to the greater happiness. These things an intellectually proficient person might be brought to understand about his own character, however much he dislikes them. But none of these constitute the recognition of vice as that is understood by Aristotle. An Aristotelian vice is injurious to one's own happiness and it rests on certain so-called unnatural or not-truly-pleasant pleasures (*N.E.* VII, 1154b14–17), which "pleasures," Aristotle says, can be recognized as problematic only by the virtuous. To the vicious they seem as straightforward as any others.

> in the case of men . . . the same things delight some and pain others. . . .
> In all such cases that which appears such to the good man is thought to to
> be really so. . . . [Thus] if virtue and the good man are the measure of
> each thing, those also will be pleasures that appear so to him. (*N.E.* X,
> 1176a10–20)[11]

In this way the vicious are systematically blinded to the knowledge that could inform them of their true condition. Vice, as vice, is behavior that is disloyal to one's own self, one's own pleasure, and one's own happiness. While the vicious can understand many things about themselves, it is precisely this that they cannot see.

That much is purely Aristotle. If we add to it the psychodynamic understanding of vice (a primitive form of which Aristotle seems actually to have accepted[12]) the matter becomes even clearer. Then the self that is hidden from the vicious is hidden by the operations of the unconscious, and the pleasures of the vicious are the pleasures of neurotic pain relief. Access to the relevant truths is systematically blocked by all the familiar operations of the Freudian unconscious, but most of all by what are called "resistance" and "denial." That is, the systematic use of willful ignorance to anaesthetize ourselves to the relevant suspected truth.

Thus, even more deeply than Aristotle understood, the knowledge of ethical truth cannot transcend the psychology of its embodiment. It is the operations of the unconscious, the peculiar human capacity for self-deception, that lies at the bottom of the corruptibility of the intellect. Nothing can convince the vicious of their vices except what unmasks their self-deceptions, and that is the role of the peculiarly therapeutic mode of discourse (or of no discourse at all). Reason does, of course, have a role to play in this discourse, but only the most optimistic rationalist expects it to be sufficient.

The interdependence of intellect and character in ethical knowledge introduces an inevitable circularity into ethical argument. We quote once again Aristotle's candid and unembarrassed acknowledgment of that fact.

It is clear that the good cannot be good without practical wisdom nor practically wise without moral virtue. (1144b30)

Consequently, disagreements about concrete issues will not be resolvable except between people of similar character. When the virtuous try to explain virtue, they are forced to use the theoretically deficient formula of the mean. The question of how to define the mean is answered, if at all, by taking it as a means to happiness, and happiness is then explained (in part) by the distinction between true and false pleasures. But no one who has not seen through at least some her own (apparently true) pleasures can be forced to see much value in the general distinction, and those wedded to false pleasures in some particular arena of behavior will not be able to agree with the virtuous on an empirically significant definition of the relevant virtue or its relationship to happiness. Hence, there is no possibility for a dialectically forced agreement about the specifics of virtue and vice. Nothing can resolve such disagreements until one of the speakers undergoes a fairly radical reassessment of his own selfhood.

We return then to the familiar facts from which the problem of ethical knowledge begins. For the reasons given, it is not to be escaped in Aristotle. Neither is it escaped by the synthesis of health and virtue. We merely come to a plausible understanding of why it must be this way. But if there is any truth at all to the proposed synthesis, we can see that whole idea of escape is misguided. To attempt it is to falsify the ethical subject matter before the discussion is begun—to twist the thing sought into an alien form to make it fit the demands of inappropriate epistemology. This too Aristotle understood, at least in outline.

Our discussion will be adequate if it has as much clearness as the subject-matter admits of, for precision is not to be sought alike in all discussions. Now fine and just actions . . . admit of much variety . . . so that they may be thought to exist only by opinion, and not by nature. We must be content then, in speaking of such subjects, to indicate the truth roughly and in outline . . . for it is the mark of an educated man to look for precision in each class of things just so far as the nature of the subject admits. (*N.E.* I, 1094b12–30)

We can invent an ethics that might better satisfy the demands of the theoretical intellect, as did Hobbes, Kant, and Mill, but the moral truths that we thereby come to are not the virtues about which we originally raised the question of knowledge.

The irresolvability of concrete ethical disagreement by purely rational means is simply a fact of human existence, but it does not entail, as seems often assumed, a radical contextualization or equalization of ethical judgement. That conclusion follows only when we assume that the Aristotelian account of virtue must boil down to a chain of circular definitions that gets its empirical content only by the wholesale importation of some concrete ethical ideal (alleged to be, in Aristotle, the ideal of the Athenian gentleman[13]).

But when we emphasize the psychodynamics of motivation in Aristotle's understanding of virtue, and when we add to them the mechanisms of the unconscious (properly understood), we escape the alleged circularity. The relief of pain in general, and unconscious anxiety relief in particular, are real, empirical matters — methodologically and conceptually imprecise, to be sure, and certainly unexplored by Aristotle in any significant detail, but undoubtedly empirical. Many kinds of behavior are certainly infected with such motivations, and many others of uncertain status may be better understood in the future. Thus there opens up the possibility of using freedom from anxiety as one of the criteria of virtue. Then the logical circle is broken by suggesting that, *all else being equal*, virtue is that state of character which belongs to the person without the need for neurotic pain relief.

This would make the theory of virtue as empirical as the basic theory of the unconscious, and while there is, of course, much debate on how empirical that is, the real problem of such theories is not that they are unempirical, but that their particular brand of empiricism does not provide criteria that are straightforwardly applicable by all rational people. The most relevant evidence is available only in peculiar circumstances (psychoanalytic interviews or other kinds of personal revelation) that are not repeatable and it is available to, or interpretable by, only a certain class of people, *some*, but not all of whom who have been trained in rather unusual ways (including their own psychoanalysis). The logical circle in the theory of virtue would thus be broken, but the inherent elitism of Aristotelian virtue would not be escaped. Virtue would not be relative, but its specifics would remain indemonstrable to all rational persons.

Elitism rather than relativism is the most serious problem of this type of theory. This is a fact that must be candidly admitted, but it is important to point out that this elitism is actually no worse, and is in some ways less of a problem, than the elitism inherent in other forms of truth.

It is inherent in the logic of virtue and the unconscious that, in general, only the virtuous can know the specifics of virtue and that they will be unable to explain themselves to others in terms that are rationally convincing. This is an elitism of character, but it is not an elitism of intellect, education, or wealth. It is an elitism that is open to anyone who for whatever reason happens to be relatively free of anxiety and self-deception. Thus it does not correspond to any social class, race, gender, economic condition, degree of education, or religious persuasion; thus its members are drawn equally from the most ordinary groups as well as from the recognized elites; and thus it is not and probably never can be an institutionally recognized group (and so can never, as a recognized group, hold political power). All this helps to mitigate the distastefulness that is inherent in any form of elitism.

The most important point, however, is that the elitism of character is a sort of democratic anti-elitism in which the most cherished possession of the traditional elites, knowledge, especially the knowledge of how to live well, exists wherever there is good character and with considerable disregard to the intellectual sophistication of its possessor. This should be compared to the elitism inherent in the enlightenment or scientific notion of ethical truth. Under enlightenment presuppositions moral truth does not really have to be demonstrable to all people, but only to those whose educations and inherent intellectual ability make them fit for the evaluation of rational argument and proof. On those presuppositions, then, the truths of morality (or the lack of them) turn out to be rather like the truths of mathematics or metaphysics, the special possession of an *intellectual* elite, an elitism, we note, that is inherently academic.

Viewed from this perspective, the insistence on the "universal" demonstrability of ethical truth, means only the insistence on its knowabilty to the entire intellectual and/or academic class. This elitism is not escaped when, as is currently the case, a large part of the intellectual class adopts the viewpoint of democratic relativism and tolerance. For the presupposition that lies behind this relativism is that if ethics is susceptible of real, objective knowledge at all, then it is *they*, the intellectuals, who must know it. If the "universal" knowability of the enlightenment ideal turns out to be unavailable, (as is now commonly accepted among intellectuals) then *they* may conclude that virtue is not a matter of "objective" or interpersonal knowledge, and so *they* may abandon the whole business of ethics to a very tolerant and democratic-sounding relativism. But all this depends on the presupposition that the intellect alone (and hence the intellectual class) is the final arbiter of what is interpersonally and/or objectively true.

This explains why such relativism, despite its inherent appeal to the oppressed, is far more popular among the intellectuals than among the people generally. Most people simply do not make the intellectualist presupposition on which it rests. Intellectuals, however, almost cannot help but make it, however great their attachment to democratic ideals.

Thus it is not a question of whether we will be elitist or egalitarian, but rather which sort of elitism is least injurious to democratic ideals. Under the elitism of character the desired knowledge is most often found in relatively untutored individuals (who are spread more or less evenly through-out the population). In this respect, the elitism of character is certainly the more democratic of them.

Nor does the indemonstrability of ethical truth make it inherently unteachable, and therefore, less available to all than intellectual truth. It does make it unteachable in the traditional academic manner, but there are other forms of education that are more appropriate to the ethical subject matter. Like the elitism of the intellect, the elitism of character has its ways, more or less effective, of bringing about an appreciation of its truths by those who do not naturally possess them. If this is not clearly seen, it is because we tend to understand education in a narrowly intellectual way, while in all other times and places it is taken for granted that what is required is a cultivation of the entire person, the *education sentimentale* referred to by MacIntyre, or what Aristotle was getting at when he spoke of the importance of acquiring good habits in childhood.

Ethical truth may, in fact, be as widely teachable as the truths of math-ematics, but the appropriate form of education is extra-intellectual and sometimes involves the acquisition of emotionally significant self-knowl-edge. To all willing to undergo this (rather painful) kind of education, ethi-cal truth would be more or less accessible, just as all willing to undergo the (frequently painful) discipline of mathematics will gain a greater or lesser comprehension.

The elitism of character is generally more democratic than the elitism of intellect. In education, the principle requirement is that the curriculum not be imbalanced in the direction of intellect—that the education of the emotions be considered a normal part of the cultivation of self that is called "liberal education." There is nothing all that unusual about this. It is a fre-quently cited fact that over the door of Plato's Academy there was a sign that barred entry to all who had not studied geometry. It is forgotten, how-ever, that in his *Republic* Plato allowed no one to talk philosophy who had not first achieved the soldier's mastery of fear.

The theoretical helplessness of the Aristotelian theory of virtue is thus partly remedied by the reunion of virtue and health. However, the problem of ethical knowledge is not solved in the terms in which it was raised. We merely come to a better understanding of its intractability. We are familiar by now with the helplessness of rational persuasion in the face of the defensive personality. The synthesis of virtue and health makes it clear that this is also the basic reason for the problem of ethical truth. This does not mean that ethical truth is relative. It means only that its appreciation often requires non-dialectical modes of persuasion—persuasion that somehow arouses the thing called "conscience."

Notes

INTRODUCTION

1. Wheelwright (1966: 54).
2. Plato, *Republic*, VI, 508e. Unless otherwise noted all passages from the *Republic* are by Paul Shorey in the Loeb Library editions.
3. *Republic*, VI, 509b.
4. Timaeus, 29e–30a. Cornford translation.
5. "primitive ontology has a Platonic structure; and in that case Plato could be regarded as the outstanding philosopher of 'primitive mentality', that is as the thinker who succeeded in giving philosophic currency and validity to the modes of life and behavior of archaic humanity." Eliade (1954: 34).
6. Kirk and Raven (1964: 114).
7. Wheelwright (1966: 54).
8. Wheelwright (1966: 71).
9. Wheelwright (1966: 75).
10. Kirk and Raven (1964: 158).
11. Kirk and Raven (1964: 273).
12. Kirk and Raven (1964: 284).
13. Genesis, 1,10, 1,12, 1,31. King James translation. Even if chapter 1 is a later redaction, the same sentiment is found in 2,13: "It is not good that man should be alone; I will make him a helpmate."
14. Russell (1918), quoted in Burtt (1924: 23).
15. Symposium, 201a–c. W. R. M. Lamb, translator. Any number of quotations to the same effect can be found throughout the *Symposium* and scattered among various other dialogues.
16. Aristotle, *Nicomachean Ethics*, I, 1099a13–15.
17. *Republic*, II, 372a–d.
18. *Republic*, 372e–373a.
19. Wheelwright (1966: 70).
20. Wheelwright (1966: 70).
21. Wheelwright (1966: 70).
22. Wheelwright (1966: 79).
23. Wheelwright (1966: 72).
24. Thomas Aquinas, *Summa Theologica*, I, Question 95, Article 2.
25. Thomas Aquinas, *Summa Theologica*, I–II, Question 82, Article 1.
26. Kuhn (1957).

27. Machiavelli (1520: chapter XV).
28. Hobbes (1651: chapter XI).
29. Kant (1785) p.15.
30. *Gorgias* 464 a–b.
31. *Republic* 444e. See also Crito 47d–e.
32. Thomas Aquinas, *Summa Theologica,* I–II, Question 82, Article 1.

CHAPTER 1

1. Nagel, Ernest (1961: chapter 12). See also Canfield (1964).
2. Moravcsik (1976). p. 1.
3. Kass (1975). Quoted in Beauchamp and Walters (1978). p. 108.
4. Englehardt (1976). p. 260.
5. Englehardt (1976: 267).
6. Margolis (1976: 241).
7. Margolis (1976: 251).
8. Margolis (1976: 253).
9. One very clear example regarding physical health is Sedgewick (1973).
10. Sedgewick (1973). p. 1.
11. "We sort things out as illnesses or disease states according to judgement bearing on what functions are proper to humans . . . , or because of pain that does not play a role in such functions, or because of judgement concerning human disfigurement and deformity." Englehardt (1976) p. 261.
12. This is not meant to imply that health is a merely negative concept—the absence of disease. Although the negative definition does in fact reflect a good deal of medical practice, that fact is more a criticism of that practice than a discovery of the real meaning of health.

Further, I do not here use the distinction between disease and illness that is advocated in some of the literature cited. Instead, I use the words in their rough, ordinary meanings. The alleged distinction between illness and disease was meant to correspond roughly to the evaluative and descriptive "elements" in the meaning of "health" (Boorse 1975: 56–7). It is an echo of the fact/value dichotomy, and that, of course, is precisely what a naturalistic theory of values must avoid. For the semantics of the matter, see Englehardt (1976: 257).

13. See for example Weinrich's study (1976) linking homosexuality to intelligence, or E. O. Wilson's suggestions (1978) about its evolutionary significance. In principle, it is possible to suggest innumerable explanations for any matter of this sort, no matter how dysfunctional it might at first appear. But to be counted as truth, there must be empirical confirmation within a coherent overall account of the body.
14. See the distinction between functions and goals in Wright (1973: 140).
15. A discussion of the complications created by the introduction of the social factor follows. By no means do these complications make function "socially constructed" as that phrase is normally understood.
16. Descartes (1641), VI, p. 197–8.
17. Englehardt (1974).

18. Wilson (1978: 144–6).

19. I take it that this is Plato's essential point when he says that a thing's function is "that which it does best" (*Republic*, I, 352e–ff.).

20. These are only the latest estimates taken from a typical anthropology textbook (Farb 1978: 51, 89). The tendency of recent anthropology is to push these dates back even farther.

21. From the poles to the equator, the percentage of meat in hunter-gatherer diet varies from almost 100% to less than 20%. But the extremes are explicable by circumstances. In the arctic there are few alternatives. On the assumption that there is a species-wide norm in the matter, attention should be focused on the conditions against which evolution occurred, which were presumably not arctic. Whether or not Eskimos have made a full and genuine adaptation to a diet that was forced on them by circumstances (i.e., just how variable health is in this matter) is an open question that can be settled only by a full investigation of all aspects of their health (Farb 1978: 91).

CHAPTER 2

1. See for example the allegation in Bettleheim (1981) that Freud was misrepresented and mistranslated by English speaking psychoanalysts in order to make him appear less of a philosopher or moralist and more of a scientist. Many psychoanalysts, including Adler and Hartmann (1960), had the same goals.

2. DSM III, p. 354.

3. DSM III, p. 354.

4. DSM III, p. 358.

5. As interpreted by Hartmann and reported by Jahoda (1958: 37).

6. Jahoda (1958) is still the classic synopsis of positive definitions of mental health, but Coan (1977) is also useful.

7. See Boorse (1976: 68ff) for a discussion of some of the reasons for so many (partly) misleading (and partly helpful) definitions.

8. Szasz (1961: chapters 7 and 8).

9. For various reasons the harmony of the soul is fundamentally more "tattered" than the harmony of the body. It is so tattered, in fact, that it contains within itself a basic contradiction that has always made the question of human nature, from Plato to Heidegger, something of a mystery. This matter is thoroughly explored in chapter 4. While it does entail that the comparison to the harmony of the body is something of an oversimplification, it is still true that the naturalistic brackets force us to the conclusion that any contradiction in the affective constitution of human beings must be a contradiction within a basic harmony, so that the essential point made here remains correct.

10. See chapters 4 and 5.

11. See, for example, Horney's criticism of Freud's "formalistic" notion of work (1950: 327).

12. See note 9.

13. A rather rough but still suggestive theory of human mental health based on adaptation to life in the hunter-gatherer society has, in fact, been suggested. Models of therapy built on it are in actual practice. See Glantz and Pearce (1989).

14. See note 9.

CHAPTER 3

1. *Nicomachean Ethics*, 1104b6.

2. My goal here is to take no sides in the dispute initiated by Ryle's *Concept of Mind*. Whatever the ultimate outcome of the philosophy of mind is, we will presumably still say things like, "He went to school just for the fun of it," wherein the fun (or the tendency to have it in school) is the alleged motive, reason or explanation for the behavior constituted by class attendance, study, writing, etc. Whether or not having fun turns out to be a private, mental event or a subtle species of public behavior is not critical. Even if what we have called the "inner man" is more truly "outer," it would still not mean that motives are not, in some important sense, responsible for actions. It would mean only that some "outer things" (motives) are responsible for others (actions). In that case, all that is said here about the relation between motivation and behavior would have to be recast entirely within the language of behavior, but the outcome would still be the same — motivation and behavior (now understood as two species of behavior) would still need to be adapted to each other.

3. It is, of course, very controversial to claim that pleasures, which are generally thought of as mental entities, are formed by biological pressures; but to assume this is no worse than to assume that behavior is so formed. Obviously, pleasure and behavior simply have to be considered together. If we are formed to eat, then we must be formed to enjoy eating and to find lack of nutrition painful. Who would deny that our capacity for feeling those particular pleasures and pains are biologically rooted, however much social conditions might produce variations on the theme? This is also true for sexual pleasure, the pain of ill health, etc. The pleasures connected with the behavior that is minimally essential for life and reproduction are at least generally formed to harmonize with the appropriate behavior. The naturalistic brackets force us to maximize this most basic point.

4. Descartes (1649: article CXXXVII, p. 392).

5. Quoted in Sidgwick (1874: 191).

6. There is little point in entering into serious debate about the existence of altruism. Despite its having been made an issue in capitalist cultures, it is obviously a non-issue. To try to prove that altruistic acts exist is almost as silly as trying to prove that sex exists. See Fromm (1956: 48) for a discussion of the psychodynamics of selfishness and generosity, wherein the point of view is not much different from Aristotle's in *Ethics* IX, 4. There are many attempts to defend these obvious truths. The shame, however, is that we even require a proof of the fact that there is pleasure in giving. How much altruism there is, and its precise relation to self-regarding activity are real questions, but they can be postponed for now.

7. Plato, *Phaedo* (60B), *Republic* (IX, 583Bff). Schopenhauer went so far as to claim all pleasure-seeking to be the relief of pain (1819: 309).

8. Plato, *Republic* II, 372 c–ff.

9. Mill too employed the notion of the knowledgeable judge to explain why the higher pleasures are to be preferred to the lower. Presumably in this he was following Hutcheson, who was himself presumably following Plato (*Republic* 582).

10. To my knowledge, Plato (*Philebus* 42d; *Republic* 583b; *Phaedo* 60b) was the first to make the distinction, but almost certainly it develops from the Parmenidean or Pythagorean religio-philosophical tradition.

11. Because Greek psychology was teleological, Plato and Aristotle were forced to confront the question of why pleasure and goodness diverged, just as we have here been forced by our "as if' teleology to ask what the disrupting factor is that upsets the harmony of pleasure and function. Their answer was to declare that normal pleasures do not diverge from goodness, but others do—those motivated by the relief of some great pain (*Republic* 586a, *Nicomachean Ethics* 1154b13ff.) Thus, the ground was laid for a broad distinction of pleasures into pure (or real) pleasures and impure (or false) pleasures (*Philebus* 40dff., *Nicomachean Ethics* 1099a12, 1173b20, 1175b20–25, 1176a8–20). Plato and Aristotle might have pushed the matter farther—classifying different kinds of pain-relieving pleasures (by virtue of the different pains involved, perhaps) and by then attempting to show in detail how those "pleasures" corresponded to the "pleasures" of vice. But their psychology was not sophisticated enough for that and they seem to have mixed up this very fertile distinction with the unproductive notion that the pleasures of vice, and hence the "pleasures" of pain relief, were the pleasures of the body. Had he not stumbled on that point, Plato might well have been the discoverer of psychoanalysis, and psychiatry might have had a moral foundation from the outset. See chapter 6 for a fuller discussion of false pleasure in Aristotle.

12. This is not meant to denigrate the real meaning of various religious teachings that have stressed living in the present as a way of escaping an ego-burdened, grasping relationship to life. Such a rejection of "worry" is common to Christianity, Hinduism and Buddhism, and it may well embody real wisdom. It is, however, to condemn the vulgar and literal-minded misunderstanding of those teachings, and also those teachers who have bought popularity for themselves by making an unhealthy and selfish disregard for cares and responsibilities appear to be a deep religious teaching.

13. Freud (1920: 341).

14. Heidegger (1927: 231).

15. Heidegger (1927: 232).

16. Freud (1920: 416).

17. Beginning with Demos (1960) there was a series of articles within the analytic tradition that attempted to explain away the paradoxes of self-deception by understanding it as a species of ordinary confusion, obstinacy, ignorance, stupidity, flightiness and/or wishful thinking (Canfield and Gustafson 1962; Siegler 1963; A. Rorty 1972). For reasons made clear by Fingarette (1969: 12–34), I believe that none of these is successful. I proceed here without logical niceties and simply

accept the peculiar fact that consciousness can, in fact, do what to our inadequate formulations seems logically impossible. I believe it is better to do this than to misrepresent the phenomena for the sake of technical propriety.

18. Possibly, the paradoxes of self-deception can be mitigated if we think in terms of degrees of consciousness. It may be that in self-deception we are not so much unaware of the offending thought as we are aware of it only dimly. Then perhaps we could understand how the self knows the offending thought enough to keep that knowledge from becoming clear, but not enough to acknowledge it. This may be strictly analogous to the way one dimly knows (i.e., both knows and does not know) what one is going to say before one writes it, but only in writing it can we say what it was that we knew. Collingwood (1938: 217, 239) is extremely suggestive on this point, and it seems to me his "corrupted consciousness" is essentially the same as "self-deception."

19. The first recognition that the pleasure of anxiety relief is simply pride belongs, so far as I know, to Karen Horney in *Neurosis and Human Growth* and follows from her genius for translating psychoanalytic insights out of their technical language and back into the ordinary language and experience in which they have their real justification. This particular translation is terribly important. It is, in fact, the key to the transition from medical to moral language. Horney is frequently seen as oversimple, but she merely returns the technically expressed insight to its workaday roots. *Pride* (understood as a vice) is the right word for this kind of pleasure.

20. Freud (1920: 421).

CHAPTER 4

1. Nietzsche (1872: 77) was quite wrong to think that this was the death of tragedy. To the contrary, it merely transferred the tragic ironies from Achilles to Socrates. It intellectualized them, and it is hard not to hear the Dionysian rhythms in the love song of the *Symposium* (223d). See Roochnik (1990).

2. Griswold calls the tame animal "a quite natural sort of being" and says of it that "as zoion Socrates would not be essentially different from anyone else or perhaps from other living animals. The tameness would seem to be a result of domestication . . . and so of an acceptance of one's limits." He says also that the tame animal lives "in harmony with the divine and that its character . . . is bestowed on it from without." (1986: 41)

3. See Bloom (1968: 347).

4. The rise of anxiety is probably coincident with the rise of religion and the notion of an afterlife (i.e, with our refusal to accept mortality, a state of affairs that seems on current archeological evidence to be about 100,000 years old—i.e., much younger than the toolmaking activity of reason that has been dated back at least several million years, not to mention the more purely animal motivations that are immeasurably older still).

CHAPTER 5

1. The idea, however, was hardly unknown until then. Plato puts it into the mouth of Thrasymachus in the *Republic*, and it, too, is presumably one of the perennial resting places of human thought.

2. Benedict (1934: 1).

3. Among the exceptions are the functionalism of Malinowski, which rested on a rough list of "basic needs," such as metabolism, reproduction, movement, growth and health. Were this idea unpacked, it would turn out to be exactly the same thing that is aimed for here. But Malinowski meant to keep the list confined to activities that were narrowly organic. In any case, he did not consider the list of basic needs something to be discovered. It was merely presupposed as biologically obvious, and society was then interpreted as a simple extension of the body in its effort to meet those needs. While oversimple and psychologically naive, Malinowski's fundamental idea of a list of basic (i.e., natural) needs and a series of social variations on those themes seems to me essentially correct (Malinowski 1944: esp. 91).

4. Aquinas, II, I, Question 95.

5. It could happen if a highly effective, late-developing characteristic supervened suddenly on an already-established, cohesive set of biological characteristics, such as we have said in fact happened to human beings vis-à-vis anxiety and self-condemnation. But then the supervening characteristics, because they are so late-coming, would most certainly not constitute the species's *basic* way of maintaining itself. I have argued that anxiety is a part of what causes us to dominate, but that in no way implies it is a part of our most basic equipment for simple self-maintenance. Rudimentary forms of education, speech and reason are such, however, and the hard palaeo-archeological evidence seems continually to show us that these functions in human beings are far older than we used to think. From the other side, we seem to be learning continually that animals are ever more truly social and that they possess a remarkably greater portion of the elements of reason than ever before suspected. While some of this is offensive to certain traditional notions of human dignity, it has the tremendous virtue of strongly suggesting that reason, speech and society are part of a longstanding natural order.

6. *Ethics*, II, 1103a24; *Politics*, I, 1253a1.

7. Aquinas, *Summa Theologica*, Question 94, A. 2.

8. Thomas Aquinas, *Summa Theologica*, Question 95, Article 2, Whether Passions Existed in the Soul of the First Man.

9. On the other hand, the question of whether there are archaic universal rights of man obviously depends on the definition of *human*. If the archaic person sees only his neighbor or fellow tribesman as human, then in his terms he does treat all people reasonably well and so may be said to recognize universal human rights. Apparently, it all depends on how much there is a felt identification with the other, which in turn presumably depends on one's capacity for sympathy. See the discussion of sympathy on page 115ff.

10. See page 42.

11. This point is developed much further in the next chapter. For the moment,

consider Aristotle's *N. Ethics*, where the point is insisted upon again and again, and the famous ladder of love in the *Symposium* where moral/intellectual/aesthetic progress is pictured entirely as a transformation of desires, an education of pleasure (*Symposium* 210). Or see Veatch (1992) for a discussion of the critically important concept of what might be called "self-enjoyment" in the truly teleological conception of virtue.

CHAPTER 6

1. MacIntyre (1981: 149).

2. See Peck (1983) for an example from popular literature, or Wallach and Wallach (1990) for a more academic gesture in the same direction. The general tradition of humanistic psychology, when not overwhelmed by relativism, has definitely led the way, but it has had no real impact on professional philosophy except insofar as the mental-health movement might have been one of the influences that gave rise to virtue ethics. See Fromm (1947), Horney (1950), and Maslow (1962). See Feuer (1955) for a sociologist's version of the synthesis of ethics and psychology.

3. I use "ethics" as the genus and "virtue" and "morality" as the species, much as one might call Newtonian and Einsteinian theory species of the genus "physics." While this usage does have a historical foundation, I do not claim that the distinction corresponds with great exactitude to any particular usage of the words *morality* and *virtue*. But these words do seem apt for naming an important distinction that seems to characterize the difference between modern and traditional ethics. G. E. M. Anscome (1958) was the first I know to use the word *moral* in this restricted way.

4. See also II, 1109b23 and IV 1126b2–4.

5. See Burnyeat (1980) and Kosman (1980) for complete elaborations of this point.

6. See also Gosling and Taylor (1982: 335), Randall (1960: 267), and Ross (1923: 189). The basic point seems noncontroversial.

7. Some other examples are II, 1104b10, 1107a9, 1107b1.

8. "Aristotle neither praises nor condemns the tendencies inherent in man. They are indifferent in themselves; they become good or bad according as they are subjugated [*sic*] or allowed to assert themselves against [*sic*] the right rule which our reasonable nature grasps of itself and seeks to impose [*sic*] on them." Only a page earlier Ross refers to the passage about our natural adaptation to virtue, but apparently he interprets this adaptation as a matter of mere possibility (as the wood has the capacity for being a house) rather than a real adaptation, a special suitability, or a natural tendency (Ross 1923: 188–9).

The harsh language of the passage, as well as its substance, seem an outstanding examples of the "intellectualist" error mentioned by Burnyeat.

9. For Plato's presentation of the matter consider again the so-called pig city of *Republic* 369b–374. This brief and often ignored part of the dialogue depicts a

small city of naturally moderate pleasures in which, without government, a pure harmony of pleasure and virtue prevails. Socrates calls this the "healthy" and "true" city. Adeimantus finds it boring and requires Socrates to upset the harmony by inserting the immoderate desire for luxury. Luxury thus functions in this story as the disturbing factor—the thing that creates the need for government and (in Aristotle's terms) for habituation. But all that habituation does is restore the original harmony, just as the philosopher kings really do nothing but struggle to restore as much as possible of the harmony of the healthy city to the republic as a whole and to the souls of the guardians in particular (416D, 419A).

10. Were Job made happy by his virtue, even in the midst of the evils rained upon him by God, he would have no complaint and there would be no need to explain how an omnipotent and benevolent God could have made an unjust world. The virtuous would already be in heaven, and the kingdom of heaven would be already among us.

11. Pain relief thus amounts to a criterion for the identification of "unnatural" or "incidental" pleasures that is independent of any general presuppositions about human nature and of any (circular) attempts to define the *phronimos*, the man of practical wisdom. In fact, if one could identify the relevant pains (which Aristotle does not do) one could use this definition to arrive empirically at the meaning of human nature and thence of the practical wisdom that fulfills it. Thus, I do not understand why Gosling and Taylor (1982: 339–42) so quickly dismiss this passage. It is true, of course, that Aristotle makes no attempt to work out the matter in detail. The passage is only a suggestion, but it is a very fertile one.

12. Note the near-perfect parallelism in Horney (1950: 37–39). "On the surface . . . it looks as though the neurotic were merely more ambitious, more concerned with power, prestige and success than the healthy person."

"While the difference between the healthy and the neurotic person is [in some] respects one of degree, . . . despite surface similarities [it is] one of quality and not of quantity."

"The difference between healthy strivings and neurotic drives is one between spontaneity and compulsion."

13. See note 10.

CHAPTER 7

1. The exact relation between our problematic emphasis on freedom and the transformation of virtue into morality, for example, is unclear, but there is external evidence of a logical connection. Few tried harder than Kant and the utilitarians to achieve the "scientization" of ethics (each in its own terms, of course), and these are also the places where the classic expressions of the modern notions of freedom are found—the negative, political freedom of liberalism in Mill's *On Liberty*, and the transcendent, "ontological," and/or existential freedom of the subject from the laws of nature in Kant (the autonomy of the self).

2. Thus the paradox that Plato loved to exploit—the inversion of "values" in

which a wise but poor man may be more powerful than the rich. Admittedly, this is an irony that prepares the way for a still more radical inversion of values—that the meek shall inherit the earth. But there is really nothing all that paradoxical about either formulation. It is simply a question of where true happiness lies in relation to the general human (mis)understanding of it.

Plato believed that this self-knowledge was achieved by philosophy through a dialectical methodology that led one farther and farther from sense perception to a world of changeless ideas at the head of which stood the idea of the good—the ultimate object of all desire. This extravagant metaphysics has obscured the good sense of his ethics, and in it we need not follow him. But we *do* desire the good (in the form of happiness) and it is reasonable to suggest that happiness is systematically obscured by what can be sensibly called "unreal appearances," i.e., the "pleasures" produced by relief of pain. But the illusion is not epistemological; it has little to do with the reliability of sense perception vis-à-vis the certainty of pure reason. It is ethical and relates only to the peculiarly deceptive nature of certain kinds of pleasure. The relief of pain does not in fact bring happiness, the bulk of human behavior and all appearances to the contrary notwithstanding. From that fact alone follows almost everything else in Plato of real ethical importance.

Apparently, we have then in Plato at least the seeds of a thoroughgoing indifference to freedom as transcendence of nature. Instead, we find a character-bound notion of freedom that in its philosophical expression boils down mostly to a species of self-knowledge and depends on the wisdom to distinguish pain relief from simple pleasure. This is echoed in Aristotle and is presumably what was meant in the tradition meant by "the truth that makes one free." It is not that the truth reveals a metaphysically higher self or a disembodied moral ought. Rather it is that the truth simply shows us what it is we really want. In relation to the difficult tasks set us by freedom so conceived (the attainment of self-knowledge), the question of whether or not that ultimate want is set by nature or chosen by our "free" will is surely unimportant.

3. Gay (1979: 42).

4. Quoted in Gay (1979: 53).

5. Foot (1957: 73).

6. Hampshire (1959: 177).

7. The same sort of thing is found in *Exodus*, where it is said with no apparent sense of incongruity both that God hardened Pharaoh's heart (and so caused his refusal to let the Jews leave Egypt) and also that the Pharaoh did it to himself (and so is presumably responsible for his obstinate character). *Exodus* 7: 13, 14, and 23; 8: 10, 15, and 28; 9: 7, 12, and 34; 9: 34–5; 10: 1.

8. Butler (1726: VII). Cited in Szabados (1976: 463).

9. Certainly few non-philosopher's would accept Himmler's grossly self-serving rationalizations as genuine examples of conscientious thought. It is less clear whether this would be so of Huck Finn's guilt feelings about helping Jim to escape from slavery, but we note that the example seems contrived by Twain to win a laugh or make a point precisely because we cannot easily imagine it happening the way it is pictured. Huck's acceptance of slavery may be a vestigial and/or largely

thoughtless acceptance of convention that is opposed by his best moral instincts. The question is whether these guilt feelings come from his very best efforts to ascertain the moral truth, or whether they rest on a thoughtless acceptance of convention and authority. To know that we need to know more than we have been given. (We need to know, for example, whether or not it has ever occurred to him that slavery might be wrong. If it has not occurred to him, why hasn't it? Hasn't he heard discussions about its possible illegitimacy? Did he give those discussions any real thought? Did he simply ignore them so as to maintain an untroubled mind? etc.) Of course, he might well be honestly confused about the matter, but then the question of his conscientiousness boils down to which part of his confusion stems from the activity of conscience and which (if any) from the kind of thoughtlessness that is precisely his *not* doing the best he could. We do not know the answers to all these questions, but the need for them shows that we do not normally just take his word for his sincerity. Consequently, sincerity is not at all so clearly compatible every form of behavior, and the diversity of conscientious action is far less obvious than at first supposed.

10. This does not mean that there cannot be non-personal knowledge of ethical tautologies ("Be moderate."), fairly useless generalizations ("Thou shall not lie.") or certain details of moral reasoning as understood by utilitarians, Kantians, or social contract theorists. One can always try to make ethics into a purely theoretical discipline, presumably with varying degrees of success. But when it comes to concrete, truly practical ethical decision making, the character of the thinker inevitably intrudes.

11. Also N.E. 113a30.

12. See page 134–139. "Owing to the excesses of pain that men experience, they pursue excessive and in general bodily pleasures as being a cure for the pain. Now curative agencies produce intense feeling—which is the reason why they are pursued—because they show up against the opposite pain" (*N.E.* VII, 27–33).

"People of excitable natures always need relief; for even their body is in torment . . . , but pain is driven out by the contrary pleasure, and by any chance pleasure if it be strong; and for these reasons they become self-indulgent and bad. *But the pleasures that do not involve pains do not admit of excess; and these are among the things pleasant by nature and not incidentally.* (*N.E.* VII, 1154b10–17)

13. But see Nussbaum (1988) for reasons why, even in the unreconstructed Aristotelian text, this is not so.

Bibliography

Adler, Mortimer J. 1958. *The Idea of Freedom: A Dialectical Examination of the Conception of Freedom*. Garden City: Doubleday and Co.

Adorno, T. W.; Frenkel-Brunswik, E.; Levinson, D. J.; and Sanford, R. N. 1950. *The Authoritarian Personality*. New York: Norton.

American Psychiatric Association. 1987. *Diagnostic and Statistical Manual of Mental Disorders*. 3d ed., rev. Washington, D.C.: American Psychiatric Association.

Annas, Julia. 1980. "Aristotle on Pleasure and Goodness." In Rorty (1980).

Anscombe, G. E. M. 1958. "Modern Moral Philosophy." *Philosophy*, Vol. 33, No. 124 (January).

Aquinas, St. Thomas. *Summa Theologica*. Anton Pegis, ed. New York: Random House (1945).

Ardrey, R. 1966. *The Territorial Imperative*. New York: Atheneum.

———. 1970. *The Social Contract*. New York: Atheneum.

Aristotle. *Nicomachean Ethics*. W. D. Ross, trans. Oxford: Clarendon Press (1925).

Ayer, A. J. 1954. *Philosophical Essays*. New York: St. Martin's Press (1963).

Barash, David. 1979. *The Whisperings Within: Evolution and the Origin of Human Nature*. New York: Harper and Row.

———. 1978. "Evolution as a Paradigm for Behavior." In Gregory (1978).

Baylis, Charles. 1964. "Conscience." *Encyclopedia of Philosophy*. New York: Macmillan.

Beauchamp, Tom and Walters, LeRoy. 1978. *Contemporary Issues in Bioethics*. Encino, CA: Dickenson Publishing Co.

Bellow, Saul. 1970. *Mr. Sammler's Planet*. New York: Viking Press.

Benedict, Ruth. 1932. *Patterns of Culture*. 11th ed. Boston: Houghton Mifflin.

Bennett, Jonathan. 1974. "The Conscience of Huckleberry Finn." *Philosophy*. Vol. 49, 123–134.

Bentham, Jeremy. 1789. *The Principles of Morals and Legislation*. New York: Hafner (1948).

Berlin, Isaiah. 1958. *Two Concepts of Liberty*. Oxford: Clarendon Press.

Bettelheim, Bruno. 1981. "Freud and the Soul." *The New Yorker* (March 1).

Bleibtreu, Herman K., ed. 1969. *Evolutionary Anthropology: A Reader in Human Biology*. Boston: Allyn and Bacon Inc.

Bloom, Alan. 1968. *The Republic of Plato*. New York: Basic Books.

Boorse, Christopher. 1975. "On the Distinction Between Disease and Illness." *Philosophy and Public Affairs*, 5 (Fall).

———. 1976. "What a Theory of Mental Health Should Be." *Journal for the Theory of Social Behavior*. Vol. 6 (April).

Brandt, Richard B. 1959. *Ethical Theory*. Englewood Cliffs, NJ: Prentice-Hall.

Budziszewski, J. 1986. *The Resurrection of Nature*. Ithaca: Cornell University Press.

Burnyeat, M. F. 1980. "Aristotle on Learning to Be Good." In Rorty (1980).

Burtt, E. A. 1924. *The Metaphysical Foundations of Modern Science*. Garden City: Doubleday.

Butler, Joseph. 1726. "Sermons." In *The Works of Joseph Butler*. Oxford: Oxford University Press (1850).

Canfield, J. and Gustafson, D. F. 1962. "Self-Deception." *Analysis*, Vol. 23.

Caplan, Arthur L., ed. 1978. *The Sociobiology Debate*. New York: Harper and Row.

Chagnon, Napoleon A. and Irons, William, eds. 1979. *Evolutionary Biology and Human Social Behavior: An Anthropological Perspective*. N. Scituate, MA: Duxbury Press.

Coan, Richard W. 1977. *Hero, Artist, Sage or Saint? A Survey of Views of What is Variously Called Mental Health, Normality, Maturity, Self-Actualization, and Human Fulfillment*. New York: Columbia University Press.

Collingwood, R. G. 1938. *The Principles of Art*. New York: Oxford University Press (1958)

———. 1945. *The Idea of Nature*. Oxford: Oxford University Press.

Cornford, F. M. 1912. *From Religion to Philosophy*. Reprinted, New York: Harper and Row (1957).

Darwin, Charles. 1871. *The Descent of Man*. London: J. Murray.

———. 1859. *On the Origin of Species by Means of Natural Selection*. London: J. Murray.

Demos, Raphael. 1960. "Lying to Oneself." *The Journal of Philosophy*. 57: 588–595.

Descartes, Rene. 1641. *Meditations*. Trans. Elizabeth Haldane and G. R. T. Ross. Dover Publications. 1931.

——. 1649. *The Passions of the Soul*. Trans. Elizabeth Haldane and G. R. T. Ross. New York: Dover Publications (1931).

Edel, Abraham. 1955. *Ethical Judgement: the Use of Science in Ethics*. New York: Macmillan. Partly reprinted as "Attempts to Derive Definitive Moral Patterns from Biology." In Caplan (1978).

Edwards, Rem. 1975. "Do Pleasures and Pains Differ Qualitatively?" *The Journal of Value Inquiry*. Vol. 9, 270–281.

Elidae, Mircea. 1954. *The Myth of the Eternal Return*. New York: Pantheon.

——. 1963. *Myth and Reality*. New York: Harper and Row.

Engelhardt, H. Tristram, Jr. 1974. "The Disease of Masturbation: Values and the Concept of Disease." *Bulletin of the History of Medicine*. Vol. 48, No. 2.

——. 1976. "Ideology and Etiology." *The Journal of Medicine and Philosophy*. Vol. 1, No. 3.

Engels, Fredrick. 1875. Letter to P. L. Lavrov, November 12–17.

Farb, Peter. 1978. *Humankind*. Boston: Houghton Mifflin Co.

Feinberg, Joel. 1969. *Moral Concepts*, Oxford: Oxford University Press.

——. 1973. *Social Philosophy*. Englewood Cliffs, NJ: Prentice-Hall.

Feuer, Lewis. 1955. *Psychoanalysis and Ethical Values*. Springfield, IL: C. C. Thomas.

Fingarette, Herbert. 1969. *Self-Deception*. New York: Humanities Press.

Fletcher, Joseph Francis. 1966. *Situation Ethics: The New Morality*. Philadelphia: Westminster Press.

Flew, Anthony. 1967. "From Is to Ought." In Hudson (1967).

——. 1973. *Crime or Disease*. London: Macmillan Co.

Foot, Philippa. 1957. "Free Will as Involving Determinism." *The Philosophical Review*, LXVI, 439–450. Reprinted in Morgenbesser and Walsh, *Free Will*. Englewood Cliffs, NJ: Prentice-Hall (1962).

——. 1978. *Virtues and Vices*. Berkeley: University of California Press.

Foucault, Michael. 1965. *Madness and Civilization: A History of Insanity in the Age of Reason*. New York: Pantheon.

Fox, Robin. 1989. *The Search for Society*. New Brunswick: Rutgers University Press.

Freud, Sigmund. 1920. *A General Introduction to Psychoanalysis*. New York: Perma Books.

——. 1923. *The Ego and the Id*. Trans. James Strachey. New York: Norton (1962).

——. 1933. *New Introductory Lectures on Psychoanalysis*. New York: Norton.

Fromm, Erich. 1947. *Man for Himself*. New York: Holt, Rinehart and Winston.

——. 1961. *Marx's Concept of Man*. New York: Fredrick Ungar.

Fuss, Peter. 1964. "Conscience." *Ethics*, LXXIV, 112.

Gardiner, Patrick. 1968. "Error, Faith, and Self-Deception." *Proceedings of the Aristotelian Society*. 70: 226.

Garnett, A. Campbell. 1969. "Conscience and Conscientiousness." In Feinberg (1969).

Gay, Peter. 1979. "Freud and Freedom." In *The Idea of Freedom*. Alan Ryan, ed. Oxford: Oxford University Press.

Geach, P. T. 1956. "Good and Evil." *Analysis*. Vol. 17.

Geertz, C. 1980. "Sociosexuality." *New York Review of Books* (January 24).

Glantz, Kalman and Pearce, John K. 1989. *Exiles from Eden*. New York: W. W. Norton and Co.

Gosling, J. C. B. and Taylor, C. C. W. 1982. *The Greeks on Pleasure*. Oxford: Clarendon Press.

Greene, Marjorie. 1978. "Sociobiology and the Human Mind." In Gregory (1978).

Gregory, Michael, ed. 1978. *Sociobiology and Human Nature*. San Francisco: Jossey-Bass.

Griswold, Charles L. 1986. *Self-Knowledge in Plato's Phaedrus*. New Haven: Yale University Press.

Haldane, J. B. S. 1932. *The Causes of Evolution*. London: Longmans, Green.

Hamilton, W. D. 1963. "The Evolution of Altruistic Behavior." *American Naturalist*. 97, 354–356.

——. 1964. "The Genetical Evolution of Social Behavior." *Journal of Theoretical Biology*. 7, 1–51.

Hampshire, Stuart. 1959. *Thought and Action*. New edition. Notre Dame, IN: University of Notre Dame Press (1983).

——. 1978. "The Illusion of Sociobiology." *The New York Review of Books* (October 12).

Hartmann, Heinz. 1960. *Psychoanalysis and Moral Values*. New York: International Universities Press.

Heidegger, Martin. 1927. *Being and Time*. New York: Harper and Row (1962).

Hobart, R. E. 1934. "Free Will as Involving Determination and Inconceivable without It." *Mind*. XLIII, No. 169 (January).

Hobbes, Thomas. 1651. *The Leviathan*. Michael Oakeshott, ed. Oxford: Basil Blackwell (1960).

Homer. *The Iliad*. Trans. Richmond Lattimore. Chicago: University of Chicago Press (1951).

Horney, Karen. 1950. *Neurosis and Human Growth*. New York: W. W.Norton.

Hudson, W., ed. 1967. *New Studies in Ethics*. New York: St. Martin's Press.

Hume, David. 1739. *A Treatise of Human Nature*. Oxford: Clarendon Press (1888).

Huxley, J. 1947. *Touchstone for Ethics*. New York: Harper's.

Huxley, T. H. 1863. *Man's Place in Nature*. Reprinted 1971 by University of Michigan Press, Ann Arbor.

Jahoda, Marie. 1950. *Current Concepts of Positive Mental Health*. New York: Basic Books.

Kant, Immanuel. 1785. *Foundations of the Metaphysic of Morals*. Trans. Lewis White Beck. Indianapolis: Liberal Arts Library (1959).

Kass, Leon. 1975. "Regarding the End of Medicine and the Pursuit of Health." *The Public Interest*. No. 40, Summer. Reprinted in Beauchamp and Walters (1978).

Kirk, G. S. and Raven, J. E. 1964. "The Presocratics." Cambridge: Cambridge University Press.

Kosman, L. A. 1980. "Being Properly Affected: Virtues and Feelings in Aristotle's Ethics." In Rorty (1980).

Kroptkin, Peter. 1903. *Mutual Aid: A Factor in Evolution*. New York: McClure Philips and Co.

Kuhn, Thomas. 1957. *The Copernican Revolution*. Cambridge: Harvard University Press.

Laing, R. D. 1967. *The Politics of Experience*. New York: Ballantine Books.

Lattimore, Richmond, trans. 1951. *The Iliad of Homer*. Chicago: University of Chicago Press.

Lee, Richard B. and DeVore, Irven, eds. 1968. *Man the Hunter*. Chicago: Aldine.

Lewontin, R. C. 1970. "The Units of Selection." *Annual Review of Ecology and Systematics*. 1, 1970, 1–18.

———. 1974. *The Genetic Basis of Evolutionary Change*. New York: Columbia University Press.

———. 1984. *Not In Our Genes*. Princeton, NJ: Princeton University Press.

Lorenz, Konrad. 1966. *On Agression*. New York: Harcourt Brace Jovanovitch.

McDougall, William. 1908. *An Introduction to Social Psychology*. Boston: J. W. Luce.

Machiavelli, Niccolo. 1520. *The Prince*. Trans. L. Ricci. New York: Random House (1924).

MacIntyre, Alasdair. 1981. *After Virtue*. Notre Dame: University of Notre Dame Press.

Malinowski, Bronislaw. 1944. *A Scientific Theory of Culture*. Chapel Hill: University of North Carolina Press.

Margolis, Joseph 1966. *Psychotherapy and Morality*. New York: Random House.

———. 1976. "The Concept of Disease." *The Journal of Medicine and Philosophy*. Vol. 1, No. 3.

Maslow, Abraham H. 1962. *Toward a Psychology of Being*. New York: Van Nostrand.

Midgley, Mary. 1978. *Beast and Man: The Roots of Human Nature*. New York: Meridian.

Mill, John Stuart. 1861. *Utilitarianism*. New York: Dutton (1910).

Moore, G. E. 1903. *Principia Ethica*. Cambridge: Cambridge University Press.

Moravcsik, Julius. 1976. "Ancient and Modern Conceptions of Health and Medicine." *Journal of Medicine and Philosophy*. Vol. 1, No. 4.

Morris, Desmond. 1967. *The Naked Ape*. New York: McGraw-Hill.

Niebhur, Reinhold. 1941. *The Nature and Destiny of Man*. New York: Scribner's (1964).

Nietzsche, Fredrich. 1872. *The Birth of Tragedy*. Trans. Francis Golffing. New York: Doubleday (1956).

———. 1883. *Thus Spoke Zarathrustra*. Trans. R. J.Hollingsdale. New York: Penguin Books (1961).

Nowell–Smith, P. H. 1948. "Freewill and Moral Responsibility." *Mind*. N.S., LVII, 45–61.

———. 1954. *Ethics*. Baltimore: Penguin Books (1967).

Nussbaum, Martha. 1988. "Non-relative Virtues: An Aristotelian Approach." In *Midwest Studies in Philosophy, Vol. XIII*. Peter French, Theodore Uehling, Jr., and Howard Wettstein, ed. Notre Dame, IN: University of Notre Dame Press.

Peck, Scott. 1980. *The Road Less Traveled*. New York: Simon and Schuster.

———. 1983. *People of the Lie*. New York: Simon and Schuster.

Plato. *Gorgias*. Trans., W. D. Woodhead. In *The Collected Dialogues of Plato*. Edith Hamilton and Huntington Cairns, ed. Princeton: Princeton University Press (1961).

———. *Symposium*. Trans. W. R. M. Lamb. Loeb Library. Cambridge: Harvard University Press (1925).

———. *Timaeus*. Trans. Rev. R. G. Bury. Loeb Library. Cambridge: Harvard University Press (1929).

Potts, Timothy. 1980. *Conscience in Medieval Philosophy*. Cambridge: Cambridge University Press.

Quinton, Anthony. 1965. "Ethics and the Theory of Evolution." In Ramsey (1966).

———. 1973. *Utilitarian Ethics*. New York: St. Martin's Press.

Ramsey, I. T., ed. 1965. *Biology and Personality*. Oxford: Basil Blackwell.

Randall, John Herman. 1960. *Aristotle*. New York: Columbia University Press.

Rogers, Carl. 1951. *Client-Centered Therapy*. Boston: Houghton Mifflin.

Roochnik, David. 1990. *The Tragedy of Reason*. New York: Routledge.

Rorty, A. O. 1980. *Essays on Aristotle's Ethics*. Berkeley: University of California Press.

Ross. W. D. 1923. *Aristotle*. Cleveland: World Publishing Co. (1959).

Rousseau, J. J. 1755. *Discourse on the Origin and Foundation of Inequality Among Men*. Trans. G. D. H. Cole. New York: Dutton (1950).

Russell, Bertrand. 1918. "Mysticism and Logic." London: Allen and Unwin (1959).

Ryle, Gilbert. 1949. *The Concept of Mind*. New York: Barnes and Noble (1965).

Sahlins, M. D. 1976. *The Use and Abuse of Biology*. Ann Arbor: University of Michigan Press.

Sartre, Jean Paul. 1943. *Being and Nothingness*. Trans. Hazel Barnes. New York: Philosophical Library (1956).

———. 1946. *The Humanism of Existentialism*. In *Essays in Existentialism*. Wade Baskin, ed. New York: Citadel Press (1968).

Scheff, Thomas J. 1966. *Being Mentally Ill*. New York: Aldine Publishing Co.

Schopenhauer, Arthur. 1818. *The World as Will and Representation*. New York: Dover (1969).

Searle, John. 1978. "Sociobiology and the Explanation of Behavior." In Gregory (1978).

Sedgewick, Peter. 1973. "Psycho-politics." *Hastings Center Studies*. Vol. 1, No. 3.

Seligman, M. E. P. 1975. *Helplessness*. San Francisco: W. H. Freeman.

Sidgwick, Henry. 1874. *The Methods of Ethics*. Chicago: The University of Chicago Press (1962).

Simpson, G. G. 1951. *The Meaning of Evolution*. New York: Mentor Books.

———. 1958. "The Study of Evolution: Methods and Present Status of Theory." In Bleibtreu, Hermann, *Evolutionary Anthropology*. Boston: Allyn and Bacon (1969).

Singer, Marcus. 1967. *Encyclopedia of Philosophy*. Vols. 3 and 4, 365–366.

Stace, W. T. 1952. *Religion and the Modern Mind*. New York. Lippincott (1952).

Steven. Leslie. 1907. *The Science of Ethics*. 2d ed. London: Smith Elder and Co.

Szabados, Bela. 1976. "Butler on Corrupt Conscience." *Journal of the History of Philosophy*. Vol. 14 (October).

Szasz, Thomas. 1960. *The Myth of Mental Illness*. New York: Harper and Row.

Tiger, L. and Fox, R. 1971. *The Imperial Animal*. New York: Holt, Rinehart and Winston.

Trivers, R. L. 1971. "The Evolution of Reciprocal Altruism." *Quarterly Review of Biology* 46, 35–57.

Veatch, Henry. 1985. *Human Rights: Fact or Fancy*. Baton Rouge: Louisiana State University Press.

———. 1992. "Modern Ethics, Teleology, and Love of Self." *The Monist*. Vol. 75, No. 1.

Waddington, C. H. 1960. *The Ethical Animal*. London: Allen and Unwin.

Wallace, James D. 1978. *Virtues and Vices*. Ithaca: Cornell University Press.

Wheelwright, Philip. 1966. "The Presocratics." New York: Macmillan.

White, R. W. 1959. "Motivation Reconsidered: The Concept of Competence." *Psychological Review*. 66, 297–333.

Williams, Bernard. 1958. *Ethics and the Moral Life*. New York: St. Martin's Press.

———. 1985. *Ethics and the Limits of Philosophy*. Cambridge, MA: Harvard University Press.

Wilson, E. O. 1978. *On Human Nature*. Cambridge, MA: Harvard University Press.

———. 1975a. *Sociobiology: The New Synthesis*. Cambridge, MA: Harvard University Press.

———. 1975b. "Human Decency is Animal." *The New York Times Magazine* (October 12). 38–50.

Wright, Larry. (1973) "Functions." *Philosophical Review*. Vol. 83.

Wynne-Edwards, V. C. 1962. *Animal Dispersion in Relation to Social Behavior*. Edinburgh: Oliver and Boyd.

Young, Robert. 1986. *Personal Autonomy: Beyond Negative and Positive Liberty*. London and Sydney: Croom Helm.

Index